# Information Orientation

# Information Orientation
## *The Link to Business Performance*

DONALD A. MARCHAND, WILLIAM J. KETTINGER,
AND JOHN D. ROLLINS

OXFORD
UNIVERSITY PRESS

# OXFORD

UNIVERSITY PRESS

Great Clarendon Street, Oxford OX2 6DP

Oxford University Press is a department of the University of Oxford.
It furthers the University's objective of excellence in research, scholarship,
and education by publishing worldwide in

Oxford  New York

Athens  Auckland  Bangkok  Bogotá  Buenos Aires  Calcutta
Cape Town  Chennai  Dar es Salaam  Delhi  Florence  Hong Kong  Istanbul
Karachi  Kuala Lumpur  Madrid  Melbourne  Mexico City  Mumbai
Nairobi  Paris  São Paulo  Shanghai  Singapore  Taipei  Tokyo  Toronto  Warsaw
and associated companies in  Berlin  Ibadan

Oxford is a registered trade mark of Oxford University Press
in the UK and in certain other countries

Published in the United States
by Oxford University Press Inc., New York

© D. Marchand, W. Kettinger, Andersen Consulting 2001

The moral rights of the authors have been asserted

Database right Oxford University Press (maker)

First published 2001

British Library Cataloguing in Publication Data

Data available

Library of Congress Cataloging in Publication Data
Marchand, Donald A.
Information orientation: the new business performance metric / Donald A. Marchand.
William J. Kettinger, and John D. Rollins.
p. cm.
1. Information technology—Management.   I. Kettinger, William J.
II. Rollins, John D.   III. Title.
HD30.3 .M3663   2000      658.4′038—dc21       00-045302

ISBN 0-19-924067-1

1  3  5  7  9  10  8  6  4  2

Typeset by Hope Services (Abingdon) Ltd.
Printed in Great Britain
on acid-free paper by
Biddles Ltd., Guildford and King's Lynn

*To the Davids in each of our lives who inspire and challenge their dad to understand the e-generation.*

David Marchand, David Kettinger, and David Rollins

# PREFACE

This book presents the major results of a twenty-eight-month research project entitled 'Navigating Business Success'. The project was conducted at IMD with the support of Andersen Consulting from September 1997 until December 1999.

When we began this research project, senior managers in European and North American companies were debating how IT and the Internet would transform business and economic life. During the course of the study, e-commerce and e-business exploded in the USA and influenced how European managers would perceive their business opportunities in the 'new economy'. At the end of this project and in writing this book, we are convinced that while the words 'e-business' and 'e-commerce' have become part of the general vocabulary of modern business, there remain some fundamental questions.

How do successful companies in diverse industries manage their people, their business information, and their IT practices to achieve superior performance? Or, more generally, why does information use in some companies lead to better business results than in other companies in the same industries or even across industries?

After completing our project and this book, we believe our answers to these two important questions today are even more relevant in the 'new economy'. Both established companies and new 'dot.coms' now compete based on the ways they leverage their people, information, and IT practices in the global marketplace. We believe that the differences between winners and losers will increasingly depend on how effectively they use information to be smarter, faster, and better than their competitors.

In pursuing this research project, we defined three unique features to our effort:

First, the research study focuses on the ideas and thinking of senior managers, who drive the strategic decisions and, therefore, impact the performance of their companies. Over 1,000 senior managers participated in our core study sample. Fifty-eight per cent were CEOs, presidents, managing directors, executive and senior vice-presidents, and directors. The balance included CFOs, CIOs and other vice-presidents of sales, marketing, operations, human resources, and technology from twenty-five industries and twenty-six countries. Most previous studies regarding the use of information and IT focused primarily on the views of the CEO and the CIO.

Second, the study makes an important distinction between the more formal management activities of information management and information technology (IT), and those activities that remain more informal in most companies—influencing the behaviors and values of people related to information use. The study seeks to better understand both the uniqueness and interactions between these three information capabilities—taking a more people-centric view of effective information use. At the outset, the study avoided the popular, but simplistic views that IT alone impacts business performance in companies, or that IT somehow encompasses all that is important about how people use information in a business. Instead, we examined how senior managers think and shape the interactions between people, information, and IT in their companies to achieve business results.

Third, and most importantly, our study addressed a key managerial concern: is there a comprehensive measure of effective information use that predicts business performance? From the beginning, our study sought to confirm or refute how the key capabilities of people's behaviors, information use, and IT practices were linked to business performance. If the research could confirm a predictive link between how senior executives manage people, information, and IT, and how they achieve superior business performance, then we could make a major contribution to management practice by providing a new business metric that linked these capabilities to business performance.

Our book presents the major findings of our research 'journey'. It contains the summarized results of several detailed unpublished IMD working papers that are currently being refined and reviewed for distribution within the academic community. The timing of the book is propitious coming at the beginning of the twenty-first century—an exciting new era when senior managers of global companies will be challenged to deal with the business realities of the information and knowledge era. What better time to discover and understand that companies can measure and manage information, people, and IT to achieve superior business performance, and master their expectations about future industry leadership in competing with information?

D.A.M.
W.J.K.
J.D.R.

# ACKNOWLEDGEMENTS

There are many dedicated people to thank in undertaking a research project of this magnitude. Joyce P. Marchand, our project manager, provided the essential coordination for all the members of the project to know what they were supposed to do and when it needed to get done. Through the project's many phases, she provided the personal and professional focus in the team to move the project forward at each turn. Our Research Associates dedicated more than two years of their professional and personal lives to completing the project. We wish to thank Katarina Paddack and Andreas Wildberger for their outstanding contributions to the book and underlying analysis. We also wish to recognize Ursula Kaltenthaler and Piero Panseri for their dedicated work in the survey administration and case development phases of the project.

There were two cooperating faculty who played key roles in developing the analytical and statistical approaches to the research: Professor Al Segars of the University of North Carolina at Chapel Hill and Professor Choong Lee of Salisbury State University in Maryland. We thank them both for their 'virtual' participation in the project through many long e-mail and phone conferences from their offices and homes.

Two administrators supported the research project. Muriel Maradan Stern helped administer the project until her marriage and relocation to Chile. Enza Alberti assumed this key role and saw the project to its conclusion.

At IMD, the project and book were always encouraged and supported by Peter Lorange, president, with his 'can do' spirit, and Philip Rosenzweig, the director of R & D. Professors Stewart Hamilton, Jacques Horovitz, and Joachim Schwass provided key assistance to us when called upon. Jim Pulcrano and Stein Jacobsen from the IMD marketing and communication staff played key roles in helping us with company contacts. Louis LeClezio and Sabaheta Basinac provided invaluable IT and database support throughout the project. John Evans in the library and Gordon Adler, senior editor, provided excellent support to us on many occasions.

At Andersen Consulting, Vernon Ellis, managing partner and international chairman, was instrumental in sponsoring this Partnership Project at IMD and involving himself personally in its evolution. We also wish to thank Liz Padmore from the London office whose early interest in the project helped guide our efforts to frame it properly. Also, Santana Fernandez, working with John, acted as a key coordinator for our many meetings and phone calls from the start to the finish of the project—always with a smile. Finally, we wish to thank the nine partners from Andersen Consulting who gave of their time to participate in a critical review meeting of the project's early research plan. These 'volunteers' helped us focus on what could make the project a real success.

The research project and book writing are journeys in which our families fully participated. To Joyce, Lynda, and Theresa and all our children who were involved in our work wherever we had to do it—on the road, in the office, and at home on many weekends—a big thank you for your love and patience.

# CONTENTS

# LIST OF FIGURES

# LIST OF TABLES

# Introduction: Managing People, Information, and Technology to Improve Business Performance

This book examines how the interaction of people, information, and technology establishes an orientation towards the use of information within a company, and how this, in turn, affects business performance. It introduces a new and comprehensive measure of effective information use that predicts business performance. We call this new metric: *Information Orientation* or *IO*. Information Orientation measures the extent to which senior managers perceive that their organizations possess the capabilities associated with effective information use to improve business performance. IO does this by determining the degree to which a company possesses competence and synergy across three vital Information Capabilities (IC):

- *Information Technology Practices* (*ITP*)—the capabilities of a company to effectively manage information technology (IT) applications and infrastructure to support operations, business processes, managerial decision making, and innovation.
- *Information Management Practices* (*IMP*)—the capabilities of a company to manage information effectively over the life cycle of information use including sensing, collecting, organizing, processing, and maintaining information.
- *Information Behaviors/Values* (*IBV*)—the capabilities of a company to instill and promote behaviors and values in its people for effective use of information.

While past scholars and consultants recognized the importance of these three information capabilities, they tended to consider them separately in isolated schools of thought. They failed to integrate these ideas and as a result did not consider the holistic view of effective information use held in the minds of senior managers. We suspect that the fundamental disconnect between these cloistered schools of thought and the picture senior managers have painted in their own minds concerning 'what effective information use looks like in a successful company', has resulted in the dissatisfaction that many executives have concerning lower than expected payoffs from Information Technology (IT) investments.

This book demonstrates that a company must achieve competence and synergy across all three information capabilities of effective information use as a precondition to achieving superior business performance. Hence, IO represents a vital new performance metric that companies must monitor and manage to determine their readiness to compete in the information age.

## 1. A NEW AGE CALLS FOR NEW METRICS

During the twentieth century, we have followed several roads to an 'information age' that has elevated the role of information to the center of market and organizational behavior.

The first road reflects the dominance of 'capitalist' economies over 'planned' economies, and the role that competitive markets play in organizing economic activity. As Peter Drucker has recognized, the 'unique feature' of the market economy is 'precisely that it organizes economic activity around information' (Drucker 1993: 181). While markets are rarely 'perfect' (markets where all participants have equal access to all available information), the growth of the global information and communication infrastructure, including the Internet, has made information that was once scarce, ubiquitous. One needs only to look at the growth of on-line financial trading by personal investors for evidence of this trend. In the information age, customers, suppliers, employees, and competitors share a common flood of business and economic data from multiple communication channels. Information ubiquity pushes business strategists to work even harder to establish 'information asymmetries', whereby their companies lead their industries in using information in unique ways for a competitive advantage. Although not easily accomplished, some companies strive to structure business situations characterized by unequal types and amounts of information among market players and customers to fight the tide of information ubiquity (Evans and Wurster 1997: 33).

The second road focuses on the central question of organization design: what is the best way of organizing human activity so that information is used most effectively in organizational decision making? During most of the twentieth century, the dominant form of business organization has been what the nineteenth century German sociologist Max Weber called 'bureaucratic management' (Gerth and Mills 1946: 196). It was only after the Second World War that the limits of bureaucratic management became clear in the form of organizational inflexibility, rigidity, and ineffectiveness in information use and decision making. As these deficiencies became more obvious, management thinkers shifted their attention to those forms of organization that could be more effective in using information to reduce uncertainty, and in focusing managerial attention on decision making that could improve speed, flexibility, and responsiveness to rapidly changing business conditions. These newer organizational forms required less hierarchy, but, in turn, demanded increases in the volume of information to be processed to coordinate the far-flung operations with growing numbers of 'equals'. Personal information usage behaviors became paramount, as 'good' information must be shared as a means to empower, enlighten, and motivate.

The third road leading to the centrality of information in modern business life is reflected in the rise of the computer and communications technologies that comprise the global IT infrastructure today. The accelerated use of these technologies has ignited unprecedented excitement in their power to transform modern business, exemplified in the rapid evolution of the Internet and e-commerce. However, a strange, if not surprising, situation has developed in connection with the relationship between IT and information use in businesses. The explosive growth of IT use in organizations has not been matched by a better understanding of the role of information in improving business performance.

While the information age has been recognized for many years, its primary manifestation has been in the deployment of, and attention to, IT in organizations, rather than how people use information to achieve organizational purposes. Similarly, while there has been much attention to the IT productivity paradox—the elusive link between IT investments and improved business performance—most senior managers have come no closer to knowing whether their company is effectively using information to achieve better business performance.

This book presents the results of a major international research project that introduces a new metric of effective information use, called Information Orientation (IO). Managers can use this metric to evaluate how effectively people use information and IT to improve business performance. The book shows how the Information Orientation of organizations shapes business performance, and how IO is connected to managerial expectations about competing with information in the future. The Information Orientation Dashboard is presented as a diagnostic tool to measure and evaluate each of the three capabilities of IO—information behaviors and values, information management practices, and IT practices—and their relationships to business performance.

## 2. HOW INFORMATION ORIENTATION IMPROVES BUSINESS PERFORMANCE

For many years, management thinkers and practitioners have treated each of the three information capabilities of effective information use separately. Often, they tried to frame them within broader themes of human decision making, organizational culture, management control, and business performance. We categorize this previous work under three broad schools of management thinking and practice: (1) the *Information Technology* or *IT* School, (2) the *Information Management* School, and (3) the *Behavior and Control* School.

The *IT* School has focused heavily on the role of IT in improving decision making. This school attempts to establish IT management practices to automate and enhance different levels and types of decisions that managers and employees must make.

The Information Managem*e*nt School emphasizes choices about what types of information organizational members should use, and how they should sense, collect, organize, process, and maintain information. These choices should be influenced by the changing business conditions confronting a company, and the decisions that must be made to define and implement strategy.

The Behavior and Control School emphasizes both the contributions of behaviors and values to organizational performance, and the significant role of 'control' in channeling human motivation and behavior into actions that contribute to business performance.

Each of these schools has significantly advanced management thinking and practices about the relationships of people's behaviors, to information use, to strategy, and to decision making. However, each school also demonstrates key weaknesses that make understanding of the integration of the three information capabilities difficult and their links to business performance elusive. In fact, each school discusses its core focus and prescriptions for management thinking and practice with little or no connection to the other schools of thought and practice.

Contrary to most of the prevailing thinking and practices advocated by each school, this book demonstrates that senior managers do not view the three capabilities of information behaviors and values, information management practices, and IT practices as separately and independently contributing to superior business performance. Instead, senior managers possess an integrated view of these three information capabilities as contributing to one high-level idea that we call Information Orientation. Senior managers recognize that successful companies must be good at all three information capabilities if they are to enjoy synergies across capabilities. Without such an integrative view of effective information use, they recognize that their companies will fail to achieve superior business performance.

## A. The people-centric view of information use

A company is constantly confronted with many changes in business conditions—opportunities, threats, and risks—which require managers to rethink their business strategies and decision making assumptions (Simons 1995: 14–16). Managers and organizational members are continually challenged to interpret events in the business world, and to focus their attention on acquiring the appropriate knowledge and information to steer and manage the business in new directions. At a fundamental level, people use information in organizations to reduce uncertainty in decision making to accomplish tasks and actions.

However, in practice, understanding the basis of effective information use is more complicated than merely viewing business organizations as 'information processing' organisms—that sense the world and translate signals into information necessary for decisions. Neither is it sufficient to view organizations as 'computing machines' where processes are programmed to automatically turn data and physical inputs such as raw materials into products and services of value to the organization's customers. While eloquent in argument, these theoretical analogies have not led to sufficient explanations in practice as to how and why certain companies use information more effectively than others to improve business performance.

In the absence of a solid theoretical basis from academe to drive the development of an information management practice, practitioners took it upon themselves to formalize the management discipline. Two broad management disciplines emerged. One discipline attempted to improve information usage by formalizing the actual activities associated with its stewardship—namely, the Information Management School. Practitioners associated with this discipline had job titles such as record manager, corpo-rate librarian, and information center specialist. The other discipline for-malized information usage activities in terms of automated information exchanges using computer and telecommunication technologies—the IT discipline. Practitioners associated with this discipline had job titles such as data processing manager, systems analyst, network administrator, and computer operations specialist.

As both disciplines formalized their management practice into estab-lished functional departments within companies (e.g. the corporate records/library department and information systems department), they gained considerable skills within their functional domains. However, miss-ing from both of their functional charges was the responsibility to actively improve the information usage behaviors and values of the company's peo-ple. This was not completely an oversight but more likely the consequence of the fact that in the initial stages of their evolution, both of these manage-ment disciplines were viewed as low-level management support functions. They possessed neither the power nor the authority to influence major changes related to people's behaviors and values—seen typically as the domain of the human resources, operations, and accounting/control departments. As a consequence, a third area affecting information use—improving people's behaviors and values related to effective information usage—was never really formalized or incorporated into any kind of man-agement discipline in a serious way. And, because improving information usage effectiveness was not a major focus of the human resources, opera-tions, and control disciplines, it remained a side issue.

As we begin the twenty-first century, improving people's information usage behaviors and values and incorporating this with effective informa-tion management and IT practices remains an informal, and incomplete, management discipline. This is an unfortunate circumstance, as business organizations involve relationships among people, and how they choose to contribute their knowledge to achieve organizational or group purposes (Simons 1995: 21–4). People are constantly balancing their own interests with the organization's interests, in deciding whether, and how, to con-tribute their personal expertise, experience, and skills to the welfare of the group or organization (Simons 1995: 24–8). A challenge to business organi-zations is to channel human attention and information use into specific tasks and decisions. To accomplish this, a business organization must define a relevant context, or orientation, to continuously convert human knowledge and learning into creative ideas and information of value to achieve organizational success. We argue that these underdeveloped man-agement activities are an integral part of how information is used and provide tremendous opportunities for improvement through direct management influence and formalized management processes.

As Fig. 1.1 emphasizes, on an aggregate level, information use in business organizations is people-centric. It is based on the decision context and the tasks that people must execute to achieve organizational purposes. It not only involves how people use IT and manage information to help improve decisions, but how they behave with information based on organizational values associated with effective information use.

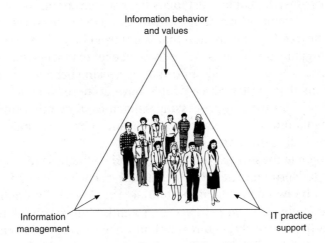

Information behavior
and values

Information
management

IT practice
support

**Fig. 1.1.  A People-centric View of Effective Information Use**

For business organizations to use information effectively, the people in them must manifest five key characteristics.

First, people must use information to support the organization's interests and not act solely on their own self-interests. People in business organizations are generally motivated to share and use information, unless they are constrained by the actions of other members or managers. The organization may constrain or block the opportunity for individuals to contribute, when people are unsure about how to contribute, or feel pressures from competing tasks, or where the organization does not provide sufficient resources to permit positive contributions (Simons 1995: 26).

Second, people must make their knowledge explicit for effective information use to occur. Keeping one's knowledge to oneself means that organizational members will not benefit from the full contribution that people can make towards attaining organizational goals. People acquire tacit knowledge through experience and interactions with others. Tacit knowledge is usually difficult to articulate and make explicit. People must be able to trust what others will do with their knowledge, feelings, and emotions before they make this knowledge explicit and shareable. The organization may block its members from making their tacit knowledge explicit, by not creating the contexts in which conversion can occur, or by not rewarding a person when they do so, or by penalizing individuals for articulating their tacit knowledge (Nonaka and Takeuchi 1995: 62).

Third, organizations cannot address all their goals simultaneously (Simons 1995: 16–17). People must focus their scarce attention and time on the 'right' or 'relevant' information and not spend their time on sensing, collecting, or processing information that is not used in decision making and executing organizational tasks. A key challenge for managers and organizational members is to focus their information seeking behavior on the goals and decisions that matter. Since people have quite severe limits on their attention and information processing capacities, they must understand over time what information seeking is relevant to improve their own performance as well as that of the organization.

Fourth, people must possess the ability and willingness to acquire new knowledge to learn and change. The learning capacity of organizations is determined by two countervailing tendencies (Argyris and Schön 1978: 17–29). One tendency is for workers to use and refine existing knowledge. The other is to proactively acquire new knowledge to respond to changes in business conditions. The more an organization can instill information use behaviors that support both types of learning, the more it builds learning capacity.

Sharing and applying existing knowledge to address problems helps organizations in detecting and correcting errors. However, organizational members must also be ready to question existing ways of solving problems. They must be prepared to rethink their assumptions for decisions in the light of changes in business conditions. Here the challenge for organizational members is a readiness to learn, the disposition to proactively sense potentially valuable information, and the willingness and disposition to employ enhanced information management practices to accommodate new ways of working. Thus, the learning capacity of people in organizations is defined by their willingness to admit errors and mistakes, share existing information, proactively sense and acquire new knowledge, challenge assumptions, and contribute to a culture whereby people 'learn to learn'.

Finally, people must accept continuous change as a natural feature of modern organizational life and be willing to respond quickly to new challenges. Companies must develop in their people openness to change and a bias for action. When people are flexible they use information sensed from the external environment as well as interpreted from existing operations to drive innovative IT solutions and enhanced decision making capabilities. In essence, people's flexibility leverages learning capacity to permit emergent situations and strategies to be addressed.

When an organization's people reflect these five characteristics for information use, we believe that the organization will use and manage its information resources more effectively. In this mature information usage culture, organizational members are energized to proactively sense and collect information to improve management support and task execution. Recognizing the information they need and how they will manage it, people are prepared to employ information technology in new ways to support decision making. Successful IT applications further energize the proactiveness of employees to use information even more effectively. A synergy is established between an organization's people, and its more established management activities for information, and technology.

Simply put, our theory of effective information use is based on the concept of a recursive spiral whereby good information usage behaviors and values drive better information definition and management; this improves the capability of a company to use IT to support decision making and problem solving, which in turn reinforces good information usage behaviors and values (see Fig. 1.2). When one of these links is derailed, the recursive aspects of the spiral are disabled and a company is less effective in using information.

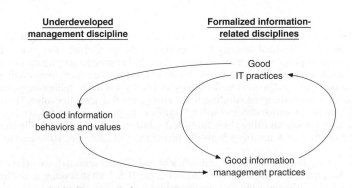

**Fig. 1.2. Spiral of Effective Information Use in Companies**

*Note*: Effective information use is based on a recursive spiral whereby good information usage behaviors and values drive good information management, which improves the capability to use IT to support decision making and problem solving, which in turn reinforces good information usage behaviors and values and information management.

## B.  The Information Orientation of senior managers

Our points of reference for this book are the perceptions of senior managers in a representative sample of international companies in diverse manufacturing and services industries. The perceptions of senior managers are important for several reasons:

First, the perceptions of senior managers drive strategic decisions within companies.[1] By examining their perceptions, we can better understand how senior managers view the deployment of people, information, and IT to achieve their business goals.[2]

Second, senior managers are continuously challenged to achieve business results for their company and business units. Previous management research has shown that the choices made by senior managers influence the performance of their companies and business units.[3]

Third, senior managers do not work alone, but are members of senior management teams or groups. For the purpose of this study, senior managers were chosen as members of senior management teams by their companies. We define a 'senior management team' as a relatively small senior leadership group of the most influential executives at the corporate, division, and/or business unit level. These managers represent the key areas of business or functional responsibility in their organizations. They are responsible for formulating the basic strategies of the organization, allocating resources, and implementing strategies to achieve appropriate business results.[4]

---

[1] Henry Mintzberg (1973) indicates that senior managers must strike the right balance, between the pursuit of intended strategy and 'emergent strategy' that arises at various levels of the organization as people search for opportunities, and engage in solving new or unexpected problems. Mintzberg observed that both views of strategy coexist in most companies, and it is senior managers who must strike the right balance between deliberate pursuit of intended strategy and creating the conditions for 'emergent strategies' to evolve. Therefore, how senior managers promote effective information use by people is conditioned by their expectations about implementing their intended strategies, versus their willingness to respond and change course resulting from the recognition of emergent strategies in their company.

[2] While the Information Management and Behavior and Control schools have been noticeably quiet on this topic, there are numerous studies in the IT School that point to the importance of the relationship between the senior executives' perceptions and information technology investment decisions and outcomes. See Jarvenpaa and Ives (1991), which was the first large-sample empirical study to examine the influence of the CEO's involvement in company success with IT. Also see Fenny, Edwards, and Simpson (1992) as well as Sambamurthy and Zmud (1992).

[3] For example, see Porter (1980); Hambrick and Mason (1984); Charkravarthy (1986); Robbins and Duncan (1988).

[4] For example: see Hambrick et al. (1996).

The core sample for the study presented in this book is 1,009 senior managers from 169 senior management teams in 98 companies as described in detail in the Appendix. The senior management teams represent companies and business units from 22 countries and 25 industries. In addition, personal and phone interviews as well as more detailed case studies were undertaken in 24 companies to better interpret the implications of our survey results.

Using a powerful set of statistical techniques described in the Appendix, the book defines the key behaviors and practices associated with each information capability of Information Orientation: information behaviors and values, information management practices, and IT practices. It demonstrates that these three information capabilities define a new strategic management concept in the minds of senior managers called Information Orientation (IO).

The book demonstrates that, in the minds of senior managers, IO is a predictor of business performance. We find that being good at information behaviors and values, information management practices, or IT practices alone does not guarantee increases to business performance. Rather it is the comprehensive concept of IO with its interactions between the three information capabilities together that constitutes the missing link to higher business performance. Thus, if the IO score of a company is high, its business performance will be high. Moreover, to achieve superior business performance, a company must score high on all information capabilities of IO. Each of the information capabilities is necessary, but not sufficient, to improve business performance.

## 3. IO: A NEW BUSINESS METRIC FOR EFFECTIVE INFORMATION USE

The book next focuses on IO as a new practical measure of effective information use in business.

If companies and industries are becoming increasingly 'information intensive' and knowledge is perceived as the new foundation for competitive advantage, then how do senior managers know whether their company is effectively using information to achieve better business performance?

In applying IO as a business measure of effective information use, we emphasize several key characteristics of IO:

1. IO incorporates a people-centric view of information use.
2. IO is causally linked to business performance.

3. IO is an organization-wide metric, not limited to the IT department or other information management support functions.
4. IO applies universally across international borders. There are no statistically significant differences between the senior manager responses in North America and Western Europe.
5. IO can be used as a key performance indicator over time to assess the effectiveness of management actions to improve information behaviors and values, information management practices, and IT practices.

The book presents and explains the use of the 'Information Orientation Dashboard' as a management tool for evaluating and benchmarking IO capabilities and practices within and across industries. Using the core benchmark sample of 169 senior management teams from diverse business units and companies, the book assesses the IO levels of other companies and business units across industries and geographic locations worldwide.

IO can be used as a benchmark measure comparing the business units and divisions of global companies across the enterprise. Companies can develop portfolio strategies using IO as a common measure of effective information use across business units worldwide.

Finally, the book shows how the IO metric positions companies to assess IO deficiencies and recommend appropriate management actions. As a new performance metric for evaluating effective information use, IO can be used to monitor the results of management actions over time to improve the company's capabilities to manage people, information, and IT to achieve better business performance.

## 4. FUTURE INDUSTRY LEADERSHIP IN COMPETING WITH INFORMATION

This book also examines how senior managers think about competing with information in the future. Companies that will be 'future industry leaders in competing with information' strive to create information asymmetries in their markets. Information asymmetries exist whenever a company leverages information about markets, customers, or its operations which is unusable or unavailable to its competitors.

We categorize the information capabilities and practices for attaining leadership in competing with information in three ways: (1) using competitive information, (2) using customer information, and (3) using operational information. Within each category, or dimension, we have identified emerging practices and trends that we believe senior managers expect to exploit to attain future industry leadership. We also demonstrate that senior managers perceive a higher-level idea that integrates the dimensions of leadership in using competitive, customer, and operational information into a single 'Industry Information Leadership' factor. Thus, our study identifies a new and integrated view of how senior managers think about achieving future industry leadership with information.

One of the key conclusions of the book is that the information orientation predicts senior manager expectations regarding their company's ability to be an industry leader in using information in the future. If the IO score of a company is high, then its expectations about future industry leadership in competing with information will also be high. Not only is it important to be good at IT practices, information management practices, and information behaviors and values, but a company must be good at IO if it is to attain future industry leadership in competing with information.

In addition, we know that companies must be better than their competitors in developing 'industry foresight' and shaping business strategies to act on their foresight (Hamel and Prahalad 1994: 73). Our research findings indicate that senior managers recognize that proactive information usage behaviors, sensing of new information needs, and innovations in using IT for management analysis and decision making are critical to competing in the future. When companies are good in all these areas they can support a company's emergent strategies.

## 5. ORGANIZATION OF THE BOOK

In the chapters that follow, the book explains how senior managers view each of the key information capabilities of information orientation and how they can manage IO to achieve superior business performance.

To set the stage for our discussion, examines how management theory and practice have evolved during the second half of the twentieth century, and addresses each of the key information capabilities of Information Orientation. As we mentioned earlier, we have summarized the key writings and management practices and called them 'schools of thought' to simplify and focus the reader on the essential strengths and weaknesses of each school. Readers who wish to skip this chapter and proceed to our major findings can review Fig. 2.1, which summarizes the major strengths and weaknesses of the IT School, the Information Management School, and the Behavior and Control School.

In Chapters 3, 4, and 5, we define each of the key information capabilities of Information Orientation, and present the findings of our study related to each. These chapters explain the concepts and practices included in each information capability based on our confirmatory factor model and statistical correlations applied to our core survey data.

Chapter 3 discusses the evolution of IT practices at four levels: IT for operational support, IT for business process support, IT for management support, and IT for innovation support. Each of these levels of IT application is tied to different types of employees and decisions in the company. In Chapter 3, we view the context for decision making as the foundation for all IT support and uses in a company.

Chapter 4 focuses on how well senior managers perceive their company is managing information to improve business performance. This chapter discusses the underlying information practices related to the five phases of the 'information life cycle'—these involve sensing, collecting organizing, processing, and maintaining information to enhance its use for decision making in a company.

Chapter 5 assesses the key behaviors and values senior managers perceive are connected to the ways people use information effectively in their companies. We have identified the six key information behaviors and values as (1) integrity, (2) formality, (3) control, (4) transparency, (5) sharing, and (6) proactiveness. These perceptions are critical to the speed and effectiveness of decisions in responding to continuously changing business conditions. In companies that are more mature in managing information behaviors and values, performance-based information about the company is interpreted and shared at all levels. This atmosphere creates a strong disposition toward sharing all types of information among organizational members. In addition, in companies where information about mistakes, errors, and failures is transparent, shared, and used constructively, there is a strong disposition to be proactive in seeking new information to respond to these problems, and resolve them quickly to improve the performance of the company.

Chapter 6 empirically shows the existence of IO as a new comprehensive measure of effective information use and then establishes a direct causal link between higher IO and higher business performance. As opposed to a parochial view derived from one of the three schools of thought discussed in Chapter 2, the integrated IO perspective demonstrates how senior managers perceive the three information capabilities contribute to a comprehensive measure of effective information use in their companies. Chapter 6 frames this discussion as an answer to an ongoing controversy over the IT productivity paradox and the elusive connection between IT investments and practices and improvements in business performance.

Chapter 7 examines the use of IO as a new metric to measure effective information use across companies and industries and within the business units of global companies. This chapter evaluates the strengths and weaknesses of the three schools of management thinking and practice related to business performance metrics. None of the schools has provided an integrated theory and empirical validation of a metric directly linking information use in companies to business performance. In this chapter, the Information Orientation Dashboard is presented as a new diagnostic tool for evaluating IO inside and across companies over time. In addition, there is an initial assessment of the types of management strategies, and actions that can be used to improve the behaviors and capabilities associated with the three information capabilities of IO within companies.

Chapter 8 explores how companies become more mature in their information usage effectiveness. Based on the theoretical underpinnings of each information capability, and the cross-capability interaction effects of the 'spiral of information effectiveness', this chapter develops the prescriptive paths that a company must follow as it becomes more IO mature. We theorize and test the causal path between dimensions of each information capability using statistical path analysis. Next, we examine the causal interaction effects across information capabilities. The paths within and between the three information capabilities of IO are discussed based on our theoretical arguments as well as five key characteristics of effective information use that surface in our interpretation of our results. Our findings indicate that in more mature IO cultures the synergy across capabilities is greater. People are energized to proactively sense and collect information to improve management support and task execution. People are prepared to employ IT in new ways to manage information in support of decision making. What emerges is a richer theoretical case for our research findings and it solidifies our people-centric view of effective information use. This chapter ends by contemplating future research benefits in further refining a comprehensive prescriptive IO maturity path model.

Chapter 9 defines the concepts and practices underlying the three key dimensions of future industry leadership in competing with information: competitive, customer, and operational information. It explains how IO is linked to these three dimensions of future industry leadership in competing with information, and how IO predicts senior manager expectations of future industry leadership with information.

Finally, Chapter 10 provides an overview of the key management conclusions that can be derived from this book. The key directions which will be pursued further regarding management practices and strategies to measure and manage IO to improve business performance in the future are presented.

The *Appendix* provides a detailed explanation of the research methods and analytical techniques underlying our study and the derivation of the major findings.

## 6. WHAT YOU CAN EXPECT FROM READING THIS BOOK

This book is primarily intended to influence management thinking and practice with competent and relevant scholarly research and theory. We combine in this study a focus on business relevance with strong empirical research and analytical methods to explore the perspectives of hundreds of senior managers in leading companies in diverse industries and countries.

The study framework presented here is derived from management theory and ongoing research in several management disciplines. It is applied to empirically derived analyses from our survey data supplemented by qualitative case research. Our approach to this research should be evaluated along five dimensions:

1. The strength and contribution of our conceptual and theoretical frameworks;
2. the reliability and validity of the data collected and analytical techniques employed;
3. the extent to which important constructs are developed, validated, and integrated into our theory;
4. the strength of the linkage between IO and business performance; and
5. the usefulness of our framework and findings to emerging management practice.

By the end of this book, readers will have a clear understanding of the significance and impact of a company's Information Orientation on current business performance, and future industry leadership in competing with information. Readers will better understand how senior managers think about and manage IO to achieve superior performance.

For academic readers, this book presents an integrated theory and our evidence and arguments for changing the way scholars examine the roles of people, information, and IT in decision making and strategy implementation.

For managers, this book provides a new managerial framework and business metric that challenges current mindsets and practices concerning how people, information, and IT can be managed to achieve business results.

# 2

# Evolution of Management Thinking and Practice about People, Information, and IT

Management thinking is influenced by the daily pressures of competition as well as by technological, and socio-economic, trends that mold the global economy. Ideas that shape business come from many intellectual sources, and develop in a seemingly haphazard fashion through real world testing of ideas, in the minds of managers, management theorists, and consultants.

This book is shaped by the confluence of several streams of management ideas and practices concerning the application of information technology, the development of information management as an organizational activity, and the understanding of the ways people behave and are managed in businesses. Each of these streams of ideas has developed over many years, from different intellectual roots and in response to diverse business challenges. However, we demonstrate in this study that ideas from these three streams are converging in the minds of senior managers today, and shaping a new mindset concerning how to manage information, technology, and people to achieve improved business performance. We have called these three streams of ideas 'schools of thought' to trace the development of related concepts that have influenced managerial strategy and action, in the past, and continue to do so today.

The first school of thought we call the Information Technology (IT) School which focuses on the evolution of IT use in business and its relationship to decision making and performance. The IT School has its roots in decision theory, operations research, and computer science. The origins of this school are strongly influenced by the application of computer and telecommunications technology in business over the last fifty years and the formalized managerial discipline that has evolved around how IT should be used in organizations.

The second school of thought we call the Information Management School. It focuses on how information as an organizational asset, or resource, should be managed throughout its life cycle, from its initial sensing, to collecting, organizing, processing, and maintaining or disposing of information. Like IT, information management has grown to be a formalized management discipline. Information management's academic school of thought has its roots in records and paperwork management, and information and library science. In addition, efforts in the 1970s to better manage the paperwork, records, and computer systems of large corporations and government agencies were implemented under the label of information resources management or IRM.

The third school of thought we call the Behavior and Control School. Unlike developments in either the IT or information management schools, there has not been development of a formal management activity directly related to people's behavior that would drive information use improvements. Two major streams of management thinking and practice, however, have provided some guidelines as to how this type of management function might be formalized within an organization. The first stream deals with how people behave in organizations, and how they should be selected, motivated, rewarded, trained, and evaluated for performing activities consistent with organizational objectives. This stream draws most directly from the organizational behavior and human resources disciplines. The second stream is concerned with the evolution of management controls as well as the information systems required in an organization to tie the company's performance directly to the performance of people doing or completing the work. Its historical roots are most closely associated with the evolution of the accounting profession, although, since the 1960s, the management control focus has evolved separately to emphasize broader measures of business performance than purely accounting and financial measures, and to link these to how managers control a company's people to achieve positive business results.

As Table 2.1 shows, each of these schools of thought has certain strengths in promoting key management ideas and practices related to IT, information use, and people, which act as the platform for our study. However, we also recognize key weaknesses related to each school that our study is designed to address and resolve.

**Table 2.1.** *Strengths and Weaknesses of the Three Schools of Management Thinking and Practice*

| Management school | Strengths | Weaknesses |
| --- | --- | --- |
| Information Technology School | This decision-centered approach focuses on the dynamics of management and positions the role of information in decision making. | While theoretically appealing, in practice, managers have not learned how to manage information to satisfy unstructured and fluid decision making contexts. |
| | Advances in IT have facilitated the use of IT for operational and tactical levels of decision making. This approach has been striving to find strategic uses for the endless proliferation of IT. | Advances in IT have not very successfully facilitated the use of IT for innovation and strategic decision making. |
| | Serious commitment to establish measures to determine the payoff of IT investments by attempting to link them to business performance. | IT professionals have emphasized the technical side of data management and often looked for the 'killer app', rather than focusing on how people use and manage information. In essence changing people's information usage behaviors has never been a high priority of the IT discipline. In addition, there has been a lack of attention dedicated to the management of non-automated and/or informal information usage. |
| Information Management School | Drawing on 'resource management' as its theoretical basis, the Information Management School emphasizes information as an important organizational resource for learning and adapting to continuous business changes. | The Information Management School has failed to draw tight links between improved management of the information resources and better business performance. |
| | The information management view focuses on information management as a 'process' or life cycle, including sensing, collecting, organizing, processing, and maintaining information. | Managing and valuing information in practice is very difficult and no well-recognized approach for doing this has become standard practice. This problem is made worse when |

**Table 2.1.** *cont.*

| Management school | Strengths | Weaknesses |
|---|---|---|
| | | people often do not have incentives to manage information for both personal and company benefit. |
| | The Information Management School seeks to address information use in all its forms and to better manage the diverse set of information-related professionals operating in different organizational units such as the corporate library, IT department, telecommunications, and knowledge management units. | Lacking legitimacy from senior management, information life cycle stewardship has often been delegated to low-level operational units or functions. With little authority this discipline did not attempt to influence behavior change of employees' information usage patterns. More recently, advocates of 'knowledge management' have tried to elevate awareness about practices surrounding how people can use and show their knowledge in a business organization. However, knowledge management efforts often fail when they cannot demonstrate direct business performance benefits. |
| Behavior and Control School Human resources (HR) stream | The human resources stream emphasizes the importance of recruiting, motivating, leading, and managing people by hiring and promoting good work behaviors and values. | The human resources stream offers general managerial prescriptions concerning human interactions and organizational behavior, but does not directly address the relationship between the management of people and how people use information and knowledge to achieve organizational goals. |
| | Human resources developed from a support function to a management function and, most recently, to a strategic management concern, as the recruitment and retention of knowledge workers have been critical to business success globally. | Human resources' prevailing 'people' functional focus has separated itself from the 'technical' IT function. Hence, the human resources stream places little emphasis on the role and impact of IT use on people and human behavior. |

| Management school | Strengths | Weaknesses |
| --- | --- | --- |
| | The human resources stream recognizes that the culture (shared values and behaviors) of a company can constrain or enhance business performance | Little is known about the relationship between good information behaviors and values and their effect on information management, decision making, and business performance. |
| Management control stream | The management control stream explicitly recognizes the role of information in managing people and linking their performance to business performance. | Too often, employees have viewed information as a 'control' with negative connotations. This stream fails to consider many key dimensions of organizational behavior, including several concepts refined in the human resources stream that are known to contribute to performance motivation in using information for the company's benefit, such as the role of personal integrity, formality, and transparency. |
| | Information is perceived as a 'positive' lever for managers to use in implementing strategy. | Control is perceived as an important lever for implementing strategy, but not as a lever for managing the relationships between people, information management practices, and IT practices to improve business performance. |
| | Controls can be used to manage the 'tensions' between individual self-interest and willingness to contribute to the company and the abundant business opportunities facing them. Controls can also focus 'attention' on the goal of improved business performance. | Optimizing a company's control mechanisms is extremely difficult and requires continual modifications to keep current. This is even more problematic when control is not integrated with the ways information is managed within the company. |

## 1. THE INFORMATION TECHNOLOGY SCHOOL

The IT School emerged in the 1950s and 1960s from the convergence of two developments. First, there was a rapid advance in the use of second and third generation computers by large businesses and government agencies seeking cost savings and efficiency benefits. Initial applications focused on large numerical and transactional tasks. At that time, many applications of computers in business were driven more by what programmers could do with the technology than by appropriate business need.

The second development arose in the 1950s from the influential work of two groups of scholars. Herbert Simon (1946, 1960) and Richard Cyert and James March (1963) of Carnegie Mellon University greatly enhanced our understanding of decision making by characterizing decisions as structured, semi-structured, and unstructured. They went on to describe the problems associated with programming the unstructured decisions made by most managers.

Meanwhile, Robert Anthony at Harvard Business School refined the concepts on management planning and control systems producing the, now famous, Anthony Pyramid of Operational Control, Managerial Control, and Strategic Planning (Anthony 1965). The early founders of the Management Information Systems (MIS) field employed Anthony's framework. For example, Gordon Davis at the University of Minnesota, in one of the earliest MIS textbooks, used Anthony's work as the foundation for tying the uses of IT to decision making in business (Davis and Olson 1974).

In 1971, in a well-known article published in the *Sloan Management Review* entitled 'A Framework for Management Information Systems,' Anthony Gorry and Michael Scott Morton recognized that business had achieved benefits from automating routine transactions. While the use of computers had grown tremendously in the 1955 to 1971 period, very few of the resulting systems had a significant impact on the way in which managers made decisions. They attributed this deficiency to the lack of management guidance about how to target computer needs and invest appropriately at the managerial and strategic level. To focus attention on managerial and strategic decision making, these scholars integrated the decision making ideas of the Carnegie Mellon scholars with Anthony's Planning and Control Framework to define how information systems and IT should be deployed in organizations. Gorry and Scott Morton's framework targeted 'managerial activities . . . looking for a characterization of organizational activity in terms of types of decisions involved' (Gorry and Scott

Morton 1989: 50).[1] To extend their framework, they used Anthony's planning and control classification of management decisions at three levels: operational control, management control, and strategic planning.

Strategic planning involves decisions about company objectives made by a small group of senior managers and staff in a non-repetitive, often creative manner: 'the complexity of the problems that arise and the non-routine manner in which they are handled, make it quite difficult to appraise the quality of this planning process' (Gorry and Scott Morton 1989: 50). Information for these decisions is mainly collected from external sources outside the business, and varied in frequency and content.

Management control focuses on the resource allocation decisions that need to be made after visions and objectives are clarified. Information for management control is often obtained through human interaction and assists in resolving uncertainty in translating strategies into reasonable work systems as well as addressing surprises presented from both within and outside the organization.

Operational control focuses on the decision processes of assuring that specific tasks are carried out efficiently and effectively. Information needs for operations are well defined, narrow in scope, and repetitive. Since this information is frequently used, its accuracy is critical.

As Fig. 2.1 suggests, the framework also differentiated decisions by whether they were well structured, semi-structured, or unstructured. Relying on Herbert Simon's earlier analysis of decision making, Gorry and Scott Morton noted that decisions could be programmed or non-programmed: 'Decisions are programmed to the extent that they are repetitive and routine, to the extent that a definite procedure has been worked out for handling them so that they don't have to be treated de novo each time they occur. . . . Decisions are non-programmed to the extent that they are novel, unstructured, and consequential' (Gorry and Scott Morton 1989: 52).

Preferring to use the terms 'structured' and 'unstructured', Gorry and Scott Morton identified three decision or problem types. Structured problems were those where the phases of intelligence gathering, option analysis, and choice were well defined. Unstructured problems were those where the three phases of a decision were ill defined. Semi-structured problems were those where one or two of the decision phases were unstructured (Gorry and Scott Morton 1971).

With this framework, Gorry and Scott Morton drew some important implications for MIS investments:

---

[1] This and the following quotes are from the 1989 reprint of Gorry and Scott Morton's article 'A Framework for Management Information Systems' (Gorry and Scott Morton 1989).

| | Operational control | Mangement control (Tactical/planning) | Stragetic planning |
|---|---|---|---|
| Structured | Accounts receivable | Budget analysis– engineered costs | Tanker fleet mix |
| | Order entry | Short-term forecasting | Warehouse and factory location |
| | Inventory control | | |
| Semi-structured | Production scheduling | Variance analysis- overall budget | Mergers and acquisitions |
| | Cash management | Budget preparation | New product planning |
| Unstructured | PERT/COST systems | Sales and production | R & D planning |

Fig. 2.1. Information Systems: A Framework

*Source*: Gorry and Scott Morton (1971)

First, they noted that most MIS investments were in support of operational control applications, and not in support of strategic or management control decisions that have a significant impact on the company.

Second, they argued that information systems should be centered on the important decisions of the business that tended to be unstructured and strategic. The authors concluded that the human skills to build systems above and below the dotted line on Fig. 2.1 were fundamentally different. To build databases and software systems that support managers took more than technical skills. MIS professionals needed a basic understanding of the business decision making context. For unstructured decisions, information needs varied significantly and managers needed to be actively involved in identifying their key decisions, and their associated information needs if MIS specialists were to properly design decision support systems.

As MIS gained academic status as a field in university business schools in the United States during the 1970s and 1980s, this decision making/planning and control framework was employed in many MIS textbooks, and used by IS professionals as the basis for both teaching and practice in business. Firms such as IBM and the large consultancies employed similar frameworks in marketing new computer applications and services to businesses globally. Information systems development techniques targeted the decisional context as the basis for information requirements analysis. And, over time, attempts were made to migrate IT applications up the decisional grid, from operational to strategic decision making.

Throughout the 1980s and into the 1990s considerable investments were made in building interactive decision support systems[2] (DSS) to assist in the unstructured decision making of middle managers, in customizing executive support systems (ESS) to help senior managers track their critical success factors,[3] and in designing experts systems[4] to convey the knowledge of the expert to the lesser informed. Following this trend Gorry and Scott Morton in 1989 reaffirmed the appropriateness of their decision-centered view as a basis for IT investment. They indicated that advances in decision support systems were highly dependent on managers taking ownership in the implementation, as well as planning, of such projects. They concluded that if IT was to have a significant impact on productivity in services sectors of the economy, then substantial progress would have to continue in applying IT for management support and innovation (Gorry and Scott Morton 1989: 59).

While some DSS success stories did emerge during the 1980s, there were many failures. Excitement waned for a DSS 'silver bullet' as it was realized that designing IT applications for unstructured decisions was far more difficult than building transactional systems. It became obvious that the dynamic nature of the business environment combined with a lack of understanding of how people behave in using information for decision making prevented widespread immediate usage of these technologies. Large investments in DSS, ESS, and experts systems began to be challenged in corporate boardrooms. The days of unbridled enthusiasm and unlimited IT budgets were drawing to an end as senior managers increasingly demanded careful justification of the payoffs derived from IT applications for managerial support.

While IT innovations continued to surface in the marketplace at a blinding pace, the number of failed or disappointing IT investments were increasingly being documented in the popular press. Failures such as the abandonment of the five-year Taurus project in the London financial markets, in this case at a cost of £80 million to the London Stock Exchange and £400 million to the City of London, provide high profile endorsement to underlying disquiet on this issue (Currie 1994). Senior managers increasingly viewed IT investments as high-risk, hidden-cost projects with a variety of factors including size and complexity of the project, the newness of the technology, the degree of 'structuredness' of the decisions, and major

---

[2] For example, see the works of Keen and Scott Morton (1979), Alter (1980), and Sprague and Watson (1986).

[3] For example, see the works of Rockart (1979), Rockart and Bullen (1986), and Rockart and Delong (1988).

[4] For example, see the works of Winston (1984), and Luconi, Malone, and Scott Morton (1986).

people, political, and cultural factors compounding risk (Willcock and Margetts 1993). Managers often complained they faced a 'Catch 22'. For competitive reasons they could not afford not to invest in IT, but economically they could not find sufficient justification, and IT measurement practice did not provide enough underpinning for making IT investment decisions (Willcock 1992b).

To answer managers' cries for better measures, the later 1980s and early 1990s saw considerable amounts of research energy expended in attempting to empirically demonstrate the positive effect of IT, and its improving practices, on business performance. Unfortunately for these researchers, little evidence surfaced indicating a direct causal link between IT investments and sustained business performance gains (Turner 1985; Weill 1989; Farbey, Land, and Targett 1992). Some researchers in the IT School refocused their attention on macro measurement of economic data to address the so-called 'productivity paradox' (Brynjolfsson and Hitt 1996; Hitt and Brynjolfsson 1996), while other researchers such as Kettinger, Grover, Guha, and Segars (1994) continued their investigation at the company unit of analysis and found that the link between IT and business performance was far more complex than many earlier IT researchers had surmised. Their research indicated that a company's IT practices were but one dimension in a set of important 'Foundation Factors' that interact with management's 'Action Strategies' to determine higher performance. Kettinger et al. (1994) moved beyond demonstrating a direct IT investment to performance linkage, taking a more integrated perspective by placing IT in the context of other company foundation factors such as: the *organizational base* (people's competence to exploit IT opportunity); *learning curve* (ability of the people in an organization to acquire and manage knowledge); and *information resources* (the richness and content of an organization's knowledge base and information management practices). Using this more contingent and integrated research approach, they found that sustained competitive advantage can be achieved in some cases.

### Strengths of the IT School

While IT has advanced significantly in the 1990s, and IT investments have grown enormously for business worldwide, the decision-centered approach to IT development retains its central role in examining IT investments in business for four key reasons.

First, the decision-centered view focuses on the changing dynamics of management decisions. Our understanding of managerial decisions and problems has increased over the years with the studies from such noted scholars as Simon (1946), Mintzberg (1973), Weick (1979), Mason and Mitroff (1981), and Schein (1985), and others, on personal managerial styles, organizational cultures, and team versus individual problem solving. Thus, the link between the type of decision and an appropriate IT response remains a strong feature of this approach, and efficiently targets IT development resources directly on a decision-based problem.

Second, IT professionals have been internal advocates for moving the onslaught of technical advances to the firm. Advances in IT have, in recent years, facilitated the development of increasing numbers of successful information systems that support business processes and tactical decision making. This continued injection of IT in support of operations and business processes has fundamentally changed the nature of companies and many industries. However, even with scientific advances in simulation, graphical presentation, and telecommunications, IT has not seen the same level of success in strategic decision making or in support of research and development.

Third, senior managers continue to be concerned about the appropriate allocation of IT resources across the strategic, tactical, and operational levels of decision making. There continues to be an imbalance between IT skills and resources in support of operations in contrast to IT support for innovation in products and services, or for improving managerial decision making. So, the decision-centered view of IT development and investments continues to be useful in pinpointing misalignments between IT resources allocations, levels of decision making, and business strategies. In this regard the IT School should be commended for their serious commitment to establishing measures to determine the payoff of IT investments.

### Weaknesses of the IT School

We believe that the IT School's decision-centered view has three weaknesses:

First, while classical management theory recognizes that good information reduces uncertainty in decision making, it has offered few real prescriptions to the managers interested in better understanding specifically how people use information in ways that go beyond the rigidity of the programmed IT system. In fact, the very strength of the decision-centered view tends to obscure the role of good information usage practices beyond the formal IT system. And, as decisions move up the organizational hierarchy and become less structured and less automated, the role of good information practices becomes even more opaque.

Second, senior managers are still perplexed concerning the ultimate pay-off for their IT-related investment and how this investment relates to their people. Managers are still asking for solid evaluation measures to determine whether their information usage is effective. Many executives' questions remain unanswered. For example, how specifically does our IT investment help our people work together to achieve our goals? How do our IT investments in a particular group affect the overall company's information practices? What is the relationship between collecting, organizing, and processing information for different levels of decision making? And how do the levels of integrity and transparency possessed by our people result in promoting the sharing of information among managers for problem solving and improved decision making?

Third, IT developments and practices have emphasized the technical aspects of data management rather than the behavioral sides of information use and IT. The focus on how people use information in daily work lives and, in particular, how their culture promotes or constrains effective information use for decision making is still poorly understood by many senior managers and IT specialists.

In sum, the IT School has made an important contribution over the years to advancing the use of IT though formalized management activities and focusing it on a decision-centered framework for developing information systems in business. While the IT School mentions the importance of information to the firm, this school has not devoted much attention to the assessment of information value, people's behaviors surrounding information use, or its management. This may explain why the connection in the minds of senior managers between IT investments and business performance remains elusive or unsatisfactory in many companies.

## 2.  THE INFORMATION MANAGEMENT SCHOOL

The Information Management School has its roots in the late nineteenth and early twentieth century when the large, diversified corporations in industries such as railroads, oil, retailing, and trading developed in the United States and Europe. As these companies grew and spread their business reach over nations and continents, the physical need to manage information across the business in the form of paper, records, mail, telegraph messages, and phone calls expanded as well (Beniger 1986).

Companies had to organize themselves to improve the efficiency for handling these physical media and tools as well as define the first policies, procedures, and disciplines focused on managing the paperwork, records, mail correspondence, office design, and directives/instructions. With the growth of the accounting and auditing professions, and increased government regulation of business during the first half of the twentieth century, came the basic practices for handling paper, records, communications, and calculations in the business.

Starting in the mid-1950s, a series of new office-based technologies were deployed in corporations to handle information. Beginning with second and third generation mainframe computers and proceeding to electronic copiers, word processing technology, mini-computers, personal computers, and further developments in telecommunications, the information handling tools entered the corporation at an increasing rate. With each set of developments, new technical professionals entered the business to manage these technologies. Much of the focus of these new people and units was on managing the new technologies rather than the information, which was largely perceived to be the responsibility of the business units.

During the late 1960s, around the same time that the IT School developed frameworks for tying IT investments to decision making, the modern Information Management School emerged (Horton 1968). This new school of consultants, academics, corporate, and government managers was concerned about treating information as an organizational resource, and better managing the proliferation of media and new technologies which were being introduced in corporations and government agencies at an accelerating rate. By the mid-1970s, the Information Management School labeled this new trend Information Resources Management or IRM, and began introducing the basic principles for managing information into the US federal government and large corporations.[5]

The first principle of IRM was that information management needed to better balance the concerns of introducing new technologies and media with the treatment of information as a key resource in the firm.[6] As a resource, information had to be managed like other important resources such as people, finances, materials, and physical technologies. In contrast to the IT School, the Information Management School argued that perhaps the pendulum had swung too far. Managers in organizations needed to focus on the use, relevance, and quality of information, as well as the management of information technologies, if the value of investments in information and IT were to achieve appropriate performance results for the organization.

---

[5] See *Managing Information Resources: U.S. Commission on Federal Paperwork* (1977).

[6] See Synnott and Gruber (1981), Horton and Marchand (1982), and Marchand and Horton (1986).

The second principle of IRM required managers to deal with information, not just as a set of objects or artifacts such as data or files, but also as a process that extended from information's identification (sensing), collection, and organization through its processing, use, and maintenance. The basic idea underlying this process is that information has a 'life cycle', from creation through use in decision making and subsequent disposal, that managers in an organization need to understand and address, if they want to capitalize on their information's potential value. Management of the information life cycle requires a company's managers to appropriately plan, budget for, evaluate, and use information efficiently and effectively (Horton 1985; Synnott 1987; McGee and Prusak 1993).

The third principle of IRM followed from the first and second. The shift to treating information as a resource implied that resource management techniques such as planning, costing, budgeting, and evaluating should be applied to information just as they were applied to other resources. To do so, required a new function that would act as the focal point for managing information resources, as well as help integrate the deployment of diverse information technologies, such as telecommunications, computing, and office technologies (Horton and Marchand 1982). During the late 1970s and 1980s, the increasing digital convergence of these technologies suggested that IRM advocates take a new look at the relationships between diverse middle management functions. The data processing or MIS department, the telecommunications unit, the duplication and mail rooms, as well as other support units, such as corporate libraries and information centers, could be integrated into more effective units, to service the overall information needs of the company or government agency (Synnott and Gruber 1981).

Such proposals for major realignments of IT and information units in a new IRM function raised significant controversy, since technical and information specialists were very protective of their professional autonomy and newly gained status in organizations.

The fourth principle of IRM was the notion that this function needed to be positioned not as a support function, but as a management function like finance and human resources management (Marchand and Horton 1986; Synnott 1987). Also, to head this new management function, there needed to be a senior manager reporting to the CEO or to another senior manager such as the chief financial officer. This individual would be called the IRM director in a public agency or the chief information officer (CIO) in a company (Marchand and Horton 1986; Synnott 1987).

This new position called for a different breed of manager, able to understand the management of information and IT in the context of the business, or mission of a government agency. During the 1980s, the CIO concept was much debated and advocated between both IRM and IT proponents, with one camp emphasizing technological, and the other camp emphasizing information, concerns. By the 1990s, many corporations in the USA had adopted the CIO concept, and had appointed managers from primarily IT backgrounds to head this function with mixed results. Where these managers could gain the credibility of the senior management team in companies, they were included in strategic decisions and problem solving, bringing in their unique blend of technology, information, and business knowledge. Where they could not gain the acceptance of senior managers, or where IT and information management were regarded as cost centers and support functions, the CIOs were relegated to middle management ranks (Grover et al. 1993). In other cases, the CIO position turned over rapidly in many companies—so much so that in some companies the abbreviation CIO came to stand for Career Is Over!

The IRM movement has evolved gradually in the public sector in the USA and other countries over the last ten to fifteen years.[7] In the private sector, the IRM movement was short lived in the 1980s, as many MIS managers began to call themselves CIOs and vice-presidents of IT or IS. In these cases, the CIO label connotes a senior officer whose principal focus is to manage IT, and let the business manage information. Some IRM critics suggested that the waning of IRM is due to the fact that information cannot be 'managed' directly or explicitly (King and Kramer 1988). Others have suggested that IRM, as a resource-based approach, was more suited to the public sector than the business context. Still others have noted that IRM may have passed, but not the importance of information management in companies or to senior managers. Finally, some argue that basic components of the popular concept of 'knowledge management' have much of their foundation in IRM and the information management school of thought.

### Strengths of the Information Management School

As executives, consultants, and academics have become more aware of the powerful role information plays in the business, the IM School has grown into a formalized management discipline in many industries. Today, the quality, relevance, and use of customer, competitive, and operational information differentiates firms in many industries from chemicals, concrete, and oil, to insurance, banking, and retailing.

---

[7] Refer to: Caudle et al. (1989) and Fletcher et al. (1992).

Thomas Davenport warns companies that have not formalized information practices that 'our fascination with technology has made us forget the key purpose of information: to inform people' (Davenport 1997: 3). A key strength of the Information Management School is the spotlight it places on managing information as a resource and formalizing this management process.

In addition, senior managers in many industries have increasingly recognized the use of information inside companies for learning and adapting to changes in competition and markets as a competitive advantage. What a company knows and how it uses its knowledge and information have, in recent years, been recognized as an essential dimension of 'knowledge management'—a movement which relies on good information management to locate, share, and leverage knowledge residing with people in a company.

Managing information as a process has highlighted the second strength of the Information Management School, which brings focus on the formal management practices employed to sense, collect, organize, process, and maintain information to enhance or constrain its use and relevance for decision making. The process management view of the information life cycle has focused on systematically improving the relevance, quality, and use of information for decision making in organizations. Treating information as a resource, with a life cycle, meant that processes had to be actively designed to link information from individual to institutional databases. It required sensing for relevant information, assignment of a relative value to the information, design of a way to continue to capture, classify, and index the information, and procedures to share and maintain its value with others in the organization.

The third strength of the Information Management School has been to identify the numerous staff and operational activities in a business that are information related. A key insight of the Information Management School is the recognition that a business uses information in many forms beyond what can be automated by IT, and that these other uses and forms of information are also important to how the business achieves results. Tom Davenport has identified four approaches to information management that have evolved over the twentieth century (Davenport 1997: 16–23).

The first approach deals with the use of 'unstructured information'. Market researchers, product developers, executive assistants, and middle managers act as the sensors, collectors, and organizers of unstructured information taken from books, reports, newsletters, and other sources of external information as well as from internal reports, memos, and special studies. These people rely heavily on the expertise of corporate librarians, marketing departments, R & D centers, and competitive intelligence units in obtaining useful information. These information professionals sift through huge amounts of printed materials and organize them in 'special collections', files, and libraries for use by diverse corporate staff and managers with ad hoc information needs. Increasingly, unstructured information is available on the Internet and through specialized on-line services. Yet the expertise and skills of information specialists (often called 'content managers' when they are responsible for managing web-based information) to search for, organize, and make available information in usable forms will remain in great demand.

The second approach to information concerns the knowledge that all members of a company have in their heads, and use within the company each day. Many firms have referred to this approach as 'knowledge management', even though the way knowledge is used by people and combined with information sources is not well understood by companies. How do people share their knowledge and develop new knowledge? How well do people convert their 'tacit' knowledge in their heads into documents, databases, and processes that other members of the business can understand and use? Davenport observes that this form of information is 'messy' and 'sprawling' across people and groups in a business. It is very difficult to 'control' in the direction of realizing business objectives and results (Davenport 1997: 18).

The third form of information is unstructured information on paper. This form was 'managed' historically as 'records management', and later as document management, which could be automated through systems for handling and communicating documents around the company. These documents recorded the actual work and notes of people in the company. In many ways, the focus on records management had more to do with storing and maintaining this type of information, than helping people in companies use it better. Most of the handling of unstructured information on paper, or in documents, is still done by individuals for themselves, or in small work groups and functional departments, such as accounting, sales, marketing, and others. Most people maintain their 'personal' filing systems, in addition to what companies and departments have available. These personal systems are used as their repositories of important knowledge to gain recognition and rewards on the job.

The fourth type of information management is 'structured information' in computer systems. For the last thirty years, IT professionals have been mostly concerned with this type of information. The information, which was automated, was the data that could be structured in computer files, records, and databases. Other forms of information often did not 'count' for

IT professionals, since they concentrated on data that was quantitative and transaction based and could be programmed for computers. Not surprisingly, most IT systems today still focus on automating data in processes that are either: (*a*) well defined and structured at the operational level; or (*b*) in summary form at the tactical level for managing processes and for exception reporting to managers.

While the Information Management School has pointed out that information management in business extends well beyond what IT can automate, the IT community of professionals, managers, industry firms, and press has been confident that, as technology advances, most approaches to information management will become susceptible to IT 'solutions'. Thus, as Davenport has wryly noted, 'we continue to ignore the real problems, re-assuring ourselves that technological progress means information progress' (Davenport 1997: 24).

### Weaknesses of the Information Management School

While the strengths of the Information Management School have been in part to focus on 'information' while the IT School in practice has focused on 'technology', key weaknesses of the Information Management School are also evident.

The first weakness of the Information Management School has been to aspire, in theory, to more than what it could do in practice. Records and paperwork managers, librarians, IRM practitioners, web content managers have all aspired to manage information as a resource in all its structured and unstructured forms; however, these aspirations have not been implemented in practice. Managing and valuing information is very difficult and no well-recognized approach for doing this has become standard practice. This problem is worsened when people in organizations do not have incentives to manage information for both personal and company benefit.

In addition, the proliferation of data in all forms throughout a company's activities and processes continues unabated and is accelerating with the use of Internet, Intranets, and Extranets in companies. Ironically, the IT industry and professionals are correct in observing that many forms of data today can be automated and used anywhere in a company by anyone. However, the central problem of managers remains—limited attention and time to search for information in advance of decisions—and more information in every form than they can process. While the gains in improved information practices by information professionals are incremental, the proliferation of IT and data in structured and unstructured forms is exponential. So the information problem continues despite the best efforts by information specialists to build awareness of and manage information as a valuable resource.

The second weakness of the Information Management School follows from the first. While the Information Management School has sought to raise senior manager perceptions of the importance of information management functions to the business, the delivery of significant business results through efforts to improve information use and IT in many companies has been disappointing.

The third major weakness of the Information Management School is that while this stream offers insight into how to effectively manage information as a resource, it never focused on testing an empirical link between effective information management and business performance. Without strong business performance improvement evidence that such an approach pays off, senior executives are not compelled to support this school's endeavors (Galliers 1995).

So, lacking focus as a senior management activity, information life cycle stewardship has often been delegated to low-level operations units or functions. More recently, advocates of knowledge management have tried to elevate the management awareness about, and call attention to, better information management practices surrounding how people can use and share their knowledge in a business organization (Nonaka and Takeuchi 1995).

## 3. THE BEHAVIOR AND CONTROL SCHOOL

Unlike the IT School's decision theory, or the Information Management School's life cycle theory, there is no comprehensive theory within the scholarly literature on instilling effective information usage behaviors. Instead, this school is less clearly defined, but draws its greatest influence from two broad streams of academic research—the human resources stream and the management control stream.

As discussed in Chapter 1, unlike the IT School and the Information Management School, there has not developed a management discipline around information usage behaviors and values. Instead, instilling good information usage behaviors and values has been tangentially treated as a component of general management or sometimes as an afterthought in personnel evaluations of employees. Yet, as Chapter 1 points out, developing a people-centric view of effective information use is necessary if we are to gain a broader understanding of how and why companies use information effectively.

We decided to tap two well-respected and related research disciplines to gain insight on behavioral and control concepts that might be tailored to the information use context. The first stream—human resources stream—focuses on the resources management function that has evolved around the management of people. Management practices dealing with people have developed in response to periodic shifts in social and business views of the relationship between employees and employers, workers, and productive processes, as well as human motivation and organizational demands. The tensions inherent in alternative approaches to organize work have fostered strong practitioner and academic views of how people should be managed in business organizations. These range from the Scientific Management perspective of Frederick Taylor, through the human relations school of the 1940s and 1950s. During the 1960s, 'organizational behavior', as a broad field of study influenced by the social sciences, especially psychology and sociology, initiated an ongoing debate about human motivation, leadership, and organizational design.

The second stream has focused on how to direct the way people behave and work to the achievement of the organizational objectives and results. This stream is most closely tied to the history of the accounting profession during the twentieth century, as well as to the specific concerns over 'management control'. During the late 1980s and 1990s, accounting and financial control practices have been criticized for losing their relevance. Now executives must assure that controls are tied to business performance related to customers, processes, and services, rather than to financial indicators alone. Having the appropriate information for control has become a key point of ongoing debate among managers and academics interested in rethinking the ways managers and employees exercise control in the new business organization of the 1990s.

## A. From administering people to mobilizing people

The history of managing people in organizations during the twentieth century can be divided into three broad phases. The first phase occurred before the Second World War and was directly tied to the rise of mass production and the industrial corporation. Labor unrest, coupled with periodic labor shortages, spawned the first personnel departments. Their main responsibilities were to hire, manage, and compensate workers in order to minimize interruptions to the mass production processes employed in large companies during this period. Personnel officers focused on labor relations to deal with the rise of unionism and worker unrest, on the one hand, and with new methods to improve productivity, on the other. This was fostered by the Scientific Management thinking of Frederick Taylor that viewed people and work as objects of study, improvement, and direct control (Caudron 1997).

During the 1930s, personnel administration developed as a function in most large companies. Personnel professionals looked beyond basic employment and labor practices to improve employment motivation and input as reflected in the 'Hawthorne studies'. This report revealed that when employees have a say in their work, they are likely to enjoy their work and be more productive.

The second phase of personnel management started during the Second World War, as the war effort required personnel departments to recruit women into the workforce, and to treat people more as individuals, better understanding their motivations and taking steps to satisfy them. After the Second World War, the human relations school became very popular as returning GIs were recruited into the workforce of a booming post-war economy (Schuler 1995).

As the large multidivisional company developed in the 1950s, personnel departments designed elaborate career ladders and training programs to reward and motivate managers and employees. Employees were in need of 'considerate supervision' which, in the 1960s, was translated into more employee involvement in decisions as well as more 'participative management'.

During the 1960s, under the strong influence of psychology, the field of organizational behavior developed and focused on understanding the sources of motivation, methods of leadership, and improved group dynamics in organizations. However, the 1960s and 1970s were contentious periods, when new social, racial, and environmental pressures were coupled with dissatisfaction over the traditional ways companies were managed and controlled.

By the late 1970s, the third phase of managing people in the business evolved as companies began to drop the term 'personnel' and focus on 'human resources' (HR) to signify efforts to better manage people to boost corporate productivity. However, just as employee empowerment and quality improvement programs were taking hold in the 1980 and 1990s, senior managers began to downsize, restructure, and delayer companies. Human resources managers now became responsible for handling outplacement, retraining, and restructuring. At the same time, they were charged with finding new ways of motivating employees to directly contribute to business performance improvements in response to the elimination or delayering of middle management ranks.

As the twenty-first century unfolds, human resources no longer considers itself a support function, but a management function, handling the strategic issues involved with people, their behaviors, and management in business.

### Strengths of the human resources stream

For the purpose of this study, there are three major strengths of this movement of personnel administration to human resource management as noted in Table 2.1.

The first strength is that 'people count' not simply as organic parts of industrial machines, methods, and processes. People are living, thinking, feeling beings with intellects, values, motivations, and need to interact as individuals and members of groups to achieve organizational purposes. Most companies today subscribe to the view that 'people are our most important asset' in a global economy, where knowledge and its use are critical to competitive survival and advantage. Senior managers recognize the importance of motivating, leading, and managing people as a critical responsibility and not as human resources' responsibility alone.

Second, the evolution of human resources from a support function to a management function and as a strategic concern of senior managers, has come when most companies are feeling the effects of three key trends. These are:

1. the increasing globalization of industries and companies;
2. the shift to knowledge- and information-based competition; and
3. the impact of intense labor shortages among knowledge workers in many industries.

These trends are challenging senior managers to focus on people at precisely the time that the availability of talented persons is likely to be the most serious constraint in achieving business growth, innovation, and customer value in the new economy.

The third strength of this shift to emphasizing people as key assets or resources is the growing recognition that a company's culture 'counts'. But, more importantly, company culture can have 'a significant impact on a firm's long-term economic performance' as John Kotter and James Heskett pointed out in their influential book entitled *Corporate Culture and Performance* (Kotter and Heskett 1992: 11). They define 'organizational culture as having two levels, which differ in terms of their visibility and their resistance to change':

> At the deeper and less visible level, culture refers to values that are shared by the people in a group and that tend to persist over time when group membership changes.

At the more visible level, culture represents the behavior patterns or style of an organization that new employees are automatically encouraged to follow by their fellow employees. (Kotter and Heskett 1992: 4)

For Kotter and Heskett, company cultures can enhance or degrade business performance by either encouraging, or inhibiting, companies from adopting or implementing key strategies or actions. While Kotter and Heskett note that cultures are always difficult to change, they can be made more 'performance enhancing': 'Such change is complex, takes time, and requires leadership. . . . That leadership must be guided by a realistic vision of what kinds of cultures enhance business performance' (Kotter and Heskett 1992: 12).

## Weaknesses of the human resources stream

While the strengths of the human resources and people-focused view of management are significant, there are, nevertheless, three weaknesses related to this stream's approach to information, technology, and people's information usage behaviors.

The first weakness of the human resources stream is that it offers general management prescriptions concerning human interactions and organizational behavior, but does little to directly address the relationship between the management of people and how people use information and knowledge to achieve organizational goals. Understanding the ways people sense, collect, organize, process, and maintain information was never a major part of studies about culture, human motivation, leadership, or human behavior in organizations.

Similarly, the second weakness follows in part from the first. Human resources professionals and academics also did not place much emphasis on the role and impacts of IT use in companies on people and human behavior. One has to look far and wide in the literature of human resources management to find studies of how IT practices have influenced work practices, human behaviors or organizational values. While a handful of researchers from the IT School did concern themselves early on with socio-technical design issues in building and implementing systems,[8] the human resources field has been fairly silent on this topic. It is only since the 1980s that studies of IT practices in companies have begun to see popular

[8] A small group of IT researchers, primarily from the UK, did some pioneering work on 'socio-technical design' whereby they focused on the reciprocal relationship that IT had on people and conversely that people had on IT use and implementation success. For example, see *The Ethics Method* of Enid Mumford and Mary Weir (1979) and Bostrom and Heinen (1977a, 1977b).

recognition. For example, Shoshana Zuboff's influential book *In the Age of the Smart Machine* (1984) highlighted the impacts of computerization on the nature of work, human behavior, and management of people. It appears that, for most of the history of personnel and human resources practice and research, there has been little or no link between IT practices and the values and behaviors of people in companies.

The third weakness of the human resources stream is associated with the organizational behavior literature's lack of practical emphasis on how people use information effectively. During the 1950s and into the 1970s, there was a theoretical focus on the nature of decision making and information processing in organizations. The debates over 'comprehensive' versus 'bounded' rationality developed by scholars such as Herbert Simon (1946, 1960), Charles Lindblom (1959) at Yale University, and later by James Cyert and James March (1963) at Carnegie Mellon University, emphasized the importance of limited human and organizational attention as critical to the ways decisions were made in organizations. Jay Galbraith, in his influential book entitled *Organization Design* in 1977, relied on these scholars and the work of James Thompson (1967) to articulate a model of organizational design based on 'information processing'. However, the links between how people in organizations make decisions, and how they use and manage information in practice, were never fully explored by these authors.

As a result, organizational behavior as it relates to information use remained an ancillary area of research. While scholars and management practitioners developed comprehensive ways to formalize both IT deployment and information management processes within their organizations, the role of people within these frameworks remained on the fringe of these two activities.

While the theories of these pioneers of decision making in organizations were no doubt influential to managers and scholars, the actual study of how people in organizations used information for decision making languished in business schools and practice. It was not until 1992 that Sharon McKinnon and William Bruns, Jr. published their book called *Information Mosaic* which empirically examined how managers in manufacturing companies actually use information (McKinnon and Bruns 1992). Interestingly, both McKinnon and Bruns were professors of accounting looking at how financial and non-financial information were actually employed by managers in decision making—the focus of our second stream in the Behavior and Control School.

## B. From financial control to control as a lever for strategy implementation

The second stream in the Behavior and Control School exhibits the strongest focus on the role of information in influencing how people act in pursuit of appropriate business objectives and results. The historical roots of this stream are in the accounting profession, and the development of performance criteria and measures that managers can use to motivate, evaluate, and reward the behaviors of people in pursuit of business success. Unlike the previous stream of human resources and organizational behavior, this stream has focused on financial information management and use since its origins in the nineteenth century. However, the value of financial performance criteria and measures, as well as the associated information use in companies, came under severe criticism from within the accounting profession in the 1980s and 1990s.

In tune with this criticism, two professors of accounting, Thomas Johnson and Robert Kaplan, published an influential book provocatively entitled *Relevance Lost: The Rise and Fall of Management Accounting* (Johnson and Kaplan 1987). Basically, the authors argued that, while bookkeeping had been invented thousands of years ago, and double entry bookkeeping 500 years ago, the demand for management accounting information—'information about transactions occurring within organizations'—had really started in the early nineteenth century. As corporations grew in scale, and required significant investments in financial capital to operate production processes and facilities, the need arose for measuring the 'conversion costs' of inputs to outputs and the costs of production, including labor, relative to prices of products sold.

During the nineteenth and first quarter of the twentieth century, management accounting approaches and information systems were created to promote efficiency in the key operating activities of the company. Owners and managers used this information to manage the company directly. Financial reporting to creditors was separate from management accounting inside the firm. By 1925, 'virtually all management accounting practices used today had been developed: cost accounts for labor, material, and overhead; budgets for cash, income, and capital; flexible budgets, sales forecasts, standard costs, variance analysis, transfer prices, and divisional performance measures' (Johnson and Kaplan 1987: 12).

After the 1920s, corporations continued to grow and change in product diversity and complexity, yet they employed largely the same management accounting approaches. One reason for this 'stagnation' was the shift in the accounting profession to 'external reporting and accounting' and the growing dominance of financial accounting over managerial accounting for operating the company. The rise of external financial reporting coupled with the stagnation of basic accounting approaches in measuring performance in manufacturing and service businesses over the next sixty years resulted in disconnecting financial performance criteria and measures from the customer, competitive, and operational information required to manage the firm.

During the 1950s to 1980s, as Thomas Johnson argues in his later book, *Relevance Regained*, the 'dark ages of relevance lost' occurred as businesses used predominantly financial information to direct management decisions at two levels:

1. 'to plan the extent and financing of the enterprise as a whole'; and
2. 'to control the work of individuals and subordinate production units' (Johnson 1992: 17).

While Johnson had no quarrel with using financial information to plan the extent and financing of the firm as a whole, he noted that using 'top-down accounting to control operations' became the central feature of 'post-1950s management accounting'. This emphasis resulted in a form of 'remote control' management focused on financial control and reporting inside and outside the firm that often overlooked basic operational or management support information to guide and run the business successfully (Johnson 1992: 18).

For Johnson and his colleagues, changing business conditions and imperatives in the 1990s such as globalization, short product cycles, responsiveness to customers, flexibility, and new IT required a radical shift from a top-down control cycle to a bottom-up empowerment cycle as Fig. 2.2 suggests. The key to competitiveness 'is management information that relates the goals and actions of company personnel to the appropriate imperatives' (Johnson 1992: 57). Thus, identifying the right management information to be responsive to customers, and to be flexible with processes and products, is important. Using information to link customers to employees with the right financial and non-financial performance metrics of the company is a major challenge for senior managers.

### Strengths of the management control stream

From the perspective of this study, this 'management control' stream of the Behavior and Control School possesses some important strengths and corresponding weaknesses.

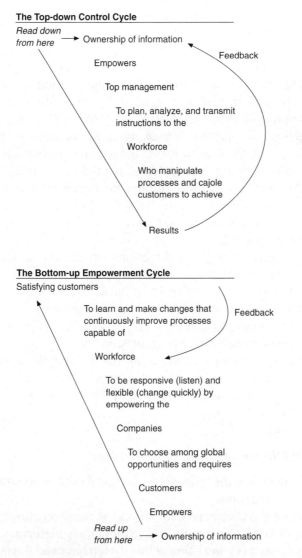

**The Top-down Control Cycle**

*Read down from here* → Ownership of information

Feedback

Empowers

Top management

To plan, analyze, and transmit instructions to the

Workforce

Who manipulate processes and cajole customers to achieve

Results

**The Bottom-up Empowerment Cycle**

Satisfying customers

To learn and make changes that continuously improve processes capable of

Feedback

Workforce

To be responsive (listen) and flexible (change quickly) by empowering the

Companies

To choose among global opportunities and requires

Customers

Empowers

*Read up from here* → Ownership of information

**Fig. 2.2. Johnson's Top-down Control vs. Bottom-up Empowerment Cycles**

*Source*: Adapted from Johnson (1992)

The first strength of this stream is the explicit emphasis on the role of information for managing people and relating their performance to the company's performance. Developing and using the right financial and non-financial performance criteria and measures are critical for the management control stream. In contrast to the Information Management School where there is no direct linkage between information management and performance, the management control stream seeks to link the right performance metrics associated with customer, competitive, and operational information to the behaviors and values of people in the company.

The second strength of this stream is that information is perceived as a 'positive' lever for managers to use for implementing strategy. Robert Simons, in his book entitled *The Levers of Control*, defines 'management control systems' as 'the formal, information-based routines and procedures that managers use to maintain or alter patterns in organizational activities' (Simons 1995: 5). For Simons, control is the way managers guide their companies towards implementing strategy and achieving a balance between control and innovation: 'Control implies managing the inherent tension between creative innovation, on the one hand, and predictable goal achievement, on the other, so that both are transformed into profitable growth' (Simons 1995: 158).

Finally, the third strength of the management control stream is the increasing recognition that appropriate controls exist to manage the tensions inherent in most companies. These tensions appear not as 'ors' but as 'ands': between individual self-interest and willingness to contribute to the company and between pursuing intended strategy diligently and still being flexible enough to incorporate 'emergent' strategies to pursue endless business opportunities. As Robert Simons has noted: 'The management of the attention of people in a company is the "scarcest" and perhaps the most precious resource that must be allocated in the direction of creating business value' (Simons 1995: 16).

### Weaknesses of the management control stream

The key weaknesses in the management control stream from the perspective of this study are three.

First, although the management control stream recognizes the role of information in managing people and relating their performance to business performance, a key weakness of this stream has been the failure to use performance-based information well to motivate people to continuously relate their personal performance to the company's business performance. Often, information for 'control' has either been poorly communicated with organizational members, or been viewed with negative connotations. For example, employees may charge that managers are only 'sharing' performance-based information of the business unit or company to get them to work harder, not better or smarter.

The second weakness of the management control stream is that, while control is perceived as an important lever for implementing strategy, it is not viewed as a lever for managing the relationships between people, information management practices, and IT practices. Most of the current efforts to improve information management for control have tended to overemphasize financial information and measures. Even where control efforts, such as the Balanced Scorecard (Kaplan and Norton 1992, 1993, 1996c) or Value-Based Management (Bannister and Jesuthasan 1997; Slater and Olson 1996; Rappaport 1992), have managed to include non-financial information such as customer satisfaction, business process performance, and personnel development and learning, the primary focus has been on measures of bottom-line business performance, rather than on including a component that examined how the company could make its people more effective in using information and IT to achieve organizational goals.

The third weakness of this stream focuses not on the 'theory' of control, but on the difficulties of optimizing control levers to keep up with rapid and continuous changes in business conditions. What the advocates of this stream have failed to realize fully is that the best business measures and controls cannot be effectively implemented without direct connections to the ways people in companies use information and IT to improve business performance. Good management of information about controls is not sufficient by itself, unless it is an integral part of the way a company manages people, information management practices, and IT practices to improve business performance.

Finally, this stream fails to consider other key dimensions of organizational behavior, including several concepts refined in the human resources stream, which contribute to performance motivation. This stream is particularly deficient in explicitly drawing out the relationships between information-based control and such behaviors as reliance on formal information and personal integrity in information sharing and use. For example, how does the role of formality influence the acceptance of information-based control? Or, what effect does control have on making organizations' members more transparent, not only in sharing performance information but also in communicating information concerning their errors and failures? In this regard, this stream has failed to fully examine the role information sharing has on motivating people to improve their performance and act as proactive employees.

In sum, while both the human resources and control streams have contributed to our understanding of behavioral motivation, neither school has developed a holistic model showing the effect that 'good' personal information usage behaviors have on improved company-wide information management or business performance. While attempts have been made to come at these issues through better understanding of the relationship between personal motivation and improved innovation and learning, neither stream has shown us how to create a workforce that is ready to proactively use information to achieve organizational purposes—to sense for reliable new competitive threats in the environment and opportunities for product and service innovation as well as to analyze this information to make informed decisions. A more integrated approach that combines the important contribution of the human resources and control streams—a people-centric viewpoint—with the more traditional and formalized management activities of IT and information management is needed if we are to have a more unified theory of how people use information effectively.

## 4. CONCLUSIONS

In this chapter, we have examined the three broad schools of management thinking and practice that have, over the course of the last century, shaped the ways people, information, and IT are viewed by managers. In reviewing the history and evolution of the IT, Information Management, and Behavior and Control schools, we have been amazed, but not surprised, that there have been so few real interactions or connections between the three schools, particularly in recent decades.

In many ways, these three schools of management thinking have promoted and, at the same time, reflected the functional views and practices associated with accounting, human resources, IT, and even information management within most companies. Managers and professionals in each domain have not sought, by and large, to find the connections or links between these three areas of management practice as they impact business performance.

Human resources professionals have generally not focused on the impact of IT and information management except in their functional areas of expertise. IT professionals have steered clear of the 'softer' and less technical concerns about how people behave with information or how information practices in the business shape how IT can or should be used. IT professionals have generally advocated that the business areas should worry about how people use information, while they focus on providing the application systems and IT infrastructure that the company's business strategy requires.

Information management professionals, on the other hand, have generally been relegated to support functions in the business, such as marketing research, web site content, or corporate information centers. They have had little impact or influence on the broader information management practices and people behaviors that shape how information is or should be used in the company, to improve business performance.

Moreover, the focus on improved 'management control' in recent years has similarly done little to highlight the importance of understanding and integrating, in practice, how people use information and IT to improve business performance. The management control stream has focused on the importance of good financial information management in support of better business measures and control systems within companies. But, this stream of management thinking and practice has not pursued the corresponding need to develop business measures of effective information use that could highlight the ways people, information, and IT can be managed to improve business performance.

If we manage what we measure, then it is not surprising that the management of the interactions between people, information, and IT to improve business performance is not well understood by executives, since effective information use in companies is seldom measured. If we manage and measure only what we see, the danger is that an important aspect of effective information use—namely people's behavior—will continue to be ignored or minimized next to the more formalized IT and information management functions that have traditionally held management attention. While in limited instances, proponents of one school refer to some relationships of ideas shared between schools, our review generally did not uncover an existing unifying theory of effective information use. In fact, the lack of a comprehensive integrated theory on how each of the three schools relate seemed to contradict what we had been hearing from senior managers over the past several years at IMD, the University of South Carolina, and at Andersen Consulting. These conversations suggested that senior managers saw competency, in key aspects of each of the schools, as being closely coupled with business success. Similar to the model presented in Fig. 1.2 in Chapter 1, these senior managers recognized the importance of the IT and information management functions but also saw the people aspects of effective information use as a critical, but often overlooked, area.

These observations led our research team to postulate that the viewpoints of senior managers concerning the effective use of information were not completely captured within the theories of one individual school of thought. It appeared that senior managers had a more complex and comprehensive view of effective information use that integrated dimensions from each of the three schools. In addition, senior managers seem to hold that this higher-level information usage effectiveness idea (or construct) better predicts business performance than did the singular perspectives of each individual school of thought.

In the following chapters, we will take an important step toward presenting an integrated theory and business approach to managing and measuring the interactive effects of IT practices, information management practices, and information behaviors to improve business performance. In addition, we will provide a new business metric called Information Orientation (IO) that can assist managers and organizational members in directly measuring and building the business capabilities and behaviors for effectively using information in their companies to achieve better business performance.

# 3

# How Senior Managers Assess Information Technology Practices

In this chapter, we examine how well senior managers perceive their company is using information technology to improve business performance. We call the capability by which a company manages information technology effectively *information technology practices*. We define IT as the hardware, software, application programs, telecommunications networks, and the technical expertise that support the information processing and communications activities at all levels of a company. We use the word 'practices' because rather than measuring how well a company specifically manages its IT architecture, we are concerned with the practical outcomes of application of IT in supporting organizational operations, processes, innovation, and managerial decision making. As a framework to delineate IT practices, we focus on how well senior managers perceive IT is used in business applications that support different levels of organizational decision making.

First we will discuss the IT research framework defining each level of IT practices in support of organizational decision making. Given recent challenges brought on by the information age, we will update this framework to better address the contemporary realities of today's business environment. Most importantly, we will empirically validate a measure of IT practice competence as held in the minds of senior managers. Finally, we pose questions that will help senior managers think about how to evaluate IT practices and priorities in companies as well as position competence in IT practices relative to other capabilities necessary to achieve effective information use within a company.

## 1. IT PRACTICES AND ORGANIZATIONAL DECISION MAKING

As we noted in Chapter 2, the IT School has for many years advocated a framework for assessing how IT is deployed to various levels and types of decision making in the company. Anthony's planning and control framework which divides organizational decision making into three levels—strategic, management control, and operational control—has been widely employed in the IT field for the past thirty years. During the 1970s and 1980s, Gorry and Scott Morton (1971), among many other IT scholars and textbook writers, employed Anthony's framework. This, combined with the work of the Carnegie Mellon scholars led by Herbert Simon on decision making, contributed to the development of an evaluative approach to IT applications in business (Simon 1946, 1960).

We use the Gorry and Scott Morton framework which integrates the idea that decisions can be classified as structured, semi-structured, or unstructured, as the point of departure for understanding how senior managers align IT applications decision making at different levels in their companies (Gorry and Scott Morton 1971). However, as we will discuss below, given the realities of an increasingly information intensive competitive environment, where simple IT applications provide fewer opportunities to create information asymmetries, we have modified and updated the Gorry and Scott Morton framework. The adapted framework integrates two of Gorry and Scott Morton's decision making activities—strategic planning and management control—into one view of IT for management support and we added two new levels—business process support and innovation support.

Today, decision making about strategy is seen as central to what senior managers do, and not as a separate function or activity as viewed by managers in earlier decades. Similarly, 'management control' is perceived as a decision making activity in which senior managers are engaged, and not exclusively a middle management responsibility. With the delayering and flattening of organizational hierarchies, senior managers have assumed greater responsibility for management control in companies. At the same time, IT advances have made it possible to monitor company processes and operations from the top as well as the bottom. Thus we have integrated two of their decision making activities—strategic planning and management control—into one view of IT for management support.

Secondly, we have added two areas of IT decision making support that have grown in importance during the 1990s—IT for business process support, and IT for innovation support. Over the last ten years, new software and database technologies, coupled with re-engineering of business processes, have opened opportunities to apply IT to business applications that help companies manage cross-functional business processes and supply chains. Known as Enterprise Systems or Enterprise Resource Planning Systems, these IT applications have been widely implemented in manufacturing and service companies. In addition, advances in computer-aided design, simulation, and modeling tools, as well as in groupware, such as Lotus Notes, have progressed to permit professional workers in companies to design new products and collaborate on projects creatively. Both of these IT practices have been widely adopted by companies in the 1990s, so were not envisioned or included in the earlier IT frameworks.

Our adapted IT practices framework is presented in Fig. 3.1 Based on Gorry and Scott Morton's decision pyramid, it consists of four levels of IT support—IT for management support, IT for innovation support, IT for business process support, and IT for operational support. The pyramid shape places management support at the top to represent fewer but more significant decisions and operational support at the bottom to represent a greater number of decisional transactions but of lower potential company-wide impact. This framework is based on two realities of modern organiza-

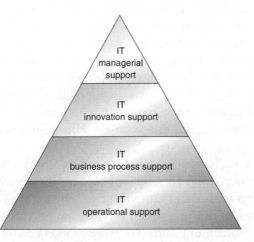

**Fig. 3.1.  IT Practices Capability Framework**

tions.

The first reality is the recognition that most work in service and manufacturing companies today is 'knowledge-based' at all levels. Workers from operational people to senior executives are expected to apply their knowledge, skills, and intelligence to their responsibilities in the company.

The second reality is that knowledge work involves different levels and types of decisions around which it is organized within companies. Four levels of knowledge workers and decision making responsibilities correspond to our four types of IT practices support.

At the highest level are the executives and senior managers, whose decision making focuses on strategic choices, analysis of options and scenarios, and management control. This is achieved by defining belief systems and monitoring the activities and behaviors of organizational members.

At the second level are the professional and technical workers, who have grown in importance and numbers in many firms as middle management ranks have been reduced. These are the R & D personnel, product designers, engineers, IT specialists, project managers, and service technicians, who often work in teams to develop new products and services or deliver them through new processes and technologies.

At the third level is the relatively recent corps of 'process managers', whose responsibilities include the coordination of cross-functional or horizontal processes, information use, and communications within companies, as well as with suppliers, partners, and customers. As many companies have re-engineered their core business processes across their value or supply chains over the last ten years, this new group of knowledge workers has assumed responsibilities for the horizontal coordination of business processes across functions such as product development, manufacturing, inventory management, distribution, marketing, and sales. These process managers have assumed bridge positions emphasizing continuous improvement of processes inside and outside their companies. Typically, these process managers operate in teams and manage projects that span two or more functions in the company's value chain to the market.

Finally, the fourth level of knowledge workers represents the 'operational' workers and supervisors. These people are responsible for executing the direct operations of the company, or for supporting the transactional systems and processes through which services are provided, or products are manufactured, distributed, and sold. These workers concentrate on getting the day-to-day business of the company done, communicate with customers and suppliers on a transactional level, and typically focus on executing the work responsibilities of their functional departments.

Corresponding to the four levels of knowledge workers and decision making responsibilities are four types of IT practices as Table 3.1 shows: IT for operational support, IT for business process support, IT for innovation support, and IT for management support. At each decision level there exist

Table 3.1. *IT Practices Support*

| Types of knowledge workers | Decision making levels | IT practice support |
|---|---|---|
| Executives/senior managers | Strategy<br>Resource allocation<br>Management control | IT for management support |
| Professional workers (e.g. R & D, engineering, product design) | New products/services<br>Improve creativity and exploration | IT for innovation support |
| Process managers | Project and process management across demand/supply chain | IT for business process support |
| Operational workers and supervisors | Transaction processing<br>Direct operations | IT for operational support |

different types of IT support (see Table 3.2). For example, IT for operational support includes systems for accounting, payroll, and personnel. On the next level, IT for business process support includes enterprise resource planning systems, or systems for sales and inventory management. IT for innovation support includes such systems as groupware, or computer-aided design. Finally, on the top level exist executive information systems, decision support systems, and data mining.

In the next section, we define and describe more fully each type of IT practice. Then we explain their relationship to decision making and business performance in the minds of senior managers.

## A. IT for operational support

We define IT for operational support as the software, hardware, telecommunication networks, and technical expertise to control business operations, to ensure that lower-skilled workers perform their responsibilities consistently and with high quality, and to improve the efficiency of operations.

Over the last forty years, computers have been employed in companies to automate and control tasks, which were previously performed by large numbers of clerical or retail workers as well as by workers in factories,

Table 3.2. *Applications Supporting Different Levels of IT Practices*

| IT practice support | Application examples |
| --- | --- |
| IT for management support | Executive information systems (EIS)<br>Decision support systems (DSS)<br>Data mining<br>On-line analytical processing (OLAP)<br>Group decision support systems (GDSS)<br>Financial management systems |
| IT for innovation support | Groupware (e.g. Lotus Notes)<br>Computer-aided design<br>Graphical simulation tools<br>Product modeling systems<br>Geographic information systems (GIS) |
| IT for business process support | Enterprise resources planning systems<br>   (e.g. SAP, People Soft)<br>Production, distribution, inventory, and<br>   sales management systems<br>Workflow automation systems |
| IT for operational support | Payment systems<br>Order processing systems<br>Policy management systems (insurance)<br>Checking, credit cards, and equity account<br>   systems (financial services)<br>Accounting, payroll, and personnel systems |

warehouses, and distribution centers. In addition, where tasks are not completely automated, computer-based systems are employed to monitor operations and to tie decisions and actions of operational workers and supervisors directly to their tasks.

There are three roles or functions that IT for operational support can play in companies:

1. to increase scale efficiencies in the operational activities of manufacturing and service firms;
2. to process basic business transactions; and
3. to monitor and record the actions and performance of operational employees in carrying out their tasks.

### Increasing scale efficiencies

IT affects the operational cost structures of companies in two different ways according to Gurbaxani and Whang (1991).

First, IT 'intensifies economies of scale in operations' by facilitating either mass production or, more recently, mass customization on a local, regional, and even global scale (Gurbaxani and Whang 1991: 66).

Second, IT 'introduces a high degree of flexibility in production (for example, through flexible manufacturing systems) and significantly reduces the cost of manufacturing a broad product line' (Gurbaxani and Whang 1991: 66). Flexibility is improved in several ways: by speeding up time to market for more products, by providing greater product choices to customers, and by lowering the overall costs of product variety.

### Processing basic transactions

In many industries, IT lowers transaction costs by automating key tasks and functions previously performed by people. The examples abound. Checkout lines in supermarkets are faster and more efficient as purchases are monitored through point-of-sale terminals where bar code devices record all products purchased by consumers. In some US locations, customers check themselves out at grocery counters, and pay with an electronic debt card, never interacting with a store employee. Automated teller machines, phone banking, and Internet banking reduce the need for bank employees and branches. Customers can execute transactions, either directly, or through operators, who efficiently handle many customer enquiries through automated call centers. Insurance claim adjusters use laptop, or pen-based notepad computers, to work at a damage site to process claims, and transmit them by modem or cellular phones to the home office. Airline reservations are processed directly over the Internet for customers. The airlines bypass the travel agent, and reduce their commission fees.

Each of these examples highlights the ways that transactions in markets and industries are increasingly being automated to reduce costs, or to speed up product and service management.

### Monitor and record the performance of lower-skilled employees

In many industries, IT not only enables companies to automate transactions, but also provides new ways to monitor the behavior and performance of lower-skilled employees while performing their operational tasks with customers, among themselves, and with other employees in partner firms. IT provides cost-effective monitoring devices such as optical scanners in retail stores, and hand-held computers for delivery agents. Optical scanners help control inventory levels, and monitor the performance of stock clerks in stores, to reduce employee theft and ensure service levels. Hand-held computers and global positioning systems help monitor the productivity and speed of express delivery services, as well as track the efficiency of delivery routes and trips.

Since direct monitoring of employees is costly to accomplish with supervisors, IT can be employed to record the actions of employees and suggest improvements in their behaviors with customers, or in cross-selling products to customers. Retail firms such as Wal-Mart and fast food chains such as McDonald's have employed IT to monitor, control, and improve the actions and behaviors of thousands of their service providers, or in-store 'associates'.

IT for operational support enables companies to improve efficiency and productivity by standardizing and controlling operations directly through automation. It also enables companies to use automation to monitor and control employee performance and behaviors associated with operational tasks and responsibilities. Information use is highly structured and well defined either as 'transactions' or as 'feedback' for monitoring and recording employee actions.

## B. IT for business process support

IT for business process support focuses on the deployment of software, hardware, networks, and technical expertise to facilitate the management of business processes and people across functions within the company and externally with suppliers and customers.

During the early 1990s, two developments occurred—one in management practice, and the second in software—that would focus manufacturing and later service companies on using IT for business process support.

The first development was the rapid and pervasive rise of 'business process re-engineering' which Michael Hammer and James Champy defined as 'the fundamental rethinking and radical redesign of business processes to achieve dramatic improvements' in performance such as 'cost, service and quality' (Hammer and Champy 1993: 32). The focus on business process re-engineering led many companies to re-examine their value chains from suppliers to customers. Managers began to focus on the horizontal, cross-functional improvements that could be made in process coordination, information use, and communications among people between functions, to improve the 'total cost', speed, flexibility, and responsiveness of the supply chain in meeting customer needs.

The second development was perhaps less visible, but equally as important. At the same time that 're-engineering' projects were launched in manufacturing companies, software companies such as SAP, People Soft, Oracle, and many others adapted database and mainframe software in financial administration, manufacturing, inventory management, distribution, and order fulfillment to support the cross-functional use of information in supply chain and sales processes. These capabilities are now known as Enterprise Systems or Enterprise Resource Planning Systems. ERP systems provide the IT platforms to permit firms to re-engineer their supply chains not only to process transactions within functions, but, more importantly, to share information across functions to improve coordination, control costs, and increase efficiency in the whole supply chain.

These two developments spread rapidly from manufacturing to service companies in the 1990s, and have not only permitted advances in IT support for process management inside companies, but have also led to the use of IT for inter-company processes with suppliers, wholesalers, distributors, and directly with customers. Moreover, with the rapid spread of the Internet worldwide, companies have begun using web technologies to link suppliers, partners, and customers through dedicated, secure 'Extranets' so that supply and demand chains can be seamlessly coordinated and managed between companies.

While ERP systems are used to process transactions and improve operational efficiencies, their primary purpose is to support cross-functional process management—the coordination of decisions and information use to optimize the whole supply or demand chain to the market or customers. In addition, with the Internet, companies are seeking to redesign their networks of suppliers, partners, and customers, and not simply their internal supply chains. This most recent development, variously called 'network competition', 'business network redesign', or 'the network value chain', emphasizes IT for business process support across competitive networks of companies, suppliers, partners, and customers within the same industries (Marchand 1999).

IT for business process support represents an important step in connecting the decisions and information flows across business processes with the decisions and transactions within functions and departments inside and outside companies. However, both IT for operational support and IT for business process support focus on institutionalizing and formalizing 'yesterday's strategic decisions'. In each case, the emphasis for decision making is in 'making things better' rather than 'making better things'—a theme that we address with the next two uses of IT for business decision making.

## C. IT for innovation support

The third way IT is used to support business decisions is to facilitate the creativity and exploration of new ideas among professional workers by improving the uses of knowledge and information inside the company as well as externally. In particular, companies have made significant progress in deploying IT for speeding up the introduction of new products and services.

In the past, research and innovation had followed a laissez-faire approach in many companies. This approach was characterized by 'finding good knowledge workers and leaving them to their own devices, only to measure how quickly and how well they produce outputs' (Davenport, 1997: 100). This approach was typical of the ways academic departments in universities, professional service consultancies, R & D departments in large companies, and asset management firms had been run.

Over the decade of the 1990s, this changed, in part due to the explosion in IT for innovation support, which was primarily driven by three types of IT developments.

### Software-based innovation

The first development occurred as a consequence of the introduction of powerful, graphic-oriented desktop computers and servers, such as those produced by IBM, Sun, and Silicon Graphics, coupled with improved software applications and databases to assist in every stage of the innovation process. Quinn, Baruch, and Zien have argued that software advances have fundamentally altered all aspects of innovation, from basic research through product introduction (Quinn, Baruch, and Zien 1996: 11).

Among basic and applied researchers, software tools influence all aspects of what researchers do including:

- literature searches and database enquiries,
- communications by e-mail and the Internet with other researchers,
- the design and execution of experiments, field studies, and lab tests,
- the modeling and simulation of complex physical, environmental, and even social phenomena,
- the statistical analysis of data and testing of ideas, to the final publication of results (Quinn, Baruch, and Zien 1996: 11–12).

Complex, powerful, software-driven graphical workstations, robust communication networks to large databases, and seamless links to distant colleagues are the essential tools of idea generation, discovery, and diffusion. In many industries, these same tools are at the center of analyzing data about the 'marketplace, user patterns, environmental trends or specific constraints to the application' of new product ideas.

In product development, almost all designs of physical systems, subsystems, components, and subcomponents are simulated with software systems and multidimensional visualization. Most physical products such as cars, ships, computer components, as well as service products such as investment funds and insurance policies, are simulated in software first, before they are released for production or distribution.

Finally, in manufacturing engineering, computer-aided engineering (CAE), design (CAD), and manufacturing (CAM) influence process design, analysis, layout, and all phases of production. From the design and production of planes such as the Boeing 777, to new car models, such as Ford's 'global' car—the Taurus—the presence and use of powerful software is critical to the process of product and service innovation.

### The Internet and the management of documents

A second development in the use of IT for innovation support has been the growth of the Internet and the widespread diffusion of document handling software technologies. These technologies have permitted the pervasive automation of documents, containing all types of structured and semi-structured information, that could be repackaged, distributed, and used by teams and professionals who shared common interests or work on projects inside and outside companies.

E-mail and the automation of documents began in the 1960s and 1970s, and were employed by large companies, universities, and government agencies to share structured and unstructured information and communications among professional workers. However, it was not until the late 1980s and early 1990s that two software and networking capabilities appeared that would revolutionize the ways information, in unstructured and structured forms, could be widely shared and used within companies and globally. These two software capabilities were the development of the World Wide Web, and the maturing of groupware packages like Lotus Notes.

The web technologies provided the capability to share all types of documents in a consistent HTML format across previously incompatible networks of servers and personal computers. In addition, with the development of standardized Internet browsers, like Netscape's Navigator, any user of the Internet could adapt his PC to easily access documents on the web.

At about the same time as the web document management capabilities appeared on the Internet, an early 1980s software product began to diffuse among large companies that were seeking to share documents among teams working in diverse locations and time zones across the world. These groupware and workflow automation packages permitted teams of dispersed professionals to develop, use, and update the same document and always see the most recent changes and updates by any member of the team. For example, Lotus Notes provided the capability called 'replication' that permitted a team member to log on, access the program, and receive automatically any updates or changes that other team members might have made during the day or night from any location on the earth. By the mid-1990s, the use of e-mail, workflow automation, and groupware packages, as well as the growing use of World Wide Web-based corporate Intranets, had become a prevalent means to exchange documents across corporate and external networks.

The ability to easily develop, share, and update documents, containing semi-structured and unstructured information of professional workers and managers, provided the impetus for rethinking the way 'knowledge work' could be done. Knowledge work could now be 'engineered' to achieve more predictable results.

### The growth of global networking and interactivity

The third development promoting IT for innovation support has been the extensive use of telecommunications networks and the digital integration of video, voice, wireless, and data communications within companies and globally. These have evolved to provide on-line navigation in real time among millions of networks operating around the world. For professional workers of all sorts, access to global networks within their companies and between companies, educational institutions, and government agencies has led to an exponential increase in interactivity.

The impact of interactivity on creating value has become known as Metcalf's Law: 'For any communications network, the number of nodes (N) on a network yields that number squared in potential value, N2' (Downes and Mui 1998: 24). Following Metcalf's Law, increased interactivity among knowledge workers has opened new opportunities for information sharing and collaboration on projects, deals, investments, and other team efforts across time zones, geographic locations, and organizational boundaries.

These developments are placing increased focus on the management of knowledge workers and information use in the 'virtual value chain' that exists alongside the physical value chains of most companies. Extracting value from information and knowledge use in the virtual value chain takes on greater importance as managers search for new sources of competitive advantage with customers and in new markets.

The Internet and global networking inside and outside of companies has opened almost unlimited opportunities for professional workers and managers to identify and focus on new markets, products, and services in the interactive, virtual 'marketspace'. However, with these abundant opportunities has come the corresponding need to manage knowledge work so that the attention, time, and resources of professional workers are focused on achieving business results (Rayport and Sviokla 1994).

## D. IT for management support

The fourth way that IT can facilitate organizational decision making is through IT for management support. We define IT for management support as the IT capabilities and expertise to assist executive and functional managers in decision making. Generally, managers are concerned with three broad types of decision making: (1) strategy; (2) resource allocation; and (3) management control.

Over the last forty years, there have been a number of efforts to develop computerized information systems for managers and executives. During the 1960s and 1970s, Management Information Systems (MIS) were developed in companies. MIS attempted to aggregate internal transaction processing of information from operational systems, and provide summaries and exception reports to managers. MIS required the specification of routine decisions in enough structure so they could be easily programmed long before the decisional context arose. These systems were not perceived as particularly useful by higher-level managers, because they focused on internal, highly structured information aggregated from existing company processes and systems, and did not accommodate the dynamic and fluid decisional context that most of these senior managers demanded. Given the complexity and rigidity of third generation mainframe hardware and software, MIS reports often presented rows of numbers and numerical indicators that proved to be of little or no value to all but tactical or production line supervisors.

During the late 1970s and early 1980s, the second wave of IT for management support emerged as Decision Support Systems (DSS). DSS were targeted at 'semi-structured' decisions typically made by functional and middle managers: 'those decisions where intuitive judgment alone will not be adequate because the solution involves some judgment and some analysis' (Keen and Scott Morton 1978: 86). These systems were often aimed at supporting ad hoc decisions and attempted to provide the appropriate data and analysis tools for assisting, but not replacing managerial judgements.

Managers were to interact with their DSS tools in an iterative fashion until they arrived at the best possible decision. However, as these systems tended to have complicated interfaces, and still required considerable programming, many managers tended not to use the expensive systems that they had purchased or developed. When the systems were used, it was often by professional workers in marketing, financial planning, forecasting, and risk assessment, rather than 'true' managers. Although sophisticated DSS still offer great promise, it is curious that some thirty years after they initially came on to the scene, the most prevalent DSS feature used today remains the 'what if' function on an Excel spreadsheet.

The third wave of IT for management support appeared in the mid-1980s and was called Executive Support Systems (ESS). ESS developed in parallel with the evolution of the desktop and portable personal computers, so from the beginning, the emphasis with ESS has concentrated on 'hands-on' IT use. ESS advocates intended to equip senior managers with the hardware, software, networking, and data retrieval capabilities to directly support their semi- and unstructured decision making and communications activities (Rockart and DeLong 1988).

Senior managers use ESS to assist them in exploring and expanding their 'mental models' underlying strategic choices. In evaluating the use of ESS for changing mental models of top managers, Rockart and DeLong have identified the following six key attributes:

- access external information;
- help combine information from multiple sources;
- present information in more meaningful formats;
- improve analytical and modeling capabilities;
- help surface and test assumptions about the business; and
- permit data access anytime, anywhere (Rockart and DeLong 1988: 135).

ESS are typically designed as highly graphical 'user friendly' executive support systems that track the key critical success factors of the firm as defined by the executive team. Initially, these systems required minimal keyboarding skills. However, during the 1990s, more senior managers began using PCs directly on their job. So, the evolution of ESS has been marked by broader use of hands-on computing, connections to the Internet as well as ubiquitous cell phone connections. Today, senior executives are literally plugged in. This has facilitated knowledge sharing among professionals and managers in companies; however, it has often resulted in a feeling of information overload.

As more of their attention has shifted to coping with the constant and unrelenting change in business conditions, senior managers have had to use IT tools to assist them in anticipating market trends, evaluating business risks, and defending their market positions. In addition, senior managers have increasingly engaged in external intelligence gathering and analysis to address rapidly developing business situations, such as mergers and acquisitions, or to prepare proactive marketplace responses to unexpected opportunities or threats.

Thus, managers today have many choices to make concerning the appropriate IT for management support. No longer confined to receiving voluminous printouts of internally focused numerical data, senior managers can personally use IT as tools to examine strategic choices, allocate resources, engage in management control, as well as test their decision making assumptions in the face of changing business conditions.

## 2. HOW SENIOR MANAGERS EVALUATE IT PRACTICES

In this section, we explain the results of our study in terms of confirmatory factor modeling as depicted in Fig. 3.2. A confirmatory factor model is a commonly used statistical technique to represent what people really think about an idea. Using well-accepted research and statistical steps, it permits researchers to determine the extent to which a theorized mental picture (model) of people's ideas actually exists in the real world. In the case of this study, confirmatory factor analysis allows us to create a picture of what senior managers really think about IT practices, as well as the other information capabilities of effective information use, which we will discuss in Chapters 4 and 5.

Our findings indicate that senior managers have a sophisticated concept of IT practices that focuses on the outcome of IT support for organizational decision making. As we expected, senior managers have an integrated view of their competence in IT practices through one high-level idea. This is demonstrated in our model presented in Fig. 3.2, by the oval located furthest to the right of the page. We call this high-level idea the 'IT practices capability'. We have statistically proven that this idea (or 'construct') does exist as a discrete and high-level evaluative construct in the minds of senior managers.

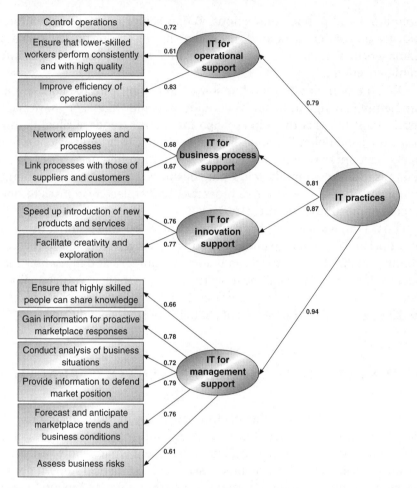

**Fig. 3.2. Confirmatory Factor Model of IT Practices**

We have also determined that this high-level idea (the IT practice capability) is comprised of four dimensions. Hence, in a factor model, the arrows point from the highest-level idea to the lower-level ideas (dimensions, e.g. IT for operational support, IT for business process support, IT for innovation support, and IT for management support). These have also been proven to be discrete in the minds of managers, and yet contribute to make up the higher-level idea. Finally, each arrow points to the left from a dimension to individual measures (actual evaluative items/questions asked of managers on our survey). These measure components of the dimension. By using this statistical modeling technique, we have moved beyond conjecture, and actually validated a model of managerial thought concerning evaluation of IT practices.

Our factor model for IT practices presented in Fig. 3.2 indicates that IT for management support (.94) is a highly recognized dimension of IT practices. This is followed by IT for innovation support (.87), IT for operational support (.81), and IT for business process support (.79).

It should be noted that the numeric value that follows each dimension, e.g. (.94) for IT for management support, represents a factor loading which is a statistical indication of the extent to which a dimension's idea is captured in the overall IT practices capability in the minds of senior managers. It should not be interpreted as a direct percentage ranking relative to the other factors. While we use numerous other statistical indicators to ultimately determine whether a factor model is valid and reliable as discussed in the Appendix, for managerial interpretation, one can assume that a factor loading above .9 is high, above .8 is moderately high, above .7 fairly strong, above .6 acceptable; and above .5 marginally acceptable, in contributing to the representation of a valid idea held by managers. If a factor score is lower, it means that we may not have captured all aspects of this idea in our measure.

In addition to looking at the individual factor scores relative to a particular dimension (such as IT for management support) or information capability (such as IT practices), we also test whether the overall model is related to all dimensions and items, and whether, as it is termed in the scholarly community, it 'fits'. While we do not present all the fit indices in the book's chapters (they are presented in the Appendix), it can be assumed that we will only present factor models that have been proven to fit, and thus represent valid and reliable models of managerial thought.

Looking at the IT for management support dimension, we see that senior managers clearly recognize this dimension of IT practices, which focuses on the principal strategic decisions that senior managers have to face, such as market positioning, competitive analysis, and exploration of business opportunities. As the factor model indicates, the strategic decisions that senior managers perceive are connected to defending the company's market position (.79), gaining information for developing proactive market responses (.78), forecasting and anticipating marketplace trends and business conditions (.76), and conducting analyses of business situations (.76).

Slightly less clearly recognized by senior managers are concerns about ensuring that highly skilled people can share knowledge (.66) and assessing business risks (.61). Both of these IT practices may be encouraged by senior managers, but are newer concerns. Understanding how to use IT to promote the sharing of knowledge by highly skilled people is a desirable, but more recent concern of 'knowledge management', which is less well defined in the minds of senior managers. Similarly, using IT to assess business risks is better understood in the financial services industry, but less familiar to manufacturing and services executives in other industries. Nevertheless, senior managers have a very high level of awareness about using IT to support strategic decisions through improved information and knowledge use.

Senior managers also regard IT for innovation support as a key idea related to facilitating creativity and exploration in the firm (.77) and speeding up the introduction of new products and services (.76). As we noted in the previous section, senior managers recognize that IT offers significant potential, if deployed appropriately. It enables collaborative work among teams, and between business units in companies, to achieve better business results from knowledge work. In addition, using IT to speed up the introduction of new products and services is already affecting product innovation practices in many industries such as autos, airplanes, computers, cellular phones, financial services, and retailing.

Senior managers clearly recognize that IT practices support the control of business operations (.72) and the need to improve the efficiency of operations (.83). Less clearly understood, but still significant, is the use of IT to ensure that lower-skilled workers perform consistently and with high quality (.61).

The differences of perception of IT for operational support may reflect a focus of senior managers to improve productivity and efficiency in operations through control processes and transactions, and only secondarily through direct control of people. That is, senior managers place priority on IT to improve transaction processing first, and regard controlling the performance of lower-skilled people in operational roles as a by-product of IT for operational support. As we noted in our examples earlier, fast food firms use point-of-sale terminals primarily to improve control of operations (inventory and cash flows). However, their design permits counter people to take orders efficiently, and to verify that each order is what the customer desired 'his or her way'. Thus, the sales behavior of people is well defined and controlled by the ergonomic design of the terminal that illustrates all product choices and prices, as well as by the data network and terminals that permit fast cooking and wrapping of customer orders.

Finally, senior managers perceive that IT can support business processes by networking employees and processes together (.68), and by connecting business processes with those of suppliers and customers (.67). The scores for these two practices confirm the recognition that managers in many manufacturing and service companies have of the importance of using IT for: (1) improving cross-functional process management; and (2) sharing information and communications across the value chains of companies with both suppliers and customers.

Thus, in interpreting Fig. 3.2, we can say that the high question (item) loadings onto each of the four IT practices dimensions indicate that senior managers view each of these dimensions of IT practices as distinct ideas. In addition, these four factors of IT practices come together as one common higher-level idea in the minds of senior managers which is the information technology practices capability. The overall significance of our statistical finding is that we can confidently say senior managers recognize the importance of a high-level idea, IT practices capability, its dimensions, and the items that make up these dimensions, and we have a clear way to reliably and validly measure the importance that managers place on each of these ideas.

## 3. IMPLICATIONS FOR MANAGERS AND RESEARCHERS

We have presented in section 2 a statistically valid model that managers and researchers can use to evaluate their own strengths and weaknesses within the context of IT practices. This model indicates that each IT practice is essential to providing superior IT support at all levels of an organization. As a measurement tool, it can be used to check the pulse of an organization's effectiveness in using IT to support its decision making at all levels. However, just because we have developed a valid measure of IT practices does not necessarily mean that we have developed a reliable indicator that will predict that 'good' IT practices or investments will result in higher overall business performance. In fact, as will be demonstrated in Chapter 6, we think quite the contrary. We believe that good IT practices are only one component of a higher-level concept of effective information use that must include 'good' information management and 'good' information behaviors. This perspective pushes us to ask the following questions:

*Is delivering 'good' IT practices in support of intended business strategies enough to achieve a competitive advantage?*

There have been many frameworks developed by IT scholars, consultants, and practitioners that have attempted to find the elusive link between IT strategy and business strategy (Rockart 1979; McFarlan 1984; Henderson and Venkatraman 1989; Reich and Benbasat 1996; Chan et al. 1997), between 'strategic information systems' and sustainable competitive advantage

(Clemons 1986), between IT enabled support and business transformation (Luftman, Lewis, and Oldach 1993; Kettinger and Grover 1995), and, most relevant to this section, between IT practices and improved organizational decision making (Rockart and Bullen 1986; Keen 1993). The common denominator among these frameworks has been the concept of 'alignment'. If only IT could be properly aligned with business strategy, then senior managers would see the 'business value' of their IT investments (Strassmann 1985; Keen 1988; Roach 1991; Brown and Magill 1994). Or, if only IT could be aligned with the pace of business change, then senior managers would recognize IT's contribution to future business success (Chan et al. 1997).

The difficulty with the concept of alignment when applied to IT practices is that it only addresses the most rational side of strategy development and implementation. This rationality attempts to align 'planned' and 'deliberate' IT practices with 'planned' or 'deliberate' business strategy. But what if strategy is 'emergent'—a pattern of decisions and behaviors that are realized, but may not have been fully intended? Recognition of the importance of emergent strategy opens up the possibility that IT practices will have to be forward-looking and focused on supporting information uses and decision making that are partly intended and partly emergent. Mintzberg has called this dual approach an 'umbrella strategy', meaning 'the broad outlines are deliberate, while the details are allowed to emerge en route' (Mintzberg, Ahlstrand, and Lampel 1998: 11).

If senior managers align IT practices only with intended strategy, then they may only support part of the business strategy (or none at all, if the intended strategy is not realized). To avoid this problem, we suggest that senior managers must ensure that IT is deployed with both intended and emergent strategy in mind. This is not an easy undertaking and means that the company must effectively balance the tensions of promoting innovation and predictable results at the same time. Or, as F. Scott Fitzgerald put it: 'The test of a first-rate intelligence is the ability to hold two opposite ideas in the mind at the same time and still retain the ability to function.'[1]

We believe that, to implement intended strategy, managers seek to formalize and institutionalize decision making and information systems to ensure predictable results. IT for business process support and operational support must be aligned with core business processes and transactional activities that directly mirror the intended strategies of senior managers. Using IT for business process support and IT for operational support well means that a company is implementing an intended strategy, which was decided at some point in the past by senior managers. It follows that a com-

---

[1] As quoted in Mintzberg, Ahlstrand, and Lampel (1998: 20).

pany must possess a culture that focuses the attention, time, and resources of its people on relevant information for intended strategy to be implemented well.

On the other hand, to permit emergent strategies to develop, we believe that senior managers seek to deploy IT to enable the making of semi-structured or unstructured decisions, or to use IT to create novel products, services, and new business concepts. In the latter case, IT for innovation support requires less formal and institutionalized uses of information and IT. The focus is on people-based discovery, creative exploration, openness to new business ideas, new uses of knowledge, and new ways of deploying IT to enable a company to navigate its future business journey successfully. Using IT for management support and innovation support well means that a company has created the tools necessary to respond to emergent or future strategy today. It seems as though a company culture must possess a high level of learning capacity and flexibility to both recognize and act on information that leads them to develop this IT support to respond to emergent strategy.

*Is providing 'good' IT for operations and process support enough to achieve a competitive advantage?*

Competitive realities in a world bombarded by the possibilities afforded by Internet technology and the opening up of new information-based markets are forcing senior managers to reassess their companies' IT competencies. In today's business environment, providing superior IT for operational or business process support that focuses primarily on structured or semi-structured decisions such as transaction processing or supply chain management will not confer sustainable competitive advantage. Managers can no longer evaluate IT investments for competitive advantage without examining the level of information asymmetry or return on information the system can provide within their industry context. Creating information asymmetry—leveraging information about customers, competitors, and operations that is unusable or unavailable to competitors—has become one of the paramount business strategies of the new decade.

To better understand how managers today are evaluating the role and relative contribution of IT to establishing information asymmetry, we have provided a managerial framework for understanding 'return on information' in Fig. 3.3. Senior managers not only base IT investment decisions on cost, but evaluate the level of information asymmetry or 'return on information' provided by different IT choices. We define 'return of information' as the degree of distinctive competence that a company expects to gain relative to its industry competitors through improving its IT practices in

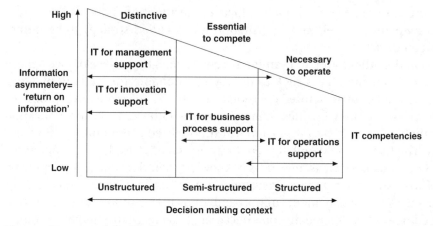

**Fig. 3.3.** Framework for Understanding Return on Information

support of all levels of decision making. If information asymmetry is low, we would expect low returns on information. However, if information asymmetry is high, we would expect high return on information and a greater ability to create a sustainable competitive advantage.

The right side of the chart represents investments in development of IT competencies that are necessary to operate a business, such as IT in support of operational processes (e.g. payment systems), and functional activities (e.g. general ledger, payroll, accounting, and external financial reporting systems). On this task level, decisions are the most structured, and can be easily supported by IT applications. Most of these systems are required to competently operate a business in an industry, but provide little or no direct competitive value or distinctive competency—being good is a necessity to survive. In most competitive industries, little or no information asymmetry can be established through IT investments in this category, since the return on information is low.

The middle of the chart represents investments in IT competencies that are essential to compete, such as those used to support business process development. These IT investments are required if a company plans to compete among the leaders in an industry. Because the decisions are less structured, or semi-structured, it is more difficult for companies to replicate these IT competencies. Companies must be 'good enough' in executing IT for business process support to be perceived as a 'player' in the industry. At best, the top five to ten companies in an industry will all receive comparable benefits from IT focused on improving business processes. For example, in the bulk chemicals industry today, all the leading chemical companies have implemented SAP's ERP software for financial administration, process control, distribution, and logistics. Senior managers in the chemicals industry believe that such systems are essential to control costs and manage information across the supply chain for on-time deliveries, and that industrial customers expect their suppliers to operate this way. Investments in this IT category may initially lead to information asymmetry for first movers. Among top competitors in the longer term, however, this technology will become essential to maintain competitive return on information levels, but not sufficient to ensure competitive advantage.

The left side of the chart represents investments in the development of IT competencies that can lead a company to be distinctive within their industry in achieving business value with information. Here a company is seeking innovative ways of using IT for the more difficult task of improving more unstructured management-level decision making, and of deploying IT to encourage innovation in new product and services, or to re-engineer the business processes and information systems that it deploys. In this case, companies are seeking to build distinctive competencies with IT to innovate or to rethink the ways it delivers current processes. At this level, IT support is difficult to replicate given the unstructured nature of the decision process. Companies that do this well can create the highest return on information. Why? Because IT investments in this category provide the greatest opportunity to create information asymmetry with competitors in competitive, customer, and operational information. How is this accomplished? As we will show in subsequent chapters, achieving industry leadership in the use of information requires more than just good IT practices at all levels; it requires equally 'good' information usage behaviors and values and 'good' information management practices.

This discussion raises many additional questions that need to be addressed if managers are to effectively manage their IT practices capability and ultimately improve a company's business performance:

- Do companies have to establish solid IT support for functional operations before they can effectively use IT to support business processes? If not, can improvements in IT operational support drive effective business process redesign?
- If IT support for operational decision making is lacking can the company acquire adequate information to effectively support innovation? Can a company continue to innovate if it does not have an adequate grasp of its current products, people, and customers?
- Does poor IT support of business processes result in a lack of good information on customers, suppliers, and logistics which prevents effective IT support of managerial decision making?

- Can a company proactively process information to support managers if it does not have adequate decision and executive support tools?
- Is there an appropriate path to improve IT practices and how does this relate to personal information usage behaviors and information management practices?
- Can a company develop a more mature IT practices culture?

These, and other ideas relative to the relationships between the dimensions of the IT practices capability, will be addressed in Chapter 8.

## 5.  CONCLUSIONS

In this chapter, we have examined how senior managers perceive information technology practices in their companies to improve business performance. We have described four levels of IT practices in support of organizational decision making.

We must state that while our rigorous identification of the IT practices capability, its dimensions, and its evaluative items indicates that we have captured the concept of IT practices support as it resides in the minds of managers, we suspect that being good at IT practices alone will not resolve the balance between intended and emergent strategy or lead to superior business performance. While rationalized and well-planned IT practices may work well to achieve intended strategy, it appears that the development of strong company-wide information behaviors will facilitate needed flexibility in information usage (e.g. proactive information searching, sensing, and sharing) to accommodate the dynamism associated with emergent strategy support. The 'Tension to do Better Things' drives for creative people-based information processing activities, and knowledge-based decision making.

Thus, while we believe that we have made important strides in isolating a measurable IT practices capability, we recognize that being 'good' at all the dimensions of IT practice will still probably not be enough to ensure high business performance payoffs. Rather, companies that want to improve business performance will also have to improve the way their people use and manage information and build appropriate information behaviors and values to attain this goal. This recognition pushes us to examine in Chapters 4 and 5 the extent to which senior managers' mindsets actually correspond with our own proposition: that good information usage behaviors and information management skills are equally as important as good IT practices in improving business performance.

In analyzing the results of our study's confirmatory factor, we have drawn a number of key conclusions related to how senior managers think about information technology practices in achieving better business performance.

A. Senior managers perceive four separate and distinct dimensions of information technology support (IT for operational support, IT for business process support, IT for innovation support, and IT for management support). They perceive these dimensions to be part of a higher-level idea we call the 'information technology practices' capability.

B. The dimensions of IT support are interrelated—focusing on managing only one or two levels well will probably lead to lower business performance.

C. IT practices must support the need for control and innovation in the business. We believe that aligning IT support for business processes and operations to implement the intended or deliberate strategy of the business is not sufficient for improving business performance. IT support for management decision making and innovation must enable the evolution of a company's emergent strategy to foster creativity and exploration of new ideas as well as targeting of new products and services for future business growth.

D. In the end, we believe that managers of successful companies recognize that to be good at IT practices alone will not be sufficient to improve business performance. We suspect that senior managers recognize that their companies must also be skilled in managing information over its life cycle and possess people-based behavioral competencies in information usage. Thus, we believe that being good at IT practices is a necessary, but not sufficient condition for achieving superior business performance.

In the next chapter we turn to information management practices—the way senior managers think about and manage information to realize business results.

# 4

# How Senior Managers Value Information Management Practices

There have been many attempts over the last twenty years to describe companies that manage information and knowledge well. Peter Drucker (1988) introduced the notion of the 'information-based organization' as an advanced development stage of companies that employ information effectively. Ikujiro Nonaka and Hirotaka Takeuchi (1995) have written about the 'knowledge-creating company' that excels at converting information into usable knowledge for innovation in products and services. Thomas Davenport (1997) has proposed 'information ecology' as a metaphor for an effective 'business model for information management'. And Chun Wei Choo (1998) has offered the concept of the 'knowing organization', which he defines as an 'organization that is able to integrate sense making, knowledge creation, and decision making effectively' (Choo 1998: 3).

While each of these authors has painted a picture of what a company looks like when it has reached an advanced state in managing and using its information, none of these authors have empirically validated these ideas or have developed an effectiveness measure to determine whether a company is actually doing a good job in managing its information. Neither have they clearly explained the link between improved information management and better business performance.

We focus on how well senior managers perceive their companies manage information to improve business performance. We call the capability of a company to manage information effectively *information management practices*. If IT practices refer to the capabilities of a company to effectively manage IT applications and infrastructure, information management practices focus on the company's capabilities to effectively manage the use of information in support of coordination and control, tactical problem solving and strategic decision making.

In this chapter, we will discuss information management practices as a process or life cycle that involves *sensing, collecting, organizing, processing,* and *maintaining* information to enhance its use for decision making. While this life cycle view of information management has received considerable attention in the writings of the Information Management School, the five phases of the information management life cycle have not been empirically validated as ideas held by managers in practice, nor have these concepts been shown to be associated with a higher-level measurement indicating whether 'a company is good at information management.' In this chapter we address these issues by first (*a*) presenting the information management life cycle framework and its individual dimensions; (*b*) next, we statistically determine the extent to which these ideas exist in the minds of managers, and finally (*c*) we discuss the implications for evaluating information management practices in companies.

## 1. THE LIFE CYCLE OF INFORMATION MANAGEMENT

As we noted in Chapter 2, scholars of the Information Management School have for many years described how the formalization of information occurs within organizations. These authors, emphasizing the importance of actively managing information as an organizational resource to achieve better business results, have described information management as a set of activities that moved through a 'logical succession of phases, each dependent on the other' (Marchand and Horton 1986: 184). The traditional view of the information life cycle included a circuitous set of phases—collecting, organizing, processing, and maintaining information (Ashby 1956; Taylor 1968). More recently, authors such as Kuhlthau (1991), Dervin (1992), and Choo (1998) have identified a newer fifth information management practice—sensing. This practice involves the active seeking and scanning of information in external environments. This newer practice has been depicted outside of the traditional circle of the information management life cycle, feeding into the information life cycle at the information collection phase—information sensed about the external competitive environment helps define information needs and thereby dictates and drives changes to what information would be collected within an organization.

With the exception of sensing, these five phases are associated in a continuous circular relationship. Information that is sensed based on some perceived information need is collected in a formalized manner, organized in a format that could be used within an organization, processed by employees before making decisions, and later maintained (updated or refreshed) for future use. Once maintained, information can be reused and continue around the path until deemed not usable and removed. This continuous path is commonly known as the 'information life cycle'.

We used the five phases of the information life cycle as the basis for our information management practices model, shown in Fig. 4.1. The purpose of this life cycle is to improve the ways information is used for decision making by managers and organizational members. We assumed that each phase is dependent on the last. Sensing information from outside the company on market shifts, customer needs, and new technology changes influences what information is collected by establishing information needs. Collecting new relevant information not only prevents information overload, it also directly determines how a company organizes it (i.e. how well a company indexes and classifies information and links databases to promote access and use by its people). Organizing information properly enables managers and their employees to process information for different decisional contexts. Finally, companies that know what information to process and how to maintain it save time and resources by effectively avoiding irrelevant information, or re-collecting the same information.

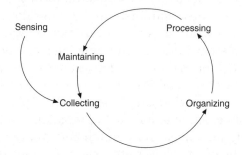

**Fig. 4.1. The Life Cycle of Information Management**

An important assumption that drove our thinking in developing our information management practices model is the simple recognition that— there is no time that information does not exist in a company. In essence, organizations do not start from totally blank information slates, creating knowledge from nothing. In contrast to our IT practices model where an organization can begin with no IT and builds it over time, our information management practices model acknowledges that information exists through the knowledge already residing within its people. Even a fledgling start-up company has information resident in the minds of its entrepreneurs. To tap this knowledge, organizations are faced with the challenge of formalizing this information, using it where needed, and then maintaining it for future organizational use.

To manage information effectively, we recognize three important properties of information use. First, information use is constructed in the minds of people; people give meaning and value to information. Second, information use is situational. The company's business context defines norms and practices that constitute the information behaviors through which people may deem information useful. Their information value judgements are determined within this context. Third, information use is dynamic: information sensing or needs determination, collecting, organizing, processing, and maintaining happen in repeated and recursive cycles that are dictated by business situations and people's abilities and desires to use information to address unique business situations. While we can paint a simpler picture of information management for discussion purposes, in reality effective information management practices represent the company's efforts to support this information life cycle within an information use context, which is personal, situational, and dynamic in nature. Thus, effectively managing information from a company perspective is a particularly challenging undertaking given the complexities of aggregating personal valuation judgements on tacit and explicit information, of varying quality and reliability, from formal and informal sources, which may be automated or manually processed.

We believe that within this circular process of the information life cycle there is continuous valuation of information at each phase of the life cycle. This evaluation is made at both the individual and company level and ultimately determines how far, if at all, any piece of information will progress through each phase of the life cycle. At the sensing phase people use cognitive judgements about their external environment to make a valuation judgement whether potentially collectable information will satisfy a new or unanswered problem or decision. At the collection phase, people decide whether the decisional benefits received from the collecting of new information are worth the associated cost of its collection. At the organizing phase decisions are made whether appropriate data structures, standards, and routings can be established to help ensure information can be used to process decisions. At the processing stage, people decide whether the information collected and organized (manually or via IT) actually satisfies analytical and decision needs. At the maintenance phase, a valuation decision is made whether information should continue to be stored and updated in anticipation of future use. To the extent that information can be reused and refreshed, we would anticipate less of a need for additional new information to be collected.

Because tacit and explicit information always exists within organizations, and is always being consciously or subconsciously valued, it is a moot point to ask: 'where does the information life cycle really begin?' Because of the model's circularity and valuation points across all five phases, it is not possible to determine where the information life cycle begins, or ends. In this way, the information management life cycle differs from the linear decisional framework that explains the dimensions of IT practices.

However, we do propose that two phases of the information life cycle are particularly important valuation points—processing and sensing. Processing is probably the most critical valuation point of the traditional circular life cycle phases because it is at this point that a determination is made by a decision maker whether the information sensed, collected, and organized really meets the problem solving needs of the business context. In essence, this is the point where the payoff of the information life cycle occurs. A valuation judgement that determines the information is deficient at the processing phase can immediately call for further collection, improved organization, reformatted presentation, or disposal.

Sensing also appears to be a particularly crucial valuation phase. Because the sensing phase lies outside the traditional life cycles' circular paths it is the least formalized and consistent information management practice. Sensing brings more cognitive elements to information valuation judgements. To effectively anticipate and begin to define new information needs, sensing demands perceptual skills to recognize changes in the competitive environment and knowing which business stimuli are relevant to an individual's business context. If these skills and judgements are weak, then new information requirements are not completely anticipated and new sources of information ill defined. Ultimately, judgements about filtering information at the sensing phase determine whether a company will be able to effectively evolve emergent competitive strategies to address changing business demands.

We will next define and explore in more depth the five phases of the information life cycle. In section 2, we present the statistical results of confirmatory factor analysis used to test this model.

## A.  Sensing information

Sensing, in English usage, means to perceive, become aware of, or detect events or a state of things, in a person's or organization's environment. During this phase people in organizations must continuously identify events, trends, and changes in business conditions, and 'make sense' out of them in order to define their information needs prior to collecting appropriate information, developing new strategies, or making decisions.

Sensing is a newer concept in information management discussions as scholars have acknowledged the importance of identifying information critical to business decisions that exists in business environments outside of immediate organizational boundaries. It has been identified as a critical activity by information resource management scholars (Marchand and Horton 1986), in environmental scanning studies (Grover, Premkumar, and Segars 1993), and emphasized by the knowledge management scholars (Kuhlthau 1991; Dervin 1992; Choo 1998).

Choo (1998: 93) has identified this phase of the information life cycle as 'information seeking' or activities related to scanning, noticing, and interpreting information in the external information environment. Sensing involves what Karl Weick perceives as 'sense making' and is an integral part of what organizations do: 'The goal of organizations, viewed as sense making systems, is to create and identify events that recur to stabilize their environments and make them more predictable' (Weick 1995: 170). Well-developed sensing practices within organizations can increase both the clarity and quality of information concerning ambiguous situations, thus making them more predictable. Research has suggested that organizations that perform environmental scanning or sensing well outperform organizations that do not scan or scan inadequately (Choo 1998: 145).

We define sensing information as the phase in the information life cycle in which information is detected and identified concerning:

- economic, social, and political changes affecting the business;
- competitors' innovations that might impact the business;
- market shifts and customer demands for new products; and
- anticipated problems with the company's suppliers and partners.

A company must be in constant touch with its environment as a precondition for decision making. It is through sensing that a company's members and managers observe: (1) changes between their current perceptions and associated ways of collecting and using information inside a company; and (2) changes in business conditions that require a reinterpretation of threats, opportunities, risks, as well as the ways information is collected and used. We can distinguish companies by how well organizational members sense changes in business conditions and respond to them.

Sensing is also closely associated with the roles of managers since they must constantly manage their attention, and those of other organizational members, to monitor potential changes in external and internal organizational conditions. Mintzberg noted over twenty years ago that the manager as 'monitor' 'perpetually scans his environment for information, interrogates his liaison contacts and his subordinates, and receives unsolicited information, much of it as a result of a network of personal contacts he has developed' (Mintzberg 1975: 56).

Knowledge workers' jobs are closely tied to decisions about what to sense, and how to sift through the overabundance of signals from inside and outside the organization. Knowledge workers must interpret the perceptions of organizational members in several ways:

1. to identify changes in the broader social, economic, and political environment;
2. to listen to customers;
3. to monitor competitors; and
4. to anticipate problems with suppliers and partners.

Failure to appropriately sense changes in business conditions can result in not collecting appropriate information to respond to these changes, as well as misreading the significance of changes for decision making, resulting in inappropriate strategies and actions. To ensure that accurate information is being sensed, thus influencing the next phase of collecting information, people must be willing and ready to learn in order to interpret changes or errors within their working environment and have the flexibility to act on what they are learning. This is important to allow for changes in information that might affect future business decisions and strategic direction.

## B. Collecting information

The next phase of the information management life cycle is the practice of systematically collecting relevant information when organizational members have sensed changes in business conditions, or in customer, competitor, partner, or supplier behaviors, and have begun to define new potential information requirements. Collecting information includes:

- profiling the information needs of employees to ensure the right information is delivered to them at the right time:
- filtering information for managers and employees to prevent information overload;
- identifying key knowledge sources so that employees can make use of the company's collective expertise; and
- training and rewarding employees for accurately and completely collecting information for which they are responsible.

While information technology has advanced the capability of organizations to collect more and more data about their customers, operations, and processes, and to share the data more broadly with networks and the Internet, the critical managerial concerns related to collecting information still involve addressing some basic questions.

### Who needs information in the company?

The first step to collecting meaningful information is to understand the information responsibilities of a company's people at various levels and for various tasks. In most organizations, the organizational structure of the company, and the lines of authority and responsibility, provide the initial definition of the information responsibilities and reporting requirements of managers and employees. Identifying what employees need for fulfilling their tasks is an important first step in assuring that business processes work effectively.

Managers have a responsibility, and must develop the capability, not only to identify their employees' information needs, but to ensure that the information is available to them when and where they need it. Normally, this responsibility involves coordinating the business functions, such as sales, marketing, product design, and manufacturing, that collect and supply information to employees, as well as the units whose primary tasks involve creating and disseminating information, such as the IT department, corporate library, and finance/accounting departments.

### What type of information is needed and how much?

Knowing the information needs of people and fulfilling them is a difficult challenge. Data does not, by itself, lead to more efficient or better work. Most companies suffer from two problems simultaneously:

First, the information that is potentially available to people today often exceeds their abilities or available time to absorb and use it effectively. Companies often collect a lot more information (or the wrong types of information) than they need. This is a consequence of the convergence of computing and communication appliances such as data mining, of terabyte plus data warehouses, as well as the Internet's 'instant overload' capabilities. Information overload can be the result of poor valuations at both the sensing and collection phases.

Second, many people in companies do not have the appropriate information to execute their duties. How does this happen? Even with the advances in formal information system development methodologies, such as formal requirements and determination procedures—businesses change, people change, and processes change. Thus, the information systems that were so carefully specified, at particular cross-sections of time, quickly become outdated. However, because they are programmed systems, they continue to produce the same volumes of information on a routine basis, even if it is out of date, or irrelevant to current problems. Conversely, the absence of relevant information often goes undetected, so that companies do not collect information that they can use. These two problems not only affect employees in carrying out their operational tasks, but also afflict managers as well.

In fact, many companies today possess very imperfect information collection procedures. 'Filtering' mechanisms often make irrelevant data available, or prevent relevant information from being collected and used by the appropriate people. These filtering mechanisms can be poorly designed business processes, and formal information systems, which do not provide employees information about customers and products when they need it to make decisions. Or the 'filters' can be cultural values and behaviors that prevent employees or managers from knowing what information should be collected before decisions are made. Thus, managers must continuously evaluate whether the right information is being sensed by the organization, and whether it is being appropriately collected through people, business processes, departments, and information technology.

### Where is the information?

Many companies today operate as if they were libraries without a catalogue. Knowledge possessed by people and information sources are available throughout the company, but the tools to tap where the expertise is, who has it, and how it might be employed are either not available, or operate very imperfectly. The 'opportunity costs' of not identifying available information and expertise mean that people in companies must collect information that others have already collected before, or they must do without the use of knowledge that the company has collected, but cannot locate (Myers 1997; Stewart 1997). Advocates of 'knowledge management' recognize that identifying knowledge sources in a company is critical to making use of the company's collective expertise residing in people (Nonaka and Takeuchi 1995; von Krogh and Roos 1996; Prusak 1997).

### Why and how should people collect information?

People are generally motivated to collect information that they will immediately put to use. The problem arises when the acts of collecting information are either separated from the acts of organizing, processing, and using the information, or carried out by different people, processes, and computerized information systems. In these cases, the people doing the collecting of the information, or the IT people designing the computerized systems, need to understand how the information will be used by other people in decision processes. In some companies, knowledge domain managers are being assigned the principal responsibility of identifying good sources of knowledge around a topic area, assigning value to the information based on an understanding of who else in the company might use this information, and then making sure that it is collected and made available to the people who need it most. While these types of positions are still most prevalent in management consulting companies, the concept is spreading throughout information intensive businesses.

It is not sufficient to assume that people will normally collect information accurately and completely as part of their position responsibilities, since, in many cases, collecting information that you may not directly use, but which others may depend on, is often perceived as a low priority on the job.

In addition, in many companies today, collecting information 'only once' for databases and operational systems requires employees to not only understand the technology that they are using, but also to take ownership of the information that they are collecting, even though it is being used by others in the company. Peter Drucker calls this 'information responsibility': 'everyone in an organization should constantly be thinking through what information he or she needs to do the job and make a contribution.' He notes that, as more and more companies become 'information-based', managers and employees in these companies must ask: 'Who in this organization depends on me for information? And on whom, in turn, do I depend?' (Drucker 1988: 9).

Instilling this sense of responsibility in many companies today requires rewarding and training employees to understand their contributions in the life cycle of information. For example, the critical role of collecting information that is as accurate and complete as possible is a responsibility for themselves, and for others who depend on them. Training people in companies to collect the information for which they are responsible accurately and completely is an important step in making sure that the information is properly organized and processed for decision making.

## C. Organizing information

The organizing phase of the information management life cycle focuses on indexing, classifying, and connecting information and databases to provide access within and across business units and functions. Like collection, assuring that information and databases are properly connected and organized requires managerial attention to the rewards and training that organizational members require to carry out this phase of the information life cycle.

Organizing information appropriately involves several critical decisions that managers and organizational members make on an ongoing basis.

First, it is necessary to know what categories to use in organizing information. Whose purposes will be served through the categorization scheme? In many companies, databases are organized by function or department. This may work well at a local level, but can create havoc on an organizational basis. In today's integrated business enterprise, other departments, functions, or even suppliers and customers, must share these databases across related business processes. Then, differences over categories, terminology, language, and indexing schemes arise. Different departments and functions have various ways of referring to the same terms such as: customer, order, shipment, or payment. Whose definition to use, and what categories of information are associated with which information systems, become critical issues that managers and organizational members must resolve.

Many organizations have attempted to deal with these problems through a standardized data dictionary, data integrity guidelines, and formal database administration functions that oversee the corporate central computer-databases. Unfortunately, these data standards have been primarily applied to the computer based transactional database applications, and have tended to disregard personal data sources, including personal computer systems and, more significantly, paper-based and informal information sources.

Second, making information 'available' through networks and databases does not always make it usable, unless organizational members can agree on shared language, terminology, and classification schemes for organizing the information sources and databases of a company. Moreover, information technology and networks may provide the technical means for organizing and connecting databases across a company, but the challenges of organizing information to share, and to use it across functions, professional domains, and different business units, are essentially human activities involving choices.

Third, like other work responsibilities, organizing information requires appropriate skills, expertise, and work habits that organizational members and managers must possess. To develop these capabilities, companies can provide appropriate training to employees in organizing information. If people are to do more than satisfy their own information needs, they must be able to recognize that information has value to others.

This is no easy task, and suggests that behavioral changes may need to occur in organizations to motivate people to want to share. As sensing and collecting are precursors to sharing, people must possess a rich enough understanding of each other's work to be able to make a value judgement whether some information they have access to might be of value to someone else. Such behavioral proactiveness towards sensing, collecting, and organizing is probably the result of formal training, as well as the institutionalization of information sharing incentives as a part of the company's overall control systems.

An important issue that we believe will affect the efficacy of collecting and organizing information is the formalization of informal and personal (tacit) knowledge to explicit, formal, and institutionalized (explicit) information. People in organizations possess two types of knowledge: tacit knowledge and explicit knowledge. Tacit knowledge is 'personal, context-specific, and therefore hard to formalize and communicate.' Explicit knowledge is 'knowledge that is transmittable in formal systematic language.' People possess both types of knowledge simultaneously. The challenge in organizations is to convert the tacit knowledge of organizational members into explicit knowledge that can contribute to the purposes of the organization (Nonaka and Takeuchi 1995: 59–61). Without this conversion process, the collecting and organizing dimensions of the information life cycle will not be as effective in providing the best information for changing decision contexts.

## D. Processing information

The next phase in the information management life cycle consists of two key steps:

First, people in an organization must be able to access appropriate information sources and databases before making decisions.

Second, people must actively engage in analyzing information sources to derive useful knowledge as inputs to decisions.

Analysis is critical in information processing. The purpose of analysis is to translate information into specific knowledge that can be used by managers and organizational members to achieve the purposes of the organization. Analysis in most organizations is an ongoing responsibility of organizational members, and not just for special occasions or 'big decisions'. Moreover, since most knowledge work is difficult to 'observe' and measure, managers must pay special attention to the hiring, ongoing training, and evaluation of employees, to assure that they have hired the right people to process information into knowledge in their companies.

Processing information is critical to decision making in organizations. Likewise, decision making by managers and organizational members has an important impact on shaping the ongoing processing of information. Changing business conditions require managers to shift the criteria and focus of their decisions. Since managers possess limited time, attention, and resources, changes in decisions that need to be made also shift the underlying processes of sensing, collecting, organizing, and processing information into useful knowledge.

This requires managers to 'satisfice' in their decisions.[1] Since they do not have the time or attention to search for new information in an unlimited manner before decisions are made, they seek information and knowledge that is 'good enough' relative to the consequences, risks, and opportunities associated with their decisions. This satisficing behavior permits managers and organizational members to focus their limited attention and search capacity on the appropriate information and knowledge for decision making. Thus, not only is decision making 'situational', so is the processing of information on which decision making rests. Rather than viewing the information management process as 'static' in organizations, we must view the information management process as 'dynamic'—requiring continuous adjustments in sensing, collecting, organizing, and processing of information to support decision making by people with limited time and attention (Davenport 1997; Drucker 1993; Weick 1995; Marchand and Horton 1986).

## E.  Maintaining information

The next phase of the information management life cycle brings us full circle in Fig. 4.1. Maintaining information involves reusing existing information to avoid collecting the same information again, updating information databases so they remain current, and refreshing data to ensure that people are using the best information possible.

---

[1] Chester I. Barnard's foreword to the second edition of Herbert Simon's *Administrative Behavior: A Study of Decision-Making Processes in Administrative Organization.*

Reusing information to avoid collecting, organizing, and processing it all over again is often advocated by managers in companies, but this admonition is more often ignored than supported. There are several reasons why reuse is difficult to practice.

First, there is a natural human tendency to go out and seek new information and assume that information already collected is stale or not useful.

Second, organizational members may not be aware that information has been already collected in one part of the organization, so they launch into new information collection activities.

Third, managers may inadvertently encourage new searches for information by redefining the decisions or problems that they face enough so that previous efforts to collect, organize, and process information look different when they may be basically the same.

Fourth, the information previously collected may not be easily accessible due to the ways it is categorized and automated.

Finally, people in a company may be reluctant to reuse information that they do not 'own'. Reuse in some companies is constrained, since people are not encouraged to share information that they have already collected, organized, and processed.

Reuse of information must be actively encouraged by managers since it requires deliberate decisions by organizational members to be aware of what information the company has already collected, organized, and processed, and to avoid collecting new information if existing information is good enough for decision making.

In contrast to the barriers facing reuse, many organizations have developed sophisticated processes to make sure that their operational information systems and databases are updated continuously. Processes and procedures for updating databases can be 'built into' the way automated systems operate for order fulfillment, customer profiling, payment processing, and purchasing. For most types of operational and process support systems, companies have learned over the last ten years to design these systems with continuous updating in mind. For most companies today, not updating information can seriously delay decisions, upset customers, degrade services, and lead to poorer business performance.

Refreshing information continuously represents the newest aspect of maintaining information. Increasingly, managers and employees work in teams on projects, special assignments, and deal making, on a regional and global basis across many time zones. The need for continuously refreshing information and documents that different members of teams are using during diverse working hours becomes critical to the speed and quality of their work.

Software tools such as Lotus Notes employ features such as 'replication' that permit team members to know when documents are modified, and by whom, each time they access the document. Similarly, when project managers of ABB are working on large power projects in South-East Asia, they can send their project plans, schedules, and drawings to London over the Internet each night to be updated and refreshed for accessing the next morning in Asia. This permits project teams to operate on a twenty-four-hour clock, and to increase their productivity as well as stay in touch with their home office. Moreover, Internet 'push' technologies permit users of these services to receive streaming updates of news, financial quotes, and weather. Not only can these services permit users to tailor their information needs for their uses, but they can also access updated information on an all day/every day basis.

In industries such as global financial services, continuously refreshing information on a second-by-second basis is the norm, not just for companies, but for the global marketplace as well. As more industries adapt to doing business in real time on a global basis, the need for continuously refreshing information will become critical to business performance.

## 2. HOW SENIOR MANAGERS EVALUATE INFORMATION MANAGEMENT PRACTICES

As we discussed in section 1, our research led us to assume that there exists a life cycle of information management that is perceived by senior managers. Based on the theories and concepts discussed in sections 1 and 2 we developed questionnaire items that measured each phase of the life cycle. As we suspected, using confirmatory factor analysis (see Fig. 4.2) we found that senior managers perceive as distinct and valid ideas each of the five separate phases of the information management life cycle. And, more importantly, we found that senior managers view these phases and associated practices as part of a higher-level idea that indicates how good they believe their company is in 'information management practices'. Our data further shows the relative strength of these ideas in the minds of senior managers at two levels.

First, we see relationships between the individual practices under each phase of the life cycle.

Second, we also see relationships between the five phases (as distinct ideas in the minds of senior managers), and the shared, or common, idea of the information management practices capability.

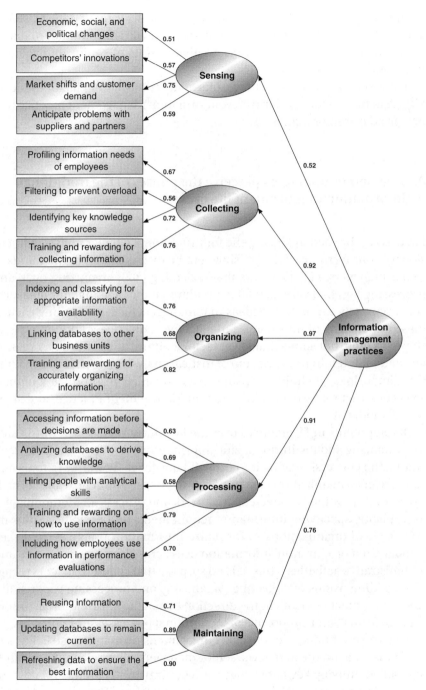

**Fig. 4.2.  Confirmatory Factor Model of Information Management Practices**

Thus, our study has, for the first time, empirically validated the existence and relative strengths of these ideas associated with information management practices in a major, representative sample of senior managers in international companies.

In this section, we explain the results of the confirmatory factor model in Fig. 4.2 in more detail to clarify how information management practices are perceived by senior managers.

## A. How senior managers perceive the phases of the traditional information management life cycle

First, as can be seen in Fig. 4.2, the four traditional circular phases (dimensions) of our factor model were shown to be discrete ideas in the minds of senior managers. Fig. 4.2 shows that collecting (.92), organizing (.97), and processing (.91) had very high factor loadings, indicating that our measures very accurately captured the ideas that managers have concerning each of these dimensions of information management practice. Maintaining (.76) showed a high, but somewhat lower factor loading than collecting, organizing, and maintaining. Second, our statistical analysis also indicates that the five dimensions (including sensing) come together to produce a higher-level construct that we term Information Management Practice, and show overall model fit.

Developments in IT practices over the last thirty years have contributed to formalizing and institutionalizing information practices as well as accelerating the conversion of tacit to explicit knowledge. Powerful IT tools and software give organizations the opportunity to institutionalize and formalize how information is collected, organized, and processed. Methodologies for explicitly specifying information requirements and designing software systems lead organizations to formalize information practices, and seek standardized or 'common' information uses across business processes and administrative activities. Thus, it is no surprise that senior managers recognize the dimensions of collecting, organizing, and processing very readily, since these practices work in the direction of making information use more explicit, formal, and supportive of institutional processes and purposes.

Based on our findings for the collecting dimension as indicated in Fig. 4.2, we can see that on the item level, senior managers have a clear understanding that 'identifying key knowledge sources' (.72) and 'training and rewarding people' (.76) result in better information collection. They may be slightly less familiar with the concepts of 'profiling the information needs of employees' (.67) or 'filtering information to prevent overload' (.56). The ability of companies to filter information to prevent information overload has developed more recently particularly in the Internet Era. Companies are now actively experimenting with improved ways of understanding information needs of employees as well as filtering information to prevent overload.

Our study also indicates that in organizing information (see Fig. 4.2), senior managers perceive indexing and classifying information for employees (.76), as well as training and rewarding them for organizing information for which they are responsible (.82), more clearly than linking databases so that other business units can access needed information (.68). Linking customer, product, and service databases together is a more recent development enabled by IT networks, Intranets, and distributed database management systems.

In processing information, each of the information practices identified seem to play a role in improving information use for decision making, although the senior managers did not recognize hiring people with analytical skills (.58) as strongly as a means to add analytical processing skills as the other items. Accessing information before decisions (.63), analyzing databases to derive knowledge (.69), evaluating (.70), and training and rewarding (.79), were all found to be strongly associated to better information processing.

Senior managers seem to perceive the practice of maintaining information slightly less clearly than collecting, organizing and processing information. Among the maintaining items, they perceive updating (.89) and refreshing (.90) information for future use as more significant than reuse of existing information (.71). We believe that there are several reasons for these perceptions.

Managers do recognize that the time and financial resources expended in collecting quality information may be wasted if it is not maintained. In fact, if maintenance slips extensively, it may prove more effective to re-collect the information than to cleanse badly neglected old data. However, the urgency to address today's critical decisions often focuses managers on having relevant information collected, organized, and processed as a first priority. Maintaining information requires a deliberate decision to allocate scarce resources and time of organizational members on activities that may be useful, but less urgent. Reusing information seems to fall into this category, since managers may believe that it is good to do, and economizes organizational resources, but is a lesser priority than having the information ready when you need it (even if it was duplicative of what the company already collected).

Another reason why managers may perceive maintaining information as being of less concern than processing information is the result of managers and technical specialists believing that storing old data is now cheap and accessing it later is no longer a problem with advanced IT. New technologies have burst on the scene such as intelligent agents, and Internet multicasting 'push' tools, which promise to make reusing, updating, and refreshing information fast, cheap, and easy. For managers faced with more urgent problems and opportunities to address, why worry about maintaining information when IT will help you do it automatically? A prevailing belief that clicking on the 'save' command, or relying on an automatic back-up program, will solve the information maintenance problem still exists in many companies.

In recent years, however, a countervailing argument for maintaining information has arisen from the knowledge management community. Maintaining information is critical to reusing and updating the company's collective knowledge and must be refreshed continuously by the organization's members. Advocates of better knowledge management have emphasized the need for a company to convert tacit knowledge into usable information, and to preserve a company's core knowledge and expertise against lose, degradation, or lack of use. Thus, this emerging school of management thought is seriously urging managers to develop improved capabilities to reuse, update, and refresh the valuable explicit knowledge and formal information that the company develops through its operations and decision making on an ongoing basis. Thus, while we believe that maintaining information will become a more important dimension in the future, a fundamental problem persists: managers and organizational members are more interested in using information than maintaining it.

## B. Understanding senior managers' mindsets concerning sensing information

The high factor loadings of our measurement model indicate that senior managers seem very comfortable in recognizing the phases (dimensions) of the traditional circular information management life cycle. Probably based on years of personal experience in making information valuation judgements at the collection, organizing, and processing phases, these managers are able to clearly recognize whether their organizations are good at collecting and organizing information that actually satisfies analytical and decisional needs. While less clear about the information maintenance dimension, these managers indicate that it is a discrete and vital valuation point within the information management life cycle.

As opposed to those phases that were contained within the traditional circular information life cycle, sensing (.52) showed an acceptable, but relatively lower factor loading than the other information management practice dimensions, indicating that we may not have fully captured all aspects of this idea as conceived by senior managers. Our data indicates that while the sensing phase does exist as a discrete dimension under the overall information management practices capability, the concept is not as well formulated in the minds of senior managers.

In interpreting our results, we have come to the conclusion that sensing information, as an activity, remains more tacit, informal, and personal and is closely tied to the ways people perceive and respond to changes in business conditions, and in their personal environment. As we discussed earlier, at the sensing phase, people use cognition to make a valuation judgement whether potentially collectable information from the external environment will satisfy a new or unanswered problem or decision. Thus, it appears that sensing information has a strong cognitive component that is more difficult to define as a set of information management practices.

Of the four practices noted on Fig. 4.2, under sensing information, senior managers seem to have recognized sensing information on market shifts and customer demands for new products (.75) most clearly. These information practices are already established through the activities of marketing departments and competitive intelligence units in most companies. Anticipating problems with suppliers and partners (.59) and identifying competitor innovations (.57) appear of lesser significance. In both these cases, the practices associated with sensing information appropriately seem to be less understood, and perhaps less developed, in companies as a set of business capabilities. Sensing information on economic, social, and political changes affecting the business (.51) seems to be the least developed, or formalized, information practice, in the minds of senior managers. In this case, the practices and responsibilities associated with sensing information seem to be less structured, more tacit, and perhaps less institutionalized than any other information practice.

We believe that sensing will remain an essential part of the cognitive and perceptual processes influencing information collection and the definition of new information requirements. Ultimately, if people do not possess the cognitive skills or an affinity to sense competitive opportunities and threats, the organization will lack needed information and IT support systems to address emerging strategic challenges. Specific practices associated with good sensing capabilities are still evolving in management thinking and practice. In future studies we need to broaden the sensing dimension's measures to better capture these cognitive aspects of its information seeking and information definition practices.

## 3. IMPLICATIONS FOR MANAGERS AND RESEARCHERS

We have presented in section 2 a statistically valid model that managers and researchers can use to evaluate their own strengths and weaknesses within the context of information management practices. This model indicates that each dimension of information management practices—sensing, collecting, organizing, processing, and maintaining—is a discrete and essential part of a company's effective management of information. As a measurement tool, it can be used to check the pulse of an organization's effectiveness in implementing and managing information management practices.

One idea that became evident during the course of our analysis was the apparent linkage between positive information usage behaviors and good information management practices. It appears that the behavioral dimension proactiveness, and the information management dimension sensing, are closely linked. As we will discuss in Chapter 5, development of proactive information behavior provides the affective response and sets the environmental preconditions for the more cognitive practice of sensing to occur. On an aggregate level, people in an organization with a propensity to actively use cognitive skills to sense for information will also make better evaluative judgements about the importance and applicability of certain information to decision contexts.

Such proactive information behavior would also seem to drive more effective information processing practices as people not only begin to understand how they can make better decisions in their own jobs, but begin to grasp a richer understanding of the work of their colleagues.

An underlying issue affecting good corporate information management practices is the extent to which managers can influence organizational members to formalize and share their knowledge. Clearly, the key asset that individuals can leverage for their benefit, or that of the organization, is their own knowledge (their expertise, experience, and skills) through information processing (the way they express, convey, and communicate their knowledge to others). Managers must encourage and provide incentives that congeal organizational members' willingness to contribute their knowledge. If organizational members perceive that their contributions to the information life cycle advance the purposes of the organization and their own 'enlightened' self-interest, then the phases of the life cycle will be effectively implemented through formal and well-articulated practices.

While the results of our research have painted a much clearer picture of good information management practices, the canvas is not yet completely covered. To move to the next level of clarity in understanding information management practices prescriptions, we will need to answer some of the following questions:

- If sensing resides outside the circle of the traditional information management life cycle and is a more cognitive element of information valuation judgements, is it directly influenced by proactive information use behaviors as we have proposed above?
- If information processing is a key information valuation point of the traditional information management life cycle, is it also influenced by more proactive information behaviors where colleagues are more willing to help define and analyze information for others?
- Does better sensing actually improve information requirements determination and thereby increase the capability to build IT management support systems that in turn improve information processing?
- Do better information maintaining practices decrease the need for information collection?
- Beyond improving information processing, where else does IT have the greatest impact on information management practices?
- Is there an appropriate path to improve information management practices and how does this relate to information use behaviors and IT practices?
- Can a company develop more mature information management practices?

These questions, along with a fuller prescriptive model, will be addressed in Chapter 8.

Finally, we have not empirically examined the relationship between good information practices and higher overall business performance. As we will demonstrate in Chapter 6, we believe that good information management practices are only one component of a higher-level concept of effective information use that must include 'good' IT support and 'good' information behaviors.

## 4. CONCLUSIONS

In this chapter, we have discussed how senior managers perceive information management practices in their companies to improve business performance. We introduced information management practices as a life cycle with five interrelated phases. We next empirically validated each phase as well as the associated information practices related to each phase.

In analyzing the results of our study's confirmatory factor model, we have drawn a number of key conclusions related to how senior managers view information management practices.

A. The traditional information life cycle phases (collecting, organizing, processing, and maintaining) are interrelated within a circular path. The fifth phase, sensing, lies outside the traditional life cycle circular path and feeds the information collection phase.

B. Senior managers do perceive these five distinct phases of the information life cycle and relate these phases to a shared higher-level idea we call the information management practices capability. This higher-level information capability represents a comprehensive measure of how well senior managers believe their organizations manage information.

C. While information valuation judgements are made throughout each phase of the information management life cycle, two key valuation points are at the sensing and processing phases.

D. Good information management, like good IT practice, should constantly focus on the decision contexts of managers and organizational members. Good information management pushes for more explicit knowledge, formalized information management solutions, and widespread institutional benefits. However, this organizational control bias should not stifle individual creativity and motivation to develop basic knowledge, operate in informal ways, or design personal information management solutions that deliver the greatest personal productivity. Individuals must be trained to see the possibilities for helping others through information sharing, and receive incentives to act in the best interest of the organization as well as themselves.

E. Sensing, while a distinct and significant dimension related to the information life cycle, is still an evolving concept in the minds of managers. It appears that the cognitive and affective nature of sensing may distinguish it slightly from the other information management practices dimensions and make it dependent on affective responses from proactive information behaviors.

F. Maintaining is a phase that is still developing and growing in recognized importance in the minds of managers and requires specific decisions as to how to build adequate incentives to encourage information reuse, updating, and refreshing.

G. Finally, while we found that senior managers recognized information management practices as a separate high-level information capability, we found no evidence indicating that managers believe this information capability alone has a profound effect on business performance. Quite the contrary was suggested in our analysis, which points to a close interrelationship with IT practices. We also found that human behaviors associated with effective information use are closely connected to many aspects of information management practices, such that behavioral adjustments are needed to be proactive in sensing information for others, and not just for one's self. Thus, while the Information Management School has much to offer in our quest for a measure of effective information use, it does not appear to be a complete paradigm.

This determination leads us to turn our attention, in the next chapter, to our proposed third information capability, which affects information use in a company—information behaviors and values—giving us a more people-centric focus.

# 5

# What Key Behaviors and Values Lead to Effective Information Use by People in Companies

As we begin the twenty-first century, improving people's information usage behaviors and values, and incorporating this with the effective management of information management and IT, remains an informal and incomplete management activity. Although the management of people as a strategic resource has been elevated to a high-level human resources management function, there has been little focus within human resources (HR) departments on developing good information usage behaviors that lead to effective information use for decision making and problem solving.

This lack of HR emphasis on building effective information behaviors is understandable. Unlike the IT and information management functions discussed in Chapters 3 and 4, where practitioners responded to their primarily information-related functional responsibilities by organizing and developing formal disciplines around information use in organizations, the human resource function's primary mission is to shepherd the management activities of people recruitment, classification, compensation, retention, and job training. Improving people's information behaviors and values is a minor, if not completely obscured priority.

Ironically, while both the IT and information management disciplines were charged with formalizing many information-related responsibilities within companies, directly improving people's usage behavior was typically outside their purview. Because the IT and information management practices evolved from low-level and non-strategic functional areas, they possessed neither the power nor the authority to influence major changes related to people's behavior—this was typically deferred to the realm of the human resources, managerial accounting, or operations functions. The next result of this fluke of organizational evolution is that academic research focusing directly on information usage behaviors is spotty at best. And, with no management disciple championing the formalization of information behavior and values improvement efforts, this area remains underdeveloped with direct measurement and management languishing.

This circumstance is very unfortunate, because information use in business organizations is inarguably people-centric. It is based on the decision context and tasks that people must execute to achieve organizational purposes. It not only involves how people use IT and manage information to help improve decisions, but how they behave with information, based on organizational values associated with effective information use.

In this chapter, we expand our discussion to include a people-centric view of information use, bringing a behavior and value focus to our discussion of effective information use. By bringing this area to the forefront of management awareness and thinking, we believe that managers will be able to better structure ways of improving this important area affecting information use, and see how a more holistic view of information use is needed to effect meaningful change within their organizations.

In this chapter, we focus on how well senior managers perceive their people behave in using information to improve business performance on an aggregate, rather than on an individual, level of analysis. We call the capability by which a company instills the set of behaviors and values that support effective information use *information behaviors and values*. As we saw in the two previous chapters, IT practices focus on the company's capabilities to manage IT applications and infrastructure to promote effective information use for decision making at all levels, and information management practices emphasize the company's capabilities to manage information as a resource to improve effective information use. Information behaviors and values, in turn, represent the company's *capabilities to instill and promote behaviors and values in its people that will result in effective information use*. Conceptually, we define values as those personally held beliefs that can be manifested in behaviors that have consequence to a company.

In this chapter, we first discuss how we derived a theory from two existing streams of literature to drive our research framework. Using ideas from the human resources and management control schools discussed in Chapter 2, we examine those behaviors and values that provide a more integrated view of enhancing effective information use—integrity, formality, control, transparency, sharing, and proactiveness. Most importantly, we will empirically validate a measure of information behaviors and values competence held in the minds of senior managers. Finally, we pose questions that will help senior managers think about how to evaluate information behaviors and values in their companies as well as position competence in information behaviors and values relative to other capabilities necessary to achieve effective information use within a company.

## 1. IDENTIFYING THE DIMENSIONS OF THE INFORMATION BEHAVIORS AND VALUES CAPABILITY

Few managers would argue that motivating people to act on information—to actively think about new products and services; to seek out new information in the competitive arena; and to use this information to respond quickly to changing business conditions—is critical to effective information use. Creating an environment to effect change in people's behaviors, however, is difficult. It is even more difficult since there exist few road maps to guide them through the difficult task of effecting appropriate behavioral change to create effective information use. An extensive search found that the management literature lacks an integrated theory of the behavioral dimensions of effective information use and how these dimensions interact with IT and information management practices.

In Chapter 2, we discussed three schools of thought that drove our overall research framework—the IT School, the Information Management School, and the Behavior and Control School. Both the IT and Information Management schools had as their principal focus the effective use of information for organizational purposes, providing us with an existing theory on which to base our model. The Behavior and Control School, however, focused exclusively on leading, managing, and motivating people. Human resources' prevailing 'people' functional focus, for example, separated itself from the 'technical' IT function resulting in little emphasis being placed on how to best modify people's behaviors to ensure they get the most out of their IT investments. Given this situation, we set out to derive a theory of effective information usage behaviors and values based on general directions provided by the behavior and control streams of thought.

Our theory of effective information usage behavior and values is based on several assumptions. First, we believe that when evaluating effective information use, managers take an organizational view, instead of an individual view, of aggregate information behaviors and values.

Second, although we believe that senior managers recognize the existence of a behavioral element when evaluating information use, the idea of effecting 'good' information behaviors and values has not been translated into structured and measurable management activities within many organizations. The act of improving information use has been managed traditionally within the domain of the more formalized IT and information management functions which have lacked the mandate to improve people's behaviors and values related to effective information use. We believe that this has contributed to the lack of formal management activities dedicated to understanding the behavioral elements of effective information use. Our research model is based on the idea that to improve information use at the organizational level, information usage behaviors and values need to be identified, measured, and formally managed. Based on this premiss, we recognize that people's dispositions and willingness to be proactive with information will help define these management activities. We believe that in companies where people are proactive in their willingness to think about, use, and improve the management of information, these management activities are more clearly defined and information is used most effectively.

We also believe that a behavioral bias for proactive information use provides the preconditions necessary for people to better sense new information needs, which helps in better defining information needs, allowing better fit of IT to decision making and problem solving. More effective decision making tools, in turn, reinforce proactive information behavior, creating an energized information environment able to make decisions accurately and rapidly, driving improvements in business performance.

Third, we assume that developing proactive information behavior is not a simple task. The development of proactive information behavior does not occur in a vacuum, but is instead dependent on a set of other information behaviors and values that influence the degree to which it is manifested in an organization.

Our research framework (as seen in Fig. 5.1) was therefore based on the theory that proactive information use was dependent on a set of other behavior and value dimensions. Drawing on incomplete behavior and control theories, we identified five additional behavior and value dimensions from the literature that we believe had direct and indirect impacts on creating proactive information use. These dimensions, drawn from both human resources and management control literature streams, included integrity, formality, control, transparency, and sharing.

A disposition to use information effectively would first demand that information be seen as truthful, accurate, and without bias. Integrity is closely related to the development of trust among organizational members within our human resources literature stream, creating the situation where people believe in and share a set of common principles about appropriate behavior in the organization (Brown 1993; Becker 1998; Kouzes and Posner 1993). Within this research area, integrity has been described as part of the

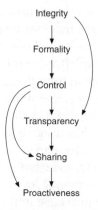

**Fig. 5.1.  A Theory of Information Behaviors and Values**

organization's 'boundary system' where senior managers define the space in which organizational members can act (Simons 1995). We believe that integrity acts as the basis for information use, setting appropriate boundaries for ethical information behavior, and influencing directly the formal use of information within an organization.

The next behavioral dimension—the use of formal information over informal information sources—would also influence a company's ability to create proactive information use by providing easier access to information and knowledge normally scattered throughout a company's people and functional areas. The discovery of the 'informal' dimension of human communications and information use relates back to the 'Hawthorne studies' during the 1940s, when researchers found that employee relationships had an important impact on worker productivity. Later, while researchers found that informal and formal information use were substitutable, they did find that formal patterns of communication and information use were generally more stable and predictable over time, and permitted the organization to better pursue its objectives than informal patterns (Rogers and Agarwala-Rogers 1976: 81).

The ability of an organization to use formal information over informal sources would improve the reliability and quality of the information used, provided that the organization possessed integrity to validate its veracity and usefulness (see Fig. 5.1). People feel more comfortable in formalizing or making information explicit when they share and trust the same ethical values related to appropriate information use. This creates confidence that formal information sources are accurate and trustworthy.

The area of information control has been a major area of study and discussion in management and control stream literature directly related to proactive information use. This stream, developing out of the accounting function, recognized the role of using performance information to manage people by linking individual performance to business performance. As discussed in Chapter 2, while control was clearly identified as a key behavioral variable affecting employee motivation and thus business performance, its definition has undergone considerable changes over the last fifty years. The 'top-down' approach to control has been replaced in more recent years by a 'bottom-up approach' that uses performance-based information to motivate people to continuously relate their personal performance to the company's business performance (Johnson 1992). Thus, the use of information for this stream is perceived as a 'positive' lever for managers to use in implementing strategy.

Both integrity and formality affect information control—by providing employees with trustworthy and formal information related to individual and organizational performance. By linking individual performance to organizational performance, managers could directly motivate employees, creating proactive information behaviors for improved information effectiveness (see Fig. 5.1).

The behavior and control literature identified two additional ideas having both a direct and indirect influence on proactiveness—transparency and sharing.

Transparency as a behavioral element of information use has been addressed primarily by the learning organization scholars. Openness and transparency with information has been discussed more generally within the work of Argyris and Schön's single and double loop learning (Argyris and Schön 1978), and more specifically with Senge's learning organization framework (Senge 1990). Transparency—treating errors, mistakes, failures, and surprises as constructive learning opportunities—accelerates the feedback loop between a company's intended strategy, its actions to implement the strategy, and its capability to correct or change course along the way.

We believe that supported by integrity and formal information use, information control has a direct influence on information transparency. By sharing trustworthy and formalized performance information with organizational members, managers show that they are willing to be open with strategic, financial, and personal performance information. We believe that the result is the creation of a more transparent and open organizational environment poised to deal constructively with mistakes, errors, and failures. A transparent information use environment would improve proactive information use by encouraging the information behavior of sharing (see Fig. 5.1).

Lastly, the business value of sharing information, like the control dimension, has been a common theme across the human resources stream's thinking and practice. It has been addressed as a key behavior by the 'total quality' movement scholars (Bell, McBride, and Wilson 1994; Hodgetts 1993), by organizational design advocates (Galbraith 1995), by advocates of networked or virtual organizations (Lipnack and Stamps 1997; Charan 1991), and more recently by information use scholars (Davenport 1997). We believe that transparency permits senior managers to build trust in sharing information across the company. If the company permits organizational members to deal with mistakes, errors, and failures positively, then organizational members are more disposed to share many other types of information as well, thus directly influencing proactive information behaviors.

Information control also has a direct influence on sharing. If senior managers provide formal, credible, and useful information about the performance of the company at each level of employees, they can build a climate of trust among organizational members regarding their willingness to share the most important information in a company—about their own and the company's performance—with employees. In companies where performance-based information is widely shared and cascaded through all teams and work groups, there is a disposition among organizational members to share many other types of information—such as competitive, customer, or operational information—in teams, across functions, and within processes. In this type of organization, there is a form of 'enlightened self-interest' that promotes the attitude that people share because it is in their best interests to share information that can improve decision making and make the company less prone to errors, mistakes, failures, and surprises.

This research theory suggests the cumulative effect of information integrity, formality, control, transparency, and sharing provides the direct and indirect influences on proactive information use. We believe that organizations that can leverage the interactions between these five information behaviors and values produce enlightened proactive information users who have recognition of the need, and a strong disposition, for thinking about how to use information for new products and services, sensing for new information in their business environments, and analyzing this information to make the best decisions possible before responding to competitive challenges.

In the next section, we will define and describe more fully each behavior and value dimension.

## A. Information integrity

Integrity is a value that plays an important part in effective information use in business organizations. Integrity is reflected in individual and organizational values as well as associated behaviors.

At the individual level, integrity involves several interrelated characteristics.

First, it is associated with 'soundness of moral principle' (Brown 1993), implying that a person practices what he preaches regardless of emotional or social pressure. The person with integrity is said to be 'principled' (Becker 1998: 157). When there are conflicts or debates over integrity, they usually involve differences over the interpretation of whose principles should define or frame actions displaying the lack of integrity.

Second, integrity is strongly related to seeking and telling the truth. This idea involves not just being honest or not deceiving, but also the characteristic of representing reality as accurately as possible. A person with integrity will present reality as they see it, and not hide the bad news or gloss over important facts or concerns that are difficult to present to others.

Third, a person with integrity will be candid or straightforward in his words and actions. But this candor will be tempered with a sense of fairness. A person with integrity can exercise good judgement, about not just what to say and do, but how to say and do it with a sense of reasonable consideration for what others will say and do as well. The concern here is not with making others feel good, but with treating others fairly.

At the organizational level, integrity is based on the notion that a company is guided by a set of key principles that have to do with 'reasonable ethical behavior'. Not only is the company expected to act ethically relative to its employees, customers, stakeholders, and the business environment, but managers and employees inside an organization will also display integrity in words and deeds with each other. Here integrity is closely related to the development of trust among organizational members: people believe in and share a set of common principles about appropriate behavior in the organization. Trust is 'usually accompanied by an assumption of an acknowledged duty to protect the rights and interests of others' (Hosmer 1995: 392).

Integrity within organizations also impacts the use of power or influence by managers and employees in getting things done. The exercise of power or influence is expected within organizations; but how they are exercised should be tempered and constrained by the ethical principles and behaviors that both managers and employees are expected to live by. Thus integrity provides managers and employees with the boundary conditions in which power and influence can be legitimately employed in an organization.

Finally, integrity is an essential 'trait' or characteristic of leadership by senior managers. Not only are senior managers expected to display integrity in their words and actions in the organization, they are also expected to establish and enforce the principles associated with integrity inside and outside the organization. Managerial credibility thus depends on whether managers display integrity in their decision making and behaviors, as well as in the exercise of influence or power, as they seek to frame and implement their intended strategies. 'Getting business results without losing integrity' has a direct impact on the credibility of leadership (Kouzes and Posner 1993).

Information integrity is an organizational value exhibited through the behavior of managers and employees that conditions the use of information and knowledge for decision making in several ways:

First, for information to be of value in decision processes, it should be free of distortions so that the information accurately reflects reality—the events, context, and actions as they occur. At a minimum, people should not knowingly pass on inaccurate information to their managers or other employees. Personal honesty and truth seeking should lead managers and employees to foster a climate in the company where people will not intentionally pass on inaccurate or distorted information.

Second, information can only contribute to decisions if it is used before decisions are made, and not just to justify decisions after the fact. The expectation in most businesses that information will be used rationally does not remove the use of information to shade analysis or arguments to favor some decisions over others. Information is a key source of personal, departmental, and managerial power and influence. Its manipulation before decisions are made to argue positions, and after decisions occur to justify intended courses of action, is restrained by principles and actions influencing information integrity within a company.

Third, effective decision making normally requires that all the pertinent information should be available before decisions are made. If managers or employees keep important pieces of information to themselves that could be used in decisions, then the integrity of information use, and decision making between individuals and the organization, is called into question. Keeping key information to oneself can occur for many reasons—fear of personal consequences for releasing it, protection of the person's perceived influence by withholding information, or hoarding information because it is difficult to share it in a particular company.

Fourth, information integrity, at a minimum, should constrain people from using the organization's information for personal gain. A basic condition for trust in an organization is that managers and employees will not use their positions or privileged access to sensitive information for personal gain. This is a sensitive issue in many companies today since the line between a person's knowledge and information that is truly personal, and what the company has a legitimate interest in controlling, not just during employment, but also upon separation from the company, is blurring. Nevertheless, information integrity requires managers to establish and enforce the boundaries beyond which using information for personal gains is not acceptable within a company.

Without clear expectations or boundaries between purely personal and organizational use of information and knowledge, managers cannot foster a climate where formal information will be viewed as accurate, honest, and trustworthy. In addition, the transparency needed to share sensitive information within a company will suffer. Organizational members will not trust each other enough to exchange information that has potential negative consequences for others, or information that may make one group look better than others within the company. As we will suggest later in our discussion, trust is a precondition for sharing information, therefore managers and employees must possess strong personal integrity if a company will share on a regular basis information that makes a difference to decisions and actions affecting the performance of the company.

## B. Information formality

The next information behavior concerns the relationship between formal and informal information use in a company. As early as the 1930s the Human Relations School began focusing on how people communicated and networked within companies, and how information use was influenced by these informal relationships and networks, in addition to the formal communications and reporting patterns defined by the organization's management structure and way of doing business (Mayo 1933).

During the 1960s and 1970s, many empirical studies were conducted to better understand the interplay between formal and informal communication patterns and people networking within companies. Basically, researchers found that both forms of communication and information use were necessary in organizations: 'Both formal and informal systems are necessary for group activity, just as two blades are essential to make a pair of scissors work' (Davis 1967). Researchers also found that not only were formal and informal ways of communicating and information use complementary, they were also substitutable. That is, informal communications and information use could supplement formal communications and information practices (and vice versa). However, formal patterns of communication and information use were generally considered more stable and predictable over time (Rogers and Agarwala-Rogers 1976: 81).

Thus, formal information use or information formality means that business organizations will push to establish formal processes and information flows to achieve predictable business results, to assure appropriate controls are in place, and to deliver products and services in a consistent manner. Managers and employees will generally use formal information sources and systems to assure efficiency in operations and process management. They will also rely, to some extent, on formal information uses for management decision making and innovation, if they believe that the information is reliable, relevant, and trustworthy. However, we also know that organizations will seek to supplement formal information for decision making using informal contacts and communications with people inside and outside the company to check the reliability of formal information, or to supplement the formal information available, if necessary.

## C.  Information control

As we observed in Chapter 2, the Behavior and Control School has emphasized the role of information in managing people, and the importance of linking their performance to the company's performance. In recent years, there has been a significant increase in managerial efforts to develop financial and non-financial metrics such as the 'balanced scorecard' and 'economic value added', and to interpret these performance criteria and measures at each level in the company. Some companies have developed 'cockpits' of key measures that are deployed within each department and work unit in the company. These are intended to build awareness among employees of the relationships between their job or work unit performance and the company's overall performance.

Historically, the field of accounting has been preoccupied with getting the 'right' financial measures in place, even when they were not always useful to senior managers in actually running the firm. As we noted in Chapter 2, the critique of the relevance of the management accounting field has come from within in recent years, and has been quite severe: 'Management accounting practice in the past forty years has had companies *control with accounting results* by having people manipulate output of processes to achieve accounting targets' (Johnson 1992: p. xi).

To overcome these shortcomings, developments in management accounting have gone in two interrelated directions.

First, there has been considerable effort to broaden and improve performance criteria and metrics to supplement financial criteria with customer-oriented, operational, service, and even 'learning and growth' measures. The 'balanced scorecard' advocated by Kaplan and Norton (1992, 1993, and 1996c) has been widely adopted in companies. The intent is not only to 'get the right measures in place', but also to 'cascade' these perform-ance criteria and measures to all levels in the company. The process of cas-cading articulates, connects, and communicates the relationship between performance criteria and measures and the intended strategy of a firm to all levels in the company, and ties employee rewards to appropriate perform-ance. A key reason for implementing such a program is to improve trans-parency and feedback at all levels in the company about what works and does not work in implementing the intended strategy of a company to improve learning. Thus, it is important that information on business per-formance is continuously presented to employees to influence their indi-vidual and group performance. In addition, the people in a company must be motivated to use the information provided about company performance to improve their individual performance as well.

The second direction in which the management accounting field has moved is to rethink the broader issue of 'control' as a lever of strategic change. A large element of management control is exercised through infor-mation control. Robert Simons has suggested that control can be exercised through four approaches. Two are positive control approaches: (1) belief sys-tems that are used to 'inspire and direct search for new opportunities'; and (2) interactive control systems that are used 'to stimulate organizational learning and the emergence of new ideas and strategies.' Two are negative control approaches: (1) boundary systems that are used 'to set limits on opportunity-seeking behavior'; and (2) diagnostic control systems that are used 'to moti-vate, monitor and reward achievement of specified goals' (Simons 1995: 7).

Managers can use these approaches in a dynamic way to promote the search for innovation and to exercise control. Belief systems inspire the search, but boundary systems define the focus and attention devoted to search by orga-nizational members. Interactive systems encourage managers to commu-nicate with employees to stimulate the emergence of new ideas and learning from mistakes, errors, and failures, while diagnostic control sys-tems help evaluate individual and unit performance consistent with the company's intended strategy.

To implement these approaches to control requires a company to be highly focused on how managers use information to control people and processes.

Companies where information about control is scattered among organizational units—each responsible for different performance criteria and different control systems—cannot exercise control over people or business processes very well. For example, in some companies, separate functional departments are responsible for different performance criteria and their control throughout the company such as: accounting controls (financial measures), service department controls (service measures), marketing and sales controls (customer satisfaction measures), and manufacturing controls (operational measures). Each of these departments develops and uses information to control its performance measures, but the information about overall company performance is so scattered in separate units that it is difficult for the senior managers to exercise appropriate controls over people and processes.

Similarly, senior managers cannot dynamically balance the four approaches to control where information is distributed on a 'need to know' basis—where people know what to do, but they do not know why they are doing the work for which they are responsible. This traditional view of management control associated with vertical, top-down control and bottom-up 'reporting' leads to rigid information flows up and down the hierarchy. These 'reporting' flows stifle the search for new opportunities and correction of errors, surprises, and mistakes, and lead a firm to become more, not less, rigid over time in pursuing intended strategy. When people do not know why they are doing what they do, and its connection to their company's performance, control is lost rather than gained.

## D.  Information transparency

Transparency is associated with four characteristics. First, transparency means being candid with one's thoughts—free from bias and accepting of the views of others. Second, transparency implies basic fairness—a person will be honest, impartial, and fair in dealing with decisions and situations that arise. Third, transparency, like sharing, requires trust between people—a sense of confidence that another person will not use your thoughts or information against you. Finally, transparency requires 'openness' to other people's thoughts and concerns even when the 'news' is negative or not good.

This suggests that high levels of personal and organizational integrity are required for being transparent about 'bad news' or surprises inside a company. People must know what information behaviors undermine integrity in a company, and within these standards act in a candid, honest manner in understanding the good and bad realities of the company to improve them. It may also be that a cultural climate of 'information selflessness' helps to create positive motivations and incentives to use information constructively to resolve hard problems.

Imagine a company environment that abhors surprises, errors, mistakes, and failures. In such companies, performance information tends to be managed from the top down and not shared or understood by organizational members. When errors, mistakes, and failures occur in such companies, they are not made formal or explicit by organizational members lest the 'messengers' are penalized. Incidents of 'shooting the messenger' are widely shared in the informal networks of such companies, and have a dampening effect on responding to emergent problems and errors that may require changes in intended strategy. Such companies foster high levels of 'political' competition among units, functions, teams, and individuals. People act in their self-interest rather than in the interest of the company as a whole. In the end, senior managers in such companies exhibit a strong bias toward certainty, but actually promote greater 'business uncertainty', since they do not know what they do not know, and their own people will not share the bad news with them.

Transparency is both a managerial value as well as an organizational value most directly associated with the disposition to listen to the 'bad news' and not just the 'good news'. Senior managers who only want to hear about organizational successes, positive numbers, and 'no surprises' are commonly viewed as lacking in transparency. Similarly, organizations that foster a climate of only focusing on the good news, positive returns, and what works often lack transparency as well. Why?

Transparency with information about failure, errors, mistakes, and surprises (We do not know why we did something, but it worked!) is required for three reasons.

First, the improvement of product and process quality is dependent on the identification and resolution of defects and mistakes. For many years, the 'total quality' movement has emphasized the need to develop attitudes and values among managers and organizational members where fear of making mistakes, identifying defects, and constructively resolving problems must be removed to continuously improve both business processes and products. Without fostering the belief among managers and workers that quality comes from continuously removing defects, failures, and mistakes, and learning from these 'opportunities', managers and their companies can only react to the inevitable problems and 'surprises' too late.

The second reason why transparency is required about errors, mistakes, and failures is that it is fundamental to managerial and organizational learning. Managers and members are continuously confronted with changes in their internal and external business environments. Changing business conditions are challenging how managers and members think about responding to these changes. In what Argyris and Schön (1978) call 'single loop learning', organizational managers and members detect errors, problems, and failures in their responses to changing business conditions that they try to correct with their intended strategy or mindset—their 'theory-in-use'. If they can resolve the sources of error or failure within their existing mindset and intended strategy, then the company stays on its course. However, if the sources of error and failure cannot be resolved within the intended strategy or mindset, then organizational members must engage in 'double loop learning' (Argyris and Schön 1978: 20). They must re-examine their intended strategy and mindset, challenge both openly, and rethink the basis for their decisions and strategies—redefine their 'theory-in-use'. To do so, managers and members must not only trust each other enough to share information about errors, failures, surprises, and mistakes, they must encourage openness in promoting effective use of the information to rethink their intended strategy and mindset. Openness to learning about changes in business conditions requires transparency among managers and members to engage in either single loop or double loop learning as required.

The third reason why transparency about errors, mistakes, surprises, and failures is important concerns the level of uncertainty that companies face, and the speed of feedback and response that they must have to confront turbulent changes in business conditions. Rarely are managers or organizational members in a position to optimize their strategic choices. More often than not, they are trying to 'satisfice' with information that is 'good enough'. Faced with increasingly turbulent business conditions, managers must focus their time on coping with uncertainty using imperfect information. If decisional choices and outcomes are always uncertain to some degree, then the capability of an organization to sense, process, and learn about the relevant sources of uncertainty is critical.

To stay on course, or even to change course in achieving business results, senior managers must leverage a company's learning capacity to identify and respond to surprises, mistakes, errors, and failures in its business environment. Surprises are unexpected consequences arising from the actions of organizational members in implementing a company's intended strategy, or from unexpected consequences of individual and group activities. Surprises may also arise from the actions of competitors that affect company performance or capabilities. Mistakes and errors occur in operational processes and in products and services that organizational members experience directly or detect from customers. Failures, both big and small, occur as organizational members innovate with new products and services, or new processes and people.

Dealing with the inevitability that surprises, mistakes, and failures will happen in rapidly changing business conditions requires openness and candor in dealing with what some companies regard as 'negative' information and what other companies regard as 'opportunities to learn'.

For the former, errors, mistakes, and even surprises imply 'failures' in intended strategy that should not happen. The information is 'bad', since it implies failure to successfully implement the intended strategy of senior managers. This mindset perceives all defects and problems as challenging the accepted direction. In these companies, there is a tendency to 'shoot the messengers of bad tidings.' Error correction and feedback are delayed in these companies, since no one has any reason to report 'bad news'.

On the other hand, treating failures, surprises, and errors constructively requires managers and organizational members to accept the inevitability of emergent strategies, and to rethink the existing strategies with the conviction that neither senior managers nor the company are 'always right'. As Peter Senge has noted: 'Nothing undermines openness more surely than certainty. Once we feel we have "the answer", all motivation to question our thinking disappears' (Senge 1990: 281). Information transparency means that information about errors, surprises, and failures are treated in an open, candid, trusting, and fair way by organizational managers and members alike. In the face of rapidly changing business conditions with high levels of uncertainty about what works and what does not work, information transparency is the litmus test of rapid, constructive, and flexible organizational learning.

## E.  Information sharing

Sharing, in English usage, means 'to divide and apportion in shares between two or more recipients.' As Tom Davenport has observed, for most of us sharing is a clear and straightforward value and set of behaviors:

We're supposed to learn how to share tangible goods like candy and toys in childhood; nevertheless, throughout our adult lives we still wrestle with how much we should share our money, property and time, probably because sharing always sounds easier to do than it is. (Davenport 1997: 87)

Sharing appears to be a 'voluntary act', but in many circumstances we are 'asked', 'encouraged', or 'urged' to share our toys with siblings or playmates, our knowledge or information with our team members or managers, and our time with our spouses and friends. What appears to be a simple and 'voluntary act', on its face, becomes more complex when we examine the preconditions for sharing, the actual acts of sharing among people, and the perceived consequences of sharing for the 'sharer' and the recipients of the act of sharing.

### Preconditions for sharing information

Sharing information must always occur in some context—among friends, within a family, and in a business organization. How individuals can share information will be affected by five preconditions for sharing information in a company.

The first precondition is the existence of some common language and shared meanings among members of an organization. People cannot share information in a company if they do not share a common language and meanings of basic ideas such as a 'customer', an 'account', an 'order', a 'shipment'. If multiple meanings are associated with common terms, then sharing information about 'customers' between sales and manufacturing may be very difficult.

The second precondition for sharing information is the existence of a prior relationship between members of an organization based on how much is known about people relative to their roles and positions in a company. We will share certain types of information with subordinates that we may not share with our boss. We will share more information with experienced members of the team versus new members.

A third precondition is the perceived level of trust among people who can share information. The assumption is that the level of perceived trust is directly proportional to the willingness to share information. The level of trust is a function of perceptions that if information is shared, it will not be used against the sharer, or it will not be used to the other person's advantage and the disadvantage of the sharer.

A fourth precondition for sharing in a business is that there needs to be a shared purpose or common stake or ownership of results. Sharing information is important to achieve improved business results. At a minimum, there needs to be a sense of the negative consequences of not sharing information.

Finally, the fifth precondition is that sharing of information must be part of the company's culture—what organizational members are expected to do with information. In some companies, the relationship between information sharing and the company's culture may be more informal than formal.

## The act of information sharing

There are many ways to share information. We may share information formally through meetings, reports, e-mails, and memos, or informally through conversations in the hallway or outside of working hours. In some cases, organizational members may be more disposed to share positive information formally and negative information informally, depending on the level of trust and perceived consequences of the act of sharing.

The act of sharing will also depend on the type of information that is shared. Public or non-sensitive information is more easily shared inside a company than sensitive, private, or confidential information. Information sharing that has risks associated with who is rewarded or blamed may be more difficult to share than information where sharer and recipient both win, or the outcome is neutral for them. Sharing information about errors, mistakes, or failures in a company may have personal disadvantages for the person, but learning advantages for the business. Sharing information about failures, errors, and mistakes may be correlated to the degree of transparency and integrity among organizational members.

## The perceived consequences of sharing information

The sharing of information is dependent on the degree of dependence or interdependence among members of the organization or outsiders such as suppliers and customers. Sharing is always associated with perceptions of gains or losses from sharing information and the degree of mutuality in sharing between people. If I share sensitive information today (where you can gain), will you do the same for me tomorrow? In an interdependent relationship, sharing is a function of perceived mutuality and win/win outcomes. In a dependent relationship, sharing may be a function of who loses or gains, or whether there is a win/win outcome possible through sharing information, for example, with suppliers.

Thus, sharing information in a business is a complex act. Information may be more freely shared among individuals or small teams than between functions or departments in a company. In addition, information may be shared inside a company, but may not be as readily shared outside the company with suppliers, customers, or partners.

## The business value of sharing information

The business value of sharing information has been a common theme across many streams of management thinking and practice. The 'total quality' movement sees information sharing among teams as central to team performance. To improve product or process quality, team members must identify and share information about the sources of defects, failures, and mistakes. To do so requires team members to share this information freely within the team, and to suggest options for solving quality problems (Bell, McBride, and Wilson 1994; Hodgetts 1993).

Similarly, the organizational design advocates (Galbraith 1995) have promoted information sharing by redesigning business organizations so that vertical lines of communication and information reporting are shifted to the background of the organization, and lateral, cross-functional processes and information flows are encouraged in the foreground of organizational activities. Advocates of continuous improvement and 're-engineering' have both supported the virtues of simplified, streamlined processes across the value chains of companies as the basis for information sharing and improved human communications across functions.

Finally, advocates of networked or virtual organizations (Lipnack and Stamps 1997; Charan 1991) have suggested that, with the help of IT, information sharing can be encouraged across virtual teams and across processes like supply chains with suppliers, customers, and partners operating in a virtual network. As Charan has observed,

Sharing information openly, visibly, and simultaneously is one of the most important dimensions of sustaining a network over time. Over time, the free flow of information allows networks to become self-correcting. (Charan 1991: 114)

Thus, sharing of information is, in many organizations, perceived as both an important value that senior managers can influence, and a set of behaviors associated with what organizational members are expected to do with information inside the company, and outside with customers, suppliers, and partners.

## F. Proactive information use

Proactive information use can be evaluated based on several branches of management and practitioner thinking—innovation researchers (Deschamps 2000), general management scholars (Hamel and Prahalad 1994), and more recently knowledge management practitioners (Sveiby 1997). Woven within the arguments of these research areas has been the acknowledgement of the need to get people thinking about and learning how to use information to create new products and services, to improve their capacity to actively seek out changes in the business environment, create industry foresight, and to create the 'capacity to act' and respond to this information and knowledge.

In the context of creating or enhancing products and services, a company must value people who actively think about using information to manage innovation in products and services effectively. This involves developing 'innovation streams' that can be leveraged for future product enhancements, or new product development. Throughout this process of enhancing or creating new products, managers must focus organizational members on using the information that the company has on hand as well as seeking new information in the form of clues, trends, and signals that provide the basis for future action (Deschamps 2000).

The first step in the innovation process is to 'identify the right customer problems' by seeking the right type of intelligence in three areas (Deschamps 2000):

- '*Market intelligence* to uncover problems customers would really like to see resolved or unarticulated needs which they "feel" without being able to express';
- '*Competitor intelligence* to zoom in on those problems which competitors have not yet discovered or satisfactorily solved';
- '*Technology intelligence* to identify those very problems which could be solved through a smart combination of existing and new technology' (Deschamps 2000).

The ability to translate thinking about innovation into the active seeking of information related to competitive trends in this area has been popularized by Hamel and Prahalad (1994) in their well-known book entitled *Competing for the Future*. Hamel and Prahalad (1994) argue that a basic responsibility of senior managers and senior management teams is to 'create the future' for their companies. To do so, this requires a company to:

1. change in some fundamental way;
2. redraw the boundaries between industries; and/or
3. create entirely new industries.

To create the future, senior managers must be willing to 'unlearn' much of the experience and strategies that made them successful and to 'develop *great* foresight into the whereabouts of tomorrow's markets' (Hamel and Prahalad 1994: 23).

Industry foresight has to do with developing a point of view about what future benefits a company should seek to provide, what competencies are needed to deliver future customer value, and what the customer interface will look like. Gaining this foresight requires managers and employees to anticipate what cues, signals, and trend lines will be important to future success before the information is well defined and known by competitors. Companies must look beyond the markets and customers they now serve to enlarge the 'opportunity horizon' by seeking to exploit their competencies in new directions. To do this effectively, senior managers and employees must actively seek out information about changes and trends in the company's business environment before their competitors. Having foresight involves anticipating the future before the 'future happens'.

Once companies acquire the insight and information to anticipate business changes and trends, will the company's managers and employees 'use the information' to respond rapidly to the changes in the competitive environment of the company? Acting on the information that is sensed and collected requires a company climate where people seek information eagerly and respond to it quickly. Managers in such a company must not only employ information in response to business changes effectively and rapidly, they must develop among organizational members a sense of urgency in sensing information that is useful, and sharing it effectively among other employees, in teams, and across functions.[1] Knowledge management scholars have begun to speak about this as the need for organizations to develop the 'capacity to act' (Sveiby 1997) that allows people the flexibility to respond to this information and knowledge.

Proactive information use involves how 'well' people think about using information to create or enhance products and services, actively seek out information about business conditions to test these ideas, and respond quickly to this information. As we have suggested in Chapter 4, together these practices create the affective response needed to set the environmental preconditions for the more cognitive practice of sensing to occur. There is research evidence that suggests the existence of a behavioral predisposition toward information scanning and looking at information for meaning and new knowledge (Vandenbosch and Huff 1997). For example, being more proactive in one's information usage behavior—willing to think about, seek

[1] According to O'Rielly (1989: 15), this company is based on a 'belief in action' shared by company employees and managers. In examining the 'norms that promote innovation', O'Rielly has identified the key traits of the 'belief in action':
- people are not obsessed with precision
- there is clear emphasis on results
- people are expected to meet their commitments
- people are anxious about timeliness
- people value getting things done
- hard work is expected and appreciated
- people feel empowered
- people emphasize quality
- there is an eagerness to get things done
- people like to cut through bureaucracy.

out, and respond to new information—creates a higher propensity to make good valuation judgements in sensing, whereby people identify and begin to define new information requirements not only for themselves, but also as being helpful to others in decision making.

Such proactive information behavior would also seem to drive more effective information processing practices as where people have a better understanding of the information required for performing their jobs, and relating to the work of their colleagues. When an organization as a whole has a better understanding of the nature of work of each of its people, it can also better deploy IT to support decision making. When IT systems help formalize an organization's knowledge, greater transparency is established throughout the company, feeding more sharing and more proactive behavior.

In the next section, we provide the empirical results used to test this unified theory of information behaviors and values.

## 2. HOW SENIOR MANAGERS EVALUATE INFORMATION BEHAVIOR AND VALUES

Based on theories and concepts discussed in sections 1 and 2, we developed questionnaire items that measured each dimension of the information behaviors and values model.

As we originally suspected, the factor loading scores from our confirmatory factor model presented in Fig. 5.2 show that senior managers perceive each of the six behaviors and values identified in our information behavior model as distinct and valid measures. More importantly, we found that senior managers view these all six values and associated behaviors as defining a higher-level common idea we call the 'information behaviors and values capability', which is supported by overall statistical model fit. The model also indicates that, while each of the six dimensions were shown to be discrete and valid ideas, the varying factor scores indicate that some of these dimensions of behaviors and values contributed more completely than others toward the higher-level, commonly held, information behaviors and values capability.

In particular, sharing (.87), transparency (.84), and control (.82) are very well recognized by senior managers followed by integrity (.68) and information proactiveness (.67) and, finally, information formality (.47). In the following subsection, we discuss factor loadings on the item level to gain a deeper understanding of the empirical model presented in Fig. 5.2.

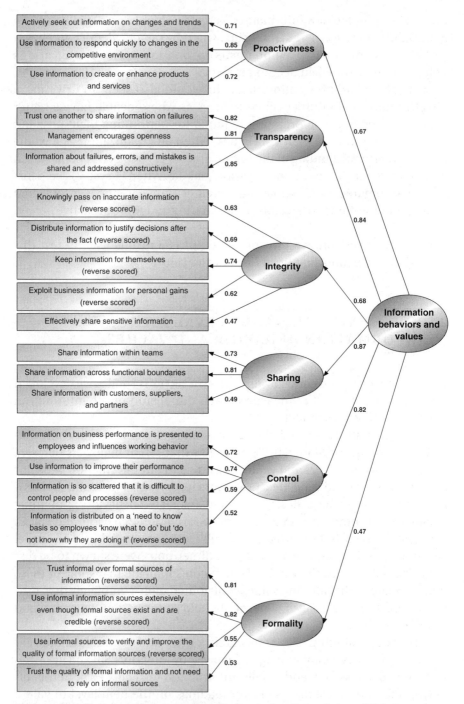

**Fig. 5.2.** Confirmatory Factor Model of Information Behaviors and Values

## A. Information integrity

Information integrity, which we defined as the use of information in a trustful and principled manner at the individual and organizational level, is recognized in management thinking today, and in the statements of guiding principles advanced by senior managers for their companies. While there may still be debates and confusion about the precise 'ethical standards' that should be linked to integrity, the views of senior managers about associated behaviors and practices connected to information integrity are fairly clear.

Information integrity is a value that defines the boundaries beyond which managers and people may not go in a company. It implies that there are ways of using information that are *not* appropriate and that will be sanctioned by managers and organizational members alike. To test this view of information integrity, we included in our survey four items (see Fig. 5.2) that were negative information behaviors and one that was a positive information behavior. However, to determine the extent to which the negative behaviors contributed to the integrity dimension, these four behaviors were reverse scored.

*Negative behaviors*

1. Frequently, our people knowingly pass on inaccurate information to their bosses or other employees (.63).
2. Our people frequently distribute information to justify decisions after the fact (.69).
3. Our people frequently keep information to themselves (.74).
4. Our people frequently exploit business information for personal gain (.62).

*Positive behavior*

5. The strong personal integrity of our people enables the effective sharing of sensitive information (.47).

It appears that information integrity is clearly recognized by the limits in which senior managers perceive organizational members and themselves should stay, rather than how they should use information (especially 'sensitive information') if they have integrity. Simons refers to this type of value and behavior as being part of the organization's 'boundary system'—senior managers define the space in which organizational members can act (Simons 1995). The boundary system does not tell you what you can do, but what you should not do. Thus, senior management's view of information integrity is important for setting the limits around appropriate information use by organizational members. Within these limits, organizational members can be very proactive with information since proactive use of information is a positive belief that senior managers may foster. Information integrity, on the other hand, can be more easily understood by what organizational members should not do to violate organizational standards, than what they should do.

## B.  Information formality

Information formality, or the willingness to use and trust institutionalized information over informal sources, seems to be the least well-represented idea of the information behaviors and values dimensions in the minds of senior managers (.47). In our earlier discussion of information formality literature, we noted that companies will try to formalize information practices and IT to provide products and services consistently, control operations and decision making by organizational members, and achieve predictable results.

In the four behaviors included in our survey (see Fig. 5.2) senior managers clearly recognized that people frequently trust informal over formal sources of information (.81), and make extensive use of informal sources of information—even though formal information sources exist and are credible (.82). Since the literature, and our own experience based on discussions with senior managers, indicates that senior managers have a 'bias for the use of formal information' in the company if the formal information is credible, we negatively scored these behaviors. Thus, to interpret the contribution of these two questions to the information behaviors and values capability, the reader should place the words 'Our people do not . . .' before each behavior. Based on the high factor loadings of these two items, we can see that senior managers clearly recognized a bias for formality as the most significant to the formality dimension.

In the same vein, we must interpret the next question as 'Our people do not use informal sources of information to verify and improve the quality of formal information sources.' The lower factor loading (.55) for this behavior seems to indicate that managers do not hold the same bias towards formality when it come to verification of formal systems. Apparently, they may see the use of informal information sources as a quality check on formal sources. Moreover, when they were asked the converse question as to whether their people trust the quality of formal information, and do not need to rely on informal sources of information, an explanation of our lower factor score of .53 seems to follow the same logic. Namely, senior managers may perceive that informal information is useful in certain situations regardless of whether formal information is trusted and credible.

In sum, while a formality dimension that emphasizes a bias for the use of trusted and credible institutional information was found to be a valid and reliable idea in the minds of senior managers, we are still somewhat unresolved as to the extent to which senior managers believe this dimension pushes for an exclusively formal information use concept.

## C.  Information control

We defined information control as the extent to which information about performance is continuously presented to people to manage and monitor their performance. Managers use information to monitor and control operational activities and decisions to achieve intended strategy and improve business performance. As we can see from our results in Fig. 5.2, managers understand the idea of information on business performance being continuously presented to employees to influence their working behaviors (.72). As we noted in the previous section, the focus on developing new performance criteria and measures of performance such as 'the balanced scorecard' (Kaplan and Norton 1996c) and 'the service profit chain' (Heskett, Sasser, and Schlesinger 1997) and cascading these measures down through the organization to influence worker behavior is not new. Neither is the related idea that people should use information provided to them to improve their performance (.74).

However, when we asked senior managers whether they understood that control of people and processes is more difficult if information is scattered around the company, they perceived this idea did not contribute as strongly (.59) to the control concept. Perhaps some senior managers did not associate this idea with information control, since the dispersion of information in a company is related to the structure and size of the company, or its geographic coverage, not simply to the difficulty of controlling information across functions, business units, and departments. In addition, some senior managers may not be as familiar with more recent advances in IT practices (e.g. data warehousing, data replication) that support centralized data management capabilities even in diverse multinational organizations.

Similarly, when we asked senior managers whether information tends to be distributed on a 'need to know' basis, so employees 'know what to do' but 'they do not know why they are doing it', the recognition of this idea as contributing to the control idea was the lowest (.52). Perhaps there is good news in this finding, since it appears that senior managers are less familiar with this information behavior as a technique for controlling information. While distributing information in companies on a need to know basis may still be done for confidential and proprietary reasons, this practice may not be as widely employed for deliberately keeping employees in the dark about why they are executing specific tasks and responsibilities on the job as we had initially proposed.

## D.  Information transparency

Information transparency can be defined as openness in reporting and presentation of information on errors, failures, and mistakes. Like sharing, we found information transparency to be a very well-recognized concept in the minds of senior managers. Information transparency permits organizational members to learn from failures, errors, and mistakes. Information transparency facilitates continuous feedback. The faster and more effective organizational members are in identifying problems, and responding to them constructively, the better they can modify or change their intended strategy and implementation paths to account for new and emergent learnings from outside and inside the company.

Not surprisingly, when we asked senior managers about the following three behaviors associated with information transparency in their companies, our factor loading scores were very high (see Fig. 5.2):

- Our employees trust one another to share information on failures openly (.82).
- Our management encourages openness to promote effective information use (.81).
- Our company fosters an environment where information about failures, errors, and mistakes is shared and addressed constructively (.85).

These high factor scores for each behavior show that our study captured most of this idea in the minds of senior managers.

## E.  Information sharing

Based on our discussion in the previous section, the concept of information sharing, as we defined it in the study, is the willingness to provide others with information in an appropriate and collaborative fashion. The value of information sharing, as we noted earlier in this chapter, has been an important part of the key management reforms over the last thirty years. The 'total quality' movement, the process redesign and re-engineering movement, and the most recent focus on virtual teams, network organizations, and knowledge management, have all emphasized the importance of freely sharing information within teams and across functional boundaries in companies. As shown in Fig. 5.2, our factor scores for these two types of behaviors were .73 for sharing with teams, and .81 for sharing across functions and departments.

However, when we asked senior managers about 'freely sharing information with customers, suppliers and partners,' their response (.49) indicated that they are uncertain whether they viewed inter-organizational information sharing in the same light as sharing information within companies. Our opinion here is that senior managers may have hesitated somewhat to view internal and external information sharing as the same concept for two reasons.

First, they may not perceive freely sharing information about internal company strategies and actions as a desirable behavior. Sharing information about company deliberations before decisions are made may send false or misleading signals to outsiders. As we observed earlier, sharing is a complex act and there may be good reasons why freely sharing information about internal company plans, decisions, and actions is not advisable.

Second, senior managers may perceive that the acts of sharing related to suppliers, customers, and partners are quite different. A company may choose to share information about product plans and projected orders with preferred suppliers, but not share information about specific negotiations with each supplier for component prices with others. A company may share sales and marketing strategies with a partner in an industry, but not its merger and acquisition planning. Finally, a company may choose to share product information with some customers rather than others, depending on the amount of business the company does with customers, or the prior relationships that the company has had with customers. While there has no doubt been a movement in management thinking during the 1990s to increase sharing of information with suppliers, partners, and customers, the attitudes of senior managers towards acts of sharing are more qualified, and not well understood by management researchers.

In sum, we can say that the information sharing dimension appears to be well recognized by senior managers, particularly as it relates to internal information sharing with team members and across functions. The jury is still out as to whether inter-organizational information sharing will be established as a strong component of this same sharing idea, or be recognized as a separate idea.

## F. Proactive information use

The dimension of proactiveness, or the active concern to think about how to use information, obtain new information, and the desire to put useful information into action, showed strength as a valid and reliable idea unto itself, and the behaviors associated with proactive use of information showed high factor loadings.

As Fig. 5.2 shows, senior managers clearly recognize that their people should use information to respond quickly in the competitive environment of the company (.85). In addition, they also recognize the value (.72) of people thinking about how to use information inside the company to create or enhance products and services and the importance (.71) of their people actively seeking out information about business changes and trends.

There is no question that senior managers associate proactive information use to responding quickly to business changes, and to more innovation in products and services. Anticipating business developments or having 'industry foresight', as Hamel and Prahalad (1994) have so strongly advocated, are behaviors that senior managers believe their people should be practicing in their companies. Moreover, perceiving that people should respond quickly to changes in the competitive environment supports the notion that senior managers have a 'belief in action'. If we proactively sense the right information, then we (ourselves and our people) should respond rapidly. In today's turbulent markets, sensing and responding to signals and cues from customers and competitors are critical to sustaining good business performance. Proactive information use is the most important element in the 'bias towards action' that many managers strive to encourage in their companies.

## 3. IMPLICATIONS FOR MANAGERS AND RESEARCHERS

Breaking new research ground, we have presented in section 2 a statistically valid and integrated model that managers and researchers can use to evaluate their own strengths and weaknesses within the context of the information behaviors and values capability. This model indicates that all six behaviors and values—integrity, formality, control, transparency, sharing, and proactiveness—are essential to developing this capability within an organization. As a measurement tool, it can be used to check the pulse of an organization's effectiveness in developing appropriate information behaviors and values to support effective information use not only with members inside organizational boundaries, but also with those outside traditional organizational boundaries, such as customers, partners, and suppliers.

One of the major managerial implications of this model concerns organizational change. Kotter and Heskett have stated that the 'single most visible factor that distinguishes major cultural changes that succeed is competent leadership at the top' (Kotter and Heskett 1992: 84). This leads us to propose that senior management leadership in shaping a company's information behaviors and values is essential. The pivotal role of 'walking the talk' to encourage appropriate information behaviors cannot be overstated. With this model, senior managers can begin to model those behaviors that we have empirically validated as essential to effective information use.

Our discussion of the information behaviors and values model, however, is not complete. First, as we have suggested in Chapters 3 and 4, valid development of an integrated information behaviors and values model does not necessarily mean that companies with good information behaviors and values will have higher overall business performance. As we will explore in Chapter 6, we believe that good information behaviors and values are only one component of a higher-level concept of effective information use that must also include 'good' IT practices and 'good' information management. Little is known about the relationship between good information behaviors and values and their effect on information management, decision making, and business performance.

Second, we have not yet empirically tested the causal relationships suggested within our research model in section 1. While we know that the individual dimensions of our model are associated with a higher-level idea called the 'information behaviors and values capability', we have not yet validated our causal model that suggests that the combined effect of information integrity, formality, control, transparency, and sharing influences proactive information use. For example, while we know that control is an important aspect of our model, we do not know if it plays as central a role as suggested in section 1. We have also not yet begun to explore how the model can be used to provide managerial prescriptions for organizational change. More generally, we have not explored other cultural issues that may affect the causal linkages between these dimensions such as the ability of a company to encourage its members to translate tacit knowledge into explicit knowledge, the importance of encouraging people to act on behalf of organizational goals, the effect of a learning culture, or the importance of flexibility to encourage action.

Third, while we have made an important step forward in providing a clearer understanding of good information behaviors and values, we still have not addressed the issue of interaction between dimensions of our three information capabilities—IT practices, information management practices, and information behaviors and values. If, as we will see in

Chapter 6, good information behaviors and values are only one component of effective information use, understanding the linkages between individual dimensions across information capabilities can give us clues as to how to best develop our behaviors and practices for maximum benefit.

Based on our research, we believe that we have begun to understand the critical role that proactive information use has within the framework of effective information use. Proactive information use creates the affective response necessary to leverage the cognitive sense making or 'framing' that takes place during the sensing phase of the information life cycle. We believe that proactiveness thus serves as a precondition for the more cognitive sensing practice, having a direct positive influence on the information life cycle. People who recognize the importance of sensing and are actively engaged in the sensing practice will demand new tools, creating the impetus for the organization to build better information systems on the management level to support higher-level decision making capabilities. We might also expect that an organizational bias for proactive behavior, coupled with the appropriate IT support for management-level data analysis, would help drive the necessary information valuation during the processing phase of the information life cycle to determine whether or not a piece of information is relevant to the decision context.

If built properly, these better systems would further support proactive information behaviors by providing tools that make easier thinking about new products and services, seeking out new information, and responding to this information through better decision making. This suggests a cumulative and recursive effect across all three information capabilities (information behaviors and values, information management practices, and IT practices) that would create an energized environment of effective information use.

These three areas leave us with some questions for further exploration and discussion:

- Do integrity, formality, control, transparency, and sharing directly and indirectly influence information proactiveness?
- Is there an appropriate path to improving people's information behaviors and values on an aggregate level?
- Does proactive behavior create the willingness and disposition of people to actively develop sensing practices?
- Does information proactiveness directly influence information valuation within the processing phase of the information life cycle?
- Does IT for management support improve the ability of a company to be proactive with information? What implication does this have on the relationship of the human resources and IT functions?

- Can a company develop more mature information behaviors and values?

These questions and a fuller prescriptive model will be addressed in Chapter 8.

## 4. CONCLUSIONS

In this chapter, we have discussed how senior managers perceive information behaviors and values to improve business performance. For the first time, we have empirically validated that certain behaviors and values do directly influence the way people use information in a company. In analyzing the results of our confirmatory model, we have reached some important conclusions about how senior managers view information behaviors and values to achieve improved business performance.

A.  Senior managers perceive six separate and distinct information values and behaviors and they relate these values and behaviors to a higher-level shared idea we call the 'information behaviors and values' capability. This information behaviors and values capability represents an integrated theoretically derived measure of how well senior managers believe their organizations behave in the use of information.

B.  Validation of a behavior and value model provides a richer understanding of behaviors that relate to effective information use than had been addressed previously in management research.

C.  We have also observed the critical role of organizational and individual integrity as a 'boundary system' in establishing appropriate standards for information use in a company. Integrity sets behavioral rules for what people should not do with information, and can improve formal information use. Companies that have a 'bias for formal information use' may supplement formal systems with informal to get the work done when necessary or to audit the quality of their institutionalized information systems.

D.  We have noted that formal information use can improve information control by ensuring that accurate performance information can be shared with employees at all levels.

E.  Companies that control by sharing performance-based information at all levels create openness and transparency where information about mistakes, errors, and failures can be dealt with in a constructive manner. This promotes a strong disposition toward sharing all types of other company-specific information among organizational members.

F. The relationships between integrity, formality, control, transparency, and sharing create a strong disposition for proactive information behavior in seeking information to respond to problems, and resolve them quickly to improve the performance of the company. This 'belief in action' translates into a disposition for sensing information and responding to changing business conditions as effectively and rapidly as possible to achieve business results.

G. While we found that senior managers recognized information behaviors and values as a separate high-level information capability that reflected a comprehensive measure of effective information behaviors and values, managers appeared to implicitly consider effective information behaviors and values as being supported by good IT practices and information management practices. There was no evidence from our findings that suggested that senior managers believe that improvements in information behaviors and values capability alone, without the accompanying support of solid IT practices or competent information management practices, will result in substantial improvements in business performance.

H. Senior manager mindsets concerning information integrity, formality, control, transparency, sharing, and proactive information use are critical to the speed and effectiveness of decisions in responding to continuously changing business conditions. This improves a company's ability to evaluate the relevance of information to different decision contexts, improving the entire information management life cycle.

I. Finally, while the Behavior and Control School has provided a solid basis for developing concepts and variables to be used in developing our measures, the school's failure to provide a comprehensive theory linking good IT practices and information management practices and good information behaviors and values leads us to suspect that pursuing improvements only in information behaviors and values will not be adequate to effect significant improvements in business performance.

These observations lead us to examine, in the next chapter, whether a comprehensive second-order factor exists that includes the information behaviors and values, information management practices, and IT practices capabilities. Furthermore, we will pursue our concern that this comprehensive measure of information effectiveness will better predict business performance than the individual capabilities will do on their own.

# 6

# Discovering the Link between Information Orientation and Business Performance

During the 1980s in the USA, a debate began in the business press and among managers, academics, and consultants over the perceived 'IT Productivity Paradox': *Why was the estimated $1 trillion invested in IT by American business in the 1980s not resulting in higher economic productivity?*

At a macro level, national productivity statistics in the USA showed little evidence to support claims that IT was transforming business and creating a productivity boom.[1] In fact, the annual rate of productivity for much of the 1980s and early 1990s in the USA showed little increase, while IT spending by the 1990s reached over two-fifths of the total investment in capital equipment by American companies. MIT economist Robert Solow captured the spirit of the debate with his famous remark: 'You can see computers everywhere but in the productivity statistics' (Lester 1998: 228). In addition to little evidence of national productivity benefits, at the micro-economic level many managers were complaining that they saw few output efficiency gains as a consequence of their expensive IT investments within their own companies (Baker 1997).

At about the same time that the IT productivity paradox debate was raging, the IT industry and business press were promoting development of 'strategic information systems'. Advocates promised that strategic IT systems were 'silver bullet' solutions with bottom-line performance benefits that could lead early adopters to sustainable competitive advantage in their industries (Wiseman 1988).

---

[1] 'Productivity: Lost in Cyberspace,' *The Economist*, Sept. 13 1997, p. 78.

So, with the IT productivity paradox on one side and the silver bullet view of strategic information systems on the other side, what should senior managers believe? Several viewpoints were advanced.

In regards to the productivity paradox, some economists argued from historical precedent, and suggested that there existed long time lags between technological breakthroughs and realized productivity gains. 'Just as inexpensive electricity radically transformed the physical layout and flows of materials in factories, transportation systems, and homes, so information technologies will radically transform the way businesses collect, process, interpret, and distribute information—in other words, the way work gets done. . . . But all of this will take time' (Lester 1998: 232). As we start the twenty-first century, strong national GDP growth rates and the continued success in raising national productivity levels in the technology-laden US 'new economy' seem to support this argument.

Some economists, including US Federal Reserve Board chairman Alan Greenspan, suggest that the IT productivity paradox at a macro level was a product of measurement problems associated with national productivity statistics that focused narrowly on the tangible outputs of manufacturing companies, rather than on the less tangible knowledge outputs of companies engaged primarily in services (Lester 1998: 230).

Regarding IT investment payoffs at a micro level, the consulting and IT research communities have come down on both sides of the silver bullet theory. Most researchers failed to find a direct relationship between increases in IT spending and business profitability (Cron and Sobol 1983; Weill 1989; Alpar and Kim 1990). Others suggest that perhaps the emphasis should shift from silver bullet investments to improved overall spending on the entire IT infrastructure that supports a company's business (Roach 1998). In both cases, the resolution of these issues at the company level has concentrated on the roles of IT managers or CIOs, to improve the alignment of IT investments with the business strategy (Willcock 1992*b*; Venkatraman 1994). Or, the spotlight has illuminated what Strassmann (1990) calls the 'Return on Management' or the judgements made by senior managers concerning their ability to leverage IT as a key business resource in the company.

Debate on the relative contribution of IT at both the macro-economic level, and at the company level, continues to challenge the management and academic communities. Many argue that the debate continues because there has been confusion as to the appropriate unit of analysis for determining IT contribution (i.e. macro-economic productivity level, macro-consumer level, company output productivity level, measures of company profitability, or some other indicators of company business performance such as market share or customer satisfaction). Others contend that the reliability and validity of the research data employed in past analyses are inappropriate, incomplete, or inaccurate. So managers are left with few definite answers or clear practical ways to measure the contribution of their information-related investments to companies.

We believe that what has been missing in these debates has been an appropriate answer to the challenge raised by MIT's Richard Lester in his book *The Productivity Edge*:

There is an old adage that you can't manage what you can't measure . . . Until better methods are found for measuring the economic value of information flows, there will be little basis for judging whether the current rate of investment in the new information technologies is too little or too great, and any correspondence between what firms are actually investing in information technology and the optimal level of these investments will be coincidental. (Lester 1998: 242)

In this chapter we directly focus on this problem at the company level by raising our major research question: *does effective information use lead to better business performance?*

In the course of answering this important research question we will determine the following:

1. Is there a comprehensive measure of overall effectiveness of information use?
2. If so, what are the capabilities that make up this measure?
3. Does a comprehensive measure better predict company business performance than the single capabilities?

In this chapter, we evaluate past attempts to link IT (investments, systems, strategic IT applications, etc.) directly to business performance. What can we conclude from almost two decades of empirical research and debate concerning this critical issue? We demonstrate through our study that past attempts to link IT at the company level with business performance may not have included a sufficiently comprehensive measure of effective information use. Further, measuring a company's IT investments (or systems contributions) alone may not sufficiently represent effective information use as it relates to improving a company's performance.

In fact, as we have shown in the previous three chapters, neither the IT School, the Information Management School, nor the Behavior and Control School has provided a comprehensive and theoretically grounded measure of effective information use. Without a measure that subsumes the relationships between how people use information, how it is managed, and how technology can support effective information use, it is understandable how the IT productivity paradox debate flourishes.

We will introduce a new comprehensive measure of effective information use that determines the degree to which a company possesses competence and synergy across all three of the information capabilities established in three previous chapters. This higher-level idea, which we call Information Orientation (IO), will be linked to business performance to determine whether it better predicts performance than the individual information capabilities of each school. We will demonstrate that within the context of a senior manager's responsibility within a firm, the use of this new metric permits him or her to move far beyond the IT productivity paradox debate.

## 1. IT INVESTMENT AND CORPORATE PROFITABILITY: DO WE HAVE A CONNECTION?

During the mid-1980s, enthusiasm for applying information technology to achieve business benefits had reached a peak (Kettinger et al. 1994). Early success stories of 'strategic information systems' (SIS), such as the American Airlines SABRE reservation systems, motivated the business press in the USA to look for other success stories of using IT for competitive advantage. These IT systems achieved mythic proportions in the IT business community as consultants, academics, and managers advanced their legendary capabilities to facilitate market access, differentiate products, achieve cost efficiencies, and transform a company's industry. Even serious IT researchers suggested that strategic users of IT should expect increases in bottom-line measures such as profitability and market share (Weill and Olson 1989; Clemons 1986).

Despite the business hype and writings of consultants and academics associated with this silver bullet view of IT value, no serious empirical studies could prove the link between IT investment and sustainable competitive advantage.

### *From strategic advantage to strategic necessity*

The early IT research on SIS tended to measure impact on business performance through indirect or surrogate measures such as the degree of IT system use, user attitudes, and perceived system success. Later, IT researchers focused on measuring IT impact through financial measures such as 'optimal levels of IT investment' (Bender 1986; Cron and Sobol 1983). Despite attempts to show the contrary, IT researchers had little success in establishing a consistent causal linkage between levels of IT investment and performance (Weill 1989; Turner 1985). When IT researchers tried to evaluate 'strategic' IT investments with financial measures such as Return on Investment, or Return on Assets or sales growth, their focus was often too narrow—either limited to individual case studies or specific uses of IT in single industries—to determine definitely any sustainable IT investment payoff (Clemons 1991; Clemons and Weber 1990; Alpar and Kim 1990; Weill 1989; Banker and Kaufman 1988). Although considerable research efforts were expended, as of the early 1990s no IT researchers had found 'sustainable competitive advantage with IT' over the long term—for example, five to ten years (Kettinger et al. 1994).

The general conclusion that could be drawn was clear: the link between IT investments in companies and their profitability was problematic.

One explanation for a company's inability to profit from IT investment was suggested by Wharton's Eric Clemons in 1986 who noted that benefits from 'externally focused' IT applications were fleeting. If there was no way to defend a company's gains in the marketplace by using IT, then competitors would be able to duplicate innovative IT systems—causing the cost structure of the entire industry to rise, but providing no company-specific competitive advantage (Clemons 1986: 134). Clemons called these applications of IT 'strategic necessities':

Such systems radically change cost structures, relative bargaining power, or the basis for competition to an extent where most competitors are compelled to imitate them . . . Many applications we have examined in financial services, retail banking, and distribution systems have proved to be strategic necessities, despite our initial expectations to the contrary. (Clemons and Row 1991: 275)

### From company profitability to industry and consumer benefits

Taking a different approach to the problem, MIT's Erik Brynjolfsson and Lorin Hitt focused on the value of IT using economic theory and econometrics. These researchers measured the relationship of IT investment to profitability, company output (as a measure of productivity), and consumer value. In this research, their measure of IT was broader than that used by previous researchers. They included the labor costs associated with the IT department, and all computer capital (the total dollar value of mainframes, mini-computers, and personal computers owned by the company) (Hitt and Brynjolfsson 1996: 127).

Based on assessing the IT investments of 370 companies in the Fortune 500 manufacturing and service list, they not only found (see Fig. 6.1) no evidence that IT led to 'supranormal' profits, but found some evidence of a 'small negative impact of profitability.' However, their study did find a significant impact on company output (as a measure of productivity), and a substantial impact on benefits to consumers of between $2 billion and $7 billion per year for these companies (Hitt and Brynjolfsson 1996: 135). Like Clemons, these researchers concluded that IT increases efficiency, and therefore productivity, intensifies industry competition by lowering barriers to entry, and eliminates market inefficiencies that enable companies to maintain a degree of monopoly over customers.

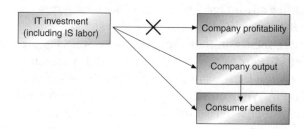

**Fig. 6.1. Findings on IT Investment's Direct Link to Company Output and Consumer Benefits: 'Productivity without Profits'**

*Note*: At an aggregate industry level, IT increases efficiency, and therefore productivity, intensifies industry competition by lowering barriers to entry, and eliminates market inefficiencies. The effect of this increased competition is to reduce prices for output and squeeze out 'fat' by reducing the consumption of other inputs such as capital and labor. For the individual company, the result is 'productivity without profit'. The winner: consumers!

However, for the individual company, the results were 'productivity without profit':

One effect of this increased competition is to reduce prices paid for firm output. A second effect is that firms will work to squeeze out 'fat' by reducing their consumption of other inputs such as ordinary capital and labor. (Hitt and Brynjolfsson 1996: 136)

Thus, lower prices of company output would lead to reduced profitability exceeding perhaps any cost savings through increased rationalization. The beneficiary would then be the consumer who benefits from IT investments in an industry through lower product prices, rather than individual companies. More recently, Bharadwaj, Bharadwaja, and Konsynski (1999: 1017), using a financial market measure of IT investment impact, determined that while IT investments did have some immediate positive effect on the market capitalization of companies this benefit is short lived as 'IT investments tend to depreciate rather quickly. Furthermore, as firms have become more sophisticated with the use of information technologies, first mover advantages are relatively short and rival firms very quickly copy IT capabilities.'

### From silver bullet optimism to distinctive competence realism

The MIT 1990s studies by Brynjolfsson and Hitt have added to a growing skepticism among senior managers and academics for silver bullet IT solutions. From a theoretical viewpoint, Brynjolfsson and Hitt and others have shown that while blanket IT investments have served to increase company productivity and consumer value, they have lowered barriers to entry, eliminated market inefficiencies that enable a firm to maintain monopoly power, and intensified market competition, thereby failing to create any sustainable lasting return for the average investing company.

Company experiences have shown that opportunities for achieving sustained competitive advantage from IT use are more difficult to realize than originally thought, and the number of sustainable strategic IT systems is few. Thus, many academics and consultants have taken the view that the competitive use of IT must be a part of an overall business strategy, and that IT applications depend more on understanding unique business opportunities, or distinctive competencies, than on any competitive benefits achieved due to technological features alone.

In an attempt to capture a broader indicator of the strategic application of IT, Kettinger et al. (1994) decided not to look at IT investment as an independent variable, but at the 'best' strategic information systems over a fifteen-year period. By looking at these strategic systems, as opposed to merely IT investments, they hoped to capture a rich indicator of effective information use that included benefits accrued in terms of people's competence to exploit IT opportunities and in acquiring and managing knowledge. They selected sixty of the most visible and highly touted strategic information systems, and examined how the strategic use of IT, or IT practices, relates not just to a company's profitability alone, but also to its relative profitability and market share within an industry. Of the sixty strategic information systems reviewed, only 50 per cent led to sustained competitive advantage. This finding is particularly noteworthy because it showed that even those IT systems that were generally accepted as being high payoffs were, in reality, only consistently contributing to the bottom line half of the time. This pushed these researchers for alternative explanations.

Kettinger et al. (1994) determined that the link between IT and business performance was far more complex than many earlier IT researchers had surmised. Their research indicated that a company's IT practices were but one capability in a set of important 'foundation factors' that interact with management's 'action strategies' to determine a company's business performance. Foundation factors are fundamental resources or capabilities that exist by virtue of a firm's infrastructure and that have evolved over time. Action strategies are factors that require definitive management strategies to leverage the foundation factors to achieve sustained competitive advantage. In essence, the action strategies were what senior managers could do to compete, such as pre-empting competitors, increasing switching costs, exploiting flexibility, and responding better to threats, risks, and opportunities. The foundation factors (resources and capabilities) of the company referred to four traditional factors such as its size, geographic coverage, product scope, and vertical integration that were useful in explaining the competitive outcomes of strategic IT systems.

Kettinger et al. (1994) also introduced four new foundation factors that had not been previously investigated relative to effective information and IT use:

1. *Technological Resources (IT practices)*: the capabilities of the IT function to deploy IT infrastructure and appropriate applications in the company.
2. *Information Resources (information management practices)*: the capability of people to acquire and manage the richness and content of the organization's knowledge base and information management practices.
3. *Learning Curve (information behaviors and values)*: the capability of the people in an organization to acquire and manage knowledge, including their skills, education, experience, and career development.
4. *Organizational Base (information behaviors and values)*: the people's competence to exploit IT opportunity. This included management commitment to IT, vision, adaptability, and previous experience with IT in the company (Kettinger et al. 1994: 35–6).

By demonstrating that there was a more complex interaction effect between IT practices and action strategies that predicted performance, these researchers determined that IT practices were only one part of the resources and capabilities that senior managers could use to implement their action strategies and improve business performance. This research pointed to the need to develop a better understanding of how IT practices, information resources, and people could lead to effective information use in the company and achieve higher business performance. Thus, these four foundation factors shaped our own thinking related to the presence of:

1. a people-related behavioral capability;
2. an information technology-related capability; and
3. a knowledge and information management capability.

These three capabilities all come together in the minds of managers to form a higher-level information use competency that, in turn, predicts positive effects on business performance.

In sum, *we believe that the elusive link between IT and company profitability may indeed be a question of measurement. IT, devoid of the context of how people behave with information, and how information is managed, will* not *explain the performance relationship.* Why?

While attributes of these three dimensions had been touched upon in previous research, past studies failed to recognize the importance of this more complex and comprehensive construct of effective information use. However, more recent studies support our position. For example, Tallon, Kraemer, and Gurbaxani (1997) have directed attention away from measurement of productivity gains at the firm level and towards multidimensional assessment of IT business value involving measures combining economic, process, and behavioral perspectives. And McKeen, Smith, and Parent (1997) proposed a similar resource-based approach to Kettinger et al. (1994) that seeks to assess the leverage effect that IT has on key, essentially human, resources in the organization.

### From interactions of behaviors, information management, and IT to an Information Orientation

Given the previous research by Kettinger et al. (1994) indicating that there is an interaction effect among the information-related foundation factors noted above and management strategies, we wanted to test the extent to which competency in these capabilities predicted higher business performance. A detailed literature review of the three different schools of thought (Chapter 2) related to the use of information in organizations only fortified our belief that these three distinct capabilities (IT practices, information management practices, information behaviors and values) of effective information use existed (this was further discussed in Chapters 3, 4, and 5).

As we have seen in Chapters 2, 3, 4, and 5, each of these schools has identified some key concepts, issues, and problems related to the effective use of information. And, in limited instances, researchers within these schools refer to relationships of ideas shared between schools; however, our literature review did not uncover an existing unifying theory of effective information use that tightly tied together all the ideas shared by each of the three schools.

Our literature review revealed that the Information Management School, where practitioners and academics focused on improving the information life cycle, has advanced management of the organization's information and knowledge bases. However, the Information Management School has never proven an empirical link between effective information management and business performance. From the Behavior and Control School we learn to place importance on human factors such as motivation and learning. However, while this school offered general management guidance, it had not addressed how organizational behavior relates to information use or how this relates to business performance. Finally, while the IT School mentioned the importance of information to the company, this school did not devote much attention to the assessments of information value, people's behaviors surrounding its use, or its management. Instead the IT research community expended considerable energy toward finding the direct link between IT and business performance. In some part, this focus was a direct response to the 'IT productivity paradox' debate questioning the bottom-line payoff of IT investments.

The absence of a comprehensive theory or construct integrating ideas of each of the three schools into a higher-level information usage competence factor seemed to contradict what we had been hearing from senior managers in classroom case discussions and in focus groups over the past several years at IMD, the University of South Carolina, and at Andersen Consulting. These conversations suggested that senior managers saw competency in key aspects of each of the three schools as being closely coupled with business performance success.

Present throughout these discussions and interviews was the importance that senior managers placed on the people or behavioral aspects of effective information use. This generally contrasted with our conversations with CIOs and information center directors who spoke of their technical and content management responsibilities and problems. The lack of focus on the behavioral aspects of effective information use by these functional managers is understandable given the fact that both the IT department and the information management function's charters typically did not include the responsibility to actively improve company-wide behaviors and values. In fact, in initial stages of their evolution, these two management disciplines were viewed as low-level management support functions that did not possess the power or authority to influence major changes related to people.

Because of this bifurcation, the behavioral element of information use has traditionally been overshadowed by a focus on the more formalized

management activities related to IT deployment and information management practices. As Fig. 6.2 suggests, these traditional information-related
disciplines have formalized their management activities in established
functional departments (e.g. the IT department or the content/data management department) within organizations. When company attention and
resources are designated for improving information effectiveness, there has
been a tendency to look to these formal departments for advice and stewardship. As a consequence, companies can easily ignore the more informal
and less developed managerial practices in place to measure and improve
information behaviors and values. An important aspect of effective information use, namely people's behaviors and values, is left out of the measurement and management equation.

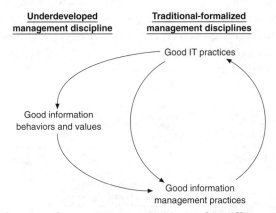

**Fig. 6.2. Formalization of Management Activities and its Effect on Improvements
to Information Use**

*Note*: Problem: if functional managers only 'see' traditional formalized activities as
avenues to improve information use in their companies, then they will ignore information behaviors and values!

The fact that many companies are not structured to formally improve
their measurement and management of information behaviors and values
seems to directly contradict the importance that senior managers are placing on a more holistic view of effective information use that includes
behavioral capabilities. These observations led the research team to postulate that the viewpoints of senior managers concerning the effective use of
information were not completely captured within the theories or practices
of each individual school of thought and that senior managers had a more
complex and comprehensive view of effective information use that integrated ideas from each of the three schools. As we stated in Chapter 1, we

suspect that the fundamental disconnect between these somewhat isolated disciplines and the pictures that senior managers had painted in their own minds concerning effective information use has resulted in much of the dissatisfaction that many executives feel concerning lower than expected payoffs from information-related investments.

What is needed is a broader theory that incorporates how people behave with information in organizations, how information is actually managed, and how IT is used to support information management, and ultimately organizational decision making. Following the conclusions of Kettinger et al. (1994) we felt that deeper research is needed to understand the extent to which senior managers perceive their organizations possess the practices and behaviors associated with effective information use to improve business performance (see Fig. 6.3). We believe this can be captured in a high-level idea that determines the degree to which a company possesses competence and synergy across the three vital capabilities (IT practices, information management practices, information behaviors and values) of effective information use.

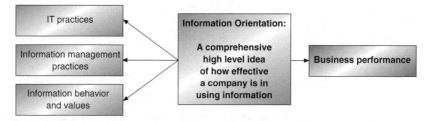

**Fig. 6.3.  The New Research Challenge**

Based on the relationships outlined in our conceptual model (Fig. 6.3), we propose that IT practices, information management practices, and information behaviors and values must all be significantly present in order to achieve superior business performance. From a practical perspective, this suggests that these information capabilities are distinct and yet significantly related. This relationship or common core of the three information capabilities is the concept or construct of Information Orientation.

*Is there a comprehensive measure of overall effectiveness of information use?* Yes, our confirmatory factor model presented in Fig. 6.4 indicates that senior managers do perceive a high-level, 'holistic' idea that characterizes 'how effective they believe their company is in using information.' We call this second-order factor Information Orientation. This finding is very exciting, because, for the first time, we have uncovered an integrated view of IT

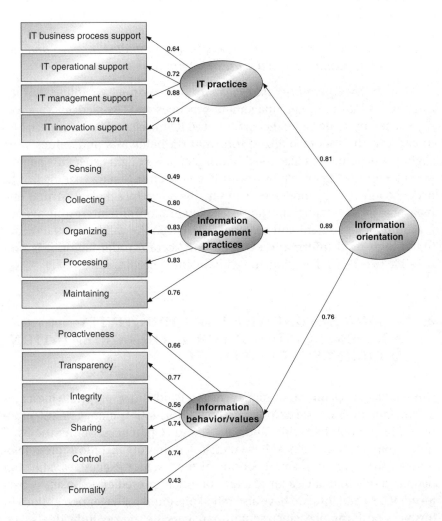

**Fig. 6.4.  Confirmatory Factor Model of Information Orientation**

practices, information management practices, and information behaviors and values in the minds of senior managers.

*The Information Orientation or IO of a business organization is composed of three capabilities:*

1. *The capability of a company to deploy appropriate IT applications and infrastructure in support of operations, business processes, management decision making, and innovation (.81).*

2. *The capability of a company to manage information effectively over its life cycle from sensing, collecting, organizing, processing, and maintaining (.89).*

3. *The capability of a company to instill and promote behaviors and values in its people for effective use of information (.76).*

*What are the capabilities that make up this measure?* We found that the established information management practices and IT practices were well recognized by senior managers within the IO measure. Since the variables to capture the less formalized information behaviors and values were slightly less refined, as discussed in Chapter 5, we might expect the slightly lower factor loading of .76. However, given the strong factor loading for the overall confirmatory model, we can say this powerful set of constructs and measures represent an important management tool and interesting avenue for future development and investigation. Given the validation of a meaningful high-level Information Orientation second-order factor, it is now possible to assess its relationship with business performance.

## 2. MOVING BEYOND THE IT PRODUCTIVITY PARADOX: LINKING INFORMATION ORIENTATION TO BUSINESS PERFORMANCE

Our study focuses on senior managers as a valid and appropriate indicator of how business organizations perceive information management practices, information behaviors and values, and IT practices. Many studies of senior managers in the past have concluded that organizations are reflections of the perceptions and actions of their senior executives, and that people in this role have a far greater potential for predicting business performance.[2] Therefore, we have also relied on senior manager perceptions of business performance, since senior managers are the key individuals who

---

[2] This study adopted the Hambrick and Mason (1984) upper-echelons perspective that the organization becomes a reflection of its top executives. They argued that understanding the characteristics of several members of top management has a far greater potential for predicting organizational performance and strategic choices than just the characteristics of the CEO. This view was based on the premiss that top managers structure decision situations to fit their view of the world. Other studies that adopt this perspective include Child's (1972) strategic choice perspective of organizational adaptation, Cyert and March's (1963) and Thompson's (1967) 'dominant coalition', and studies by Bourgeois (1984), Hrebiniak and Joyce (1985), and Stubbart (1989) which suggest that choices made by top managers influence organizational design outcomes and firm performance. Schoemaker (1990) also views executive judgement as an important source of competitive advantage.

are uniquely accountable for the overall performance of companies. In this section, we first explain how business performance is measured in this study in contrast to previous studies that tried to link IT investments to performance. Then, we will present the results of two tests to determine if Information Orientation best predicts business performance.

## A. Measuring business performance

As discussed earlier, many past studies linking IT investments to business performance used a single financial performance measure of profitability such as ROA as their sole measure of business performance. However, management studies of business strategy suggest that multiple measures of business performance should be used, given the different perceptions of key stakeholders, such as employees, customers, shareholders, and, particularly, senior managers (Venkatraman 1985; Venkatraman and Ramanujam 1986). In their study of strategic information systems and performance, Kettinger et al. (1994) included a second indicator of business performance—market share growth. Based on suggestions of more recent strategy research for additional measures of flexibility and intangibles (Chan et al. 1997), two additional indicators were added to the business performance measure—improvements in reputation and in product/service innovations—to round out our overall multiple indicator measure of business performance. In their study, Chan et al. (1997) tested these same four perceptual measures of business performance and determined that they showed reasonably strong reliability and validity.

Our next measurement challenge was to establish a broad, representative sample of senior managers from a diverse set of industries, countries, and sizes of companies, including both publicly held and privately held firms. While we have developed a broad, international sample of companies and senior managers, we have also faced some serious research challenges in using a uniform measure of business performance. We needed to resolve three major research issues:

First, there are wide variations in reporting requirements on the performance of an international sample of companies drawn from twenty-two countries. The main comparison issue in performance analysis in international business is the wide variations among accounting standards and practices from one country to another. Based on previous studies of these variations in reporting and accounting practices, these differences are caused by the diversity of capital markets, the role of governments, business and tax laws, and the processes of setting the accounting standards themselves.[3]

Second, there are important differences in what privately held versus publicly held firms divulge about performance. Since owners of privately held firms severely restrict disclosure of results, it was clear that, with our mix of companies, acquiring consistent financial information from family-owned and privately held businesses in diverse countries was not feasible.[4]

Third, we were interested in a multi-year measure of past performance. To ensure accurate reporting by senior managers and based on previous studies, we wanted a five-year measure of performance.[5]

[3] One of the research challenges in using a uniform measure of performance was to resolve the issue of a broad, multinational sample with varying reporting requirements on company performance. The main comparison issue in performance analysis in an international context was the differences in accounting standards and practices. Meek and Saudagaran (1990) acknowledge substantial differences among accounting principles, standards, regulations, and legal requirements among countries. Gray (Gray and Radebaugh 1997) asserted that no two accounting systems are alike across countries, stemming from differences in the amount of private ownership, the degree of industrialization, the rate of inflation, and the level of economic growth. Higgins (1998) attributes differences in national accounting standards to the great diversity of capital markets, the role of government, business and tax laws, and the process of setting accounting standards. Hamilton (1998) warned of serious practical consequences of accounting and reporting differences and tried to explain why such differences exist: 'In both the US and the UK, serving the needs of investors has been the driving force in the development of accounting standards . . . In Germany the principal traditional purpose of accounts is to establish the basis of collecting tax and therefore the basis of accounting was highly legalistic. There was every incentive for companies to keep their reported level of profits down . . . The professional accounting bodies in mainland Europe are much smaller and with less influence.'

[4] Another research challenge was the large number of privately held firms and family-owned businesses.

The inherent difficulties in obtaining financial information from these types of firms are obvious. Dess and Robinson (1984) contend that 'access to performance data on privately-held firms is severely restricted. Such information is not publicly available. Owners, very sensitive about releasing any performance data, are the sole gatekeepers to such information on individual firms.'

The magazine *Forbes* provided further evidence of the difficulty in gathering financial information from private companies. Every year, *Forbes* publishes a list of the largest private US companies. In 1997, only 57 of *Forbes's* 500 largest private US companies filed profit and loss statements with the Securities and Exchange Commission. The rest of the companies, who did not have to file their annual reports, sometimes volunteered financial data, and sometimes they did not. For this last group of companies, *Forbes* estimated revenues and operating income from data pieced together from industry analysts, competitors, trade associations, and present or former employees. 'It is impossible to tell whether private companies are more profitable than public companies' (Kichen and Russo McCarthy 1997: 183). In 1995, *Forbes* encountered the same problems, in fact 'some private companies disclose information on their revenues but not on their profits.' *Forbes* estimated operating and net income by looking at financial data of similar companies and by talking to competitors and industry analysts (Kichen and Russo McCarthy 1995: 171).

[5] The third research challenge concerned multi-year performance measure. To ensure an accurate measure, we followed Bourgeois (1980) and Friedrickson and Mitchell's (1984) five-year financial average, and Dess and Robinson (1984), Robinson and Pearce (1988), and Kettinger et al.'s (1994) relative five-year measure. Given the other two comparison constraints mentioned above, it would have been impractical to get secondary data.

To resolve these constraints in our sample of international companies, and to achieve the five-year measure, it was apparent that the additional use of 'objective' measures of performance was not possible, nor advisable, given these quality constraints. Thus, we chose to focus on a perceived multi-indicator of business performance that has been considered superior in previous management research under these circumstances, rather than 'objective' or secondary measures.[6] In making this decision, we recognized that multi-indicators' performance measures contain inherently more measurement error than other perceptual measures, and that our factors loadings on our confirmatory model would be slightly lower.

As we expected, a multi-level measure of performance showed slightly lower factor scores than our other dimensions. The obvious reason for this is that senior managers may perceive their company as high on one or more of the indicators (e.g. market share) of business performance, and lower on another (e.g. reputation) at any given interval along the five-year measure of performance. This would lower the internal consistency of the aggregate measure. We were willing to live with this slight drawback in exchange for the explanatory power that a multi-indicator measure gave the study's results. Actual CFA modeling of our four-item business performance measure (results presented in Fig. 6.5) were strong and supportive of our business performance measure's construct validity and reliability.

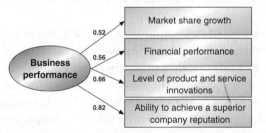

**Fig. 6.5. Perceived Business Performance Measure and Confirmatory Factor Model**

*Perceived Performance Measure for the Study*
Relative to our competitors . . .
(very disappointing to extremely exceptional)
1. Our market share growth has been . . .
2. Our financial performance has been . . .
3. Our level of product and service innovation has been . . .
4. Our ability to achieve a superior company reputation has been . . .

[6] Given these three research constraints, we opted to follow Chan et al. (1997) and their perceived performance measure. When these conditions are present, perceptual measures are superior to secondary measures of business performance.

## B.  Information Orientation and business performance

To address our major research question—*Does effective information use lead to better business performance?*—we adopted a statistical analysis approach that has been shown successful in determining whether the presence of first-order factors (IT practices, information management practices, information behaviors and values) or a second-order factor best (IO) predicts an increase in a business performance criterion (Venkatraman 1989, 1990; Segars and Grover 1998).

The primary premiss for testing a higher-level construct such as Information Orientation is to establish a direct link between IO and business performance. The basic premiss of our measurement model is that IT practices, information management practices, and information behaviors and values together, through a shared and more comprehensive indicator (Information Orientation), are better predictors of business performance than any one or subset of these capabilities. From a practical perspective, the contention is that superior business performance is predicted by high levels of IT practices, information management practices, and information behaviors and values as captured in the common variation among these dimensions. This common variance forms a core that we term Information Orientation that is directly associated with higher levels of business performance.

To assess the validity of this contention, two path models must be tested. The first model implies that information management practices, information behaviors and values, and IT practices independently and directly are predictors of business performance. The alternative model suggests that the three dimensions are coaligned or associated in their prediction of performance. This common core of variation is itself a definable source of variation (a second-order factor) that predicts performance more accurately than any unique variation among the first-order factors. Practically, this model suggests that an organization must score high on all three dimensions to realize superior performance. In other words, each of the capabilities is necessary but not sufficient for higher business performance. The dimensions form an orientation that is measured as the common core of the set of three distinct information capabilities. This orientation, i.e. Information Orientation, is causally related to business performance.

*Does a comprehensive high-level idea of how effective a company is in using information (IO) better predict business performance than the single information capabilities of IT practices, information management practices, and information behaviors and values?* The answer is Yes. Our test of the

Direct Effects Model, which tests the strength of direct causal paths between IT practices, information behaviors and values, and information management practices individually did not produce significant results, nor did this test result in a statistically acceptable model fit. The implication of this finding is that the three capabilities alone do not predict higher business performance. Alternatively, as Fig. 6.6 shows, our test of the coalignment model demonstrates that through Information Orientation a strong causal link is established which predicts business performance much more powerfully than the three capabilities independently. In contrast to the Direct Effects Model, the Coalignment Model's paths between the three information capabilities and IO and between IO and business performance are significant with good overall model fit—confirming that Information Orientation is an important link in explaining business performance.

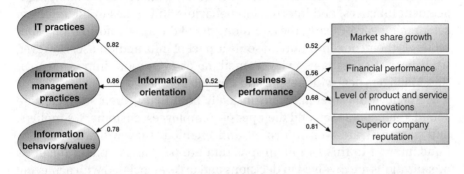

**Fig. 6.6. Coalignment Model: Information Orientation Predicting Business Performance**

This important finding means that the predictive relationship between IT practices and performance does not exist directly and helps to explain why so many previous studies found the link between IT practices and business performance so problematic. Interestingly, a direct link between information behaviors and values, or information management practices, and business performance fails to appear as well.

Based on these exciting results, we can confidently say that: *effective information use does lead to better business performance but the link is through IO*. From a practical perspective, this means that while IT practices, information management practices, and information behaviors and values are distinct and valid capabilities, organizations that are more mature in managing IT practices, managing information practices, and creating behaviors and values that leverage the use of information tend to form a core of Information Orientation that is a major contributing factor to superior business performance. Second, these results show that Information Orientation represents a superior measure of effective information use and should be practically applied in companies to diagnose and benchmark their current levels of effectiveness in information use. Finally, we can conclude that if a firm sub-optimizes by over- or under-investing in any of these three information capabilities, at the expense of one of the other capabilities, then sub-par business performance may result.

## 3. INFORMATION ORIENTATION: THE MISSING METRIC?

What binds the information capabilities of IT practices, information management practices, and information behaviors and values in the minds of senior managers? Clearly, the common core of the three information capabilities is their concentration on some aspect of information use. However, we believe that managers view something as even more important than this. Managers deal with people and through people.

We believe that managers intrinsically hold that if their strategies are sound, their course set, and their people (employees, customers, suppliers, and partners) are well informed and enabled, they will win the day. Fundamental to this simple proposition are people. People in business organizations are involved in decisions and tasks associated with achieving the organization's purposes. People use information in organizations to reduce uncertainty in decision making to accomplish tasks or actions.

As we have touched on earlier in our discussions of the three schools of thought, organizations involve relationships among people, and how people choose to contribute their knowledge to achieve organizational purposes. People are constantly balancing their own interests against the group and organization's interests, in deciding whether and how to contribute their personal expertise, skills, and experience to the welfare of the group or organization. The organization defines a relevant context to continuously convert human knowledge and learning into creative ideas and innovations of value to achieving organizational success in the future, rather than for today alone.

We have found that information use in business organizations is multidimensional in nature. Perceiving organizational information use from only one point of view, as an information processing organism, as a technical programmable process, or as a collection of knowing and thinking people, yields an incomplete view of how people use information effectively in business organizations.

Our perspective on effective information use in business organizations is people-centric, based on the decision context and tasks that people must execute to achieve organizational purposes. As Fig. 6.7 suggests, our research validates this people-centric viewpoint and points to the need for companies to formalize and integrate the behavioral aspects of information usage with the existing and more formalized IT and information management practices.

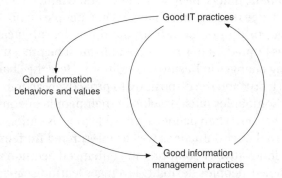

**Fig. 6.7. Through their Understanding of IO, Senior Managers Hold a People-centric View of Effective Information Use**

*Note*: Senior managers recognize the importance of the good information behaviors and values and the interrelatedness of the three capabilities of IO.

From a more general cultural perspective, we believe that for business organizations to use information effectively, people must use information in support of the organization's interest. For example, people are generally motivated to share. However, the organization may 'block' the opportunity for individuals to contribute, when people are unsure about how to contribute, or feel pressures from competing tasks, or where the organization does not provide sufficient resources to permit positive contributions. Nonaka and Takeuchi (1995) note that the first critical step in their model of knowledge creation is 'sharing tacit knowledge'. Thus, people must be able to trust what others will do with their tacit knowledge, feelings, and emotions before they make this knowledge explicit and shareable.

Organizations channel the attention of people through learned routines, behaviors, and decision making. Depending on the work that people must do, the mix of structured versus less structured tasks and decisions will vary a great deal. A key challenge for managers is to focus personal information behaviors on the goals and decisions that matter. Since people have severe limits on their attention and information processing capacities, they must understand over time what information seeking is relevant to improve their individual performance, as well as the performance of the organization. Newcomers find it difficult to 'learn their way around' an organization since they do not yet understand the formal and informal information practices that more experienced organizational members invoke each day to get the work done. Knowing where to look or who to ask for information is a sign of experience and information use.

Effective information use is influenced by the learning capacity of organizational members; that is, people's abilities and willingness to acquire and use new knowledge to learn and change. When people do not detect errors, fail to respond, or do not learn from them, the learning capacity of the organization is limited. In this regard, people must be proactive in learning and addressing changes in business conditions. Here the challenge is both a readiness to learn, and the disposition to proactively acquire and use new information. Companies must develop in their people openness to change and a bias for action. When people are flexible they use information sensed from the external environment as well as interpreted from existing operations to drive innovative IT solutions and enhanced decision making capabilities. In essence, people's flexibility leverages learning capacity to permit emergent situations and strategies to be addressed.

Clearly such an integrated, people-centric view of effective information use is not easily subsumed within the existing three schools of thoughts discussed in Chapters 3, 4, and 5. As Table 6.1 outlines, the three schools, while vital in their own rights in contributing key aspects of what we now know is 'good' practice for information use, have failed to provide an integrated measure of information use that fosters a mature information usage culture. Only when the appropriate information usage behaviors are natured with unselfish and focused information management practices are people prepared to employ IT effectively in support of decision making and task achievement at a magnitude great enough to improve its business performance.

In the end, it is quite simple. Senior managers recognize that, through the high-order IO measure, they must be good at all three information capabilities if their people, and ultimately their company, are to be effective in using information to improve business performance. They must create a mature information usage culture whereby IT systems not only support operations, business processes, and product innovation, but also management-level decision-making. Information must be managed across all units in a consistent, timely way while ensuring that the information is accurate and high quality. In addition to collecting, organizing, and maintaining information well, their companies must be good at proactively sensing new information to meet changing business opportunities. Senior managers perceive that they must instill in their employees precisely those information behaviors and values that affect how the company uses information for customer interaction and internal management.

We believe that high IO companies understand the importance of a higher synergy established when they are good at all three information capabilities, creating what we call the 'IO Interaction Effect'. It means that one strong capability cannot compensate for a weak one. All three capabilities should be maintained at a high level. This perspective raises some interesting questions. Are there prescriptive maturity paths that organizations must follow to improve their effectiveness in information use within each capability? If so, do these paths follow the same theoretical paths and explanations previously discussed in the individual schools of thought? How can companies ensure that they benefit from cross-capability synergies? What can managers do to take advantage of what we have learned to advance their own companies? We will address these points in Chapter 8.

## 4.  CONCLUSIONS

In this chapter, we have discussed the controversy over the IT productivity paradox, and the elusive connection between IT investments and practices and improvements in business performance. We have noted that previous research by academics in business and economics had little success in drawing a direct link between IT investments and company business performance. But the research has made a convincing case that IT investments often increase company output, lower barriers to competition in industries, and improve consumer value by lowering market prices for goods and services. Thus, companies are compelled to invest in IT to satisfy a 'strategic necessity'. However, rarely do IT investments and practices alone result in sustained business performance benefits.

Our research model recognized that the link between IT and business performance was not direct, and that a more complex interaction effect between behavioral, information management, and IT foundation factors, combined with management strategies, is most likely to directly predict improvements in performance.

We have, in this chapter, empirically demonstrated that information behaviors and values, information management practices, and IT practices are key information capabilities defining a new strategic management

**Table 6.1.** *How IO Addresses Weaknesses of the Schools of Thought*

| Management school | Major weaknesses | How IO resolves problem |
| --- | --- | --- |
| Information Technology School | The IT school has tended to emphasize the formalization of the technical side of data management rather than how people use and manage information. In addition, there has been a lack of attention on the management of non-automated and/or informal information usage. This tendency may explain why advances in IT have not been very successful in the use of IT for innovation and strategic decision making. | The IO model takes a more inclusive perspective on the measurement of effective information use that covers behaviors and values related to all types of company information including automated and non-automated, communication and sharing, and formal and informal sources. This more encompassing and people-centric orientation towards effective information use may lead companies to better capitalize on IT support for innovation and decision making. |
| Information Management School | The Information Management School has tended to emphasize the formalization of the resource management aspects of information but offers little insight on how to effectively change human behavior related to how people use or manage information effectively. This problem is made worse because the Information Management School has not instituted a well-recognized approach for valuing information in practice, nor has it developed workable schemes to provide people with incentives to manage information for personal or company benefit. | The IO model recognizes that information valuation is done by people and therefore a measure of effective information use must include both good information management practices and appropriate controls and incentives to motivate people to serve both their own and their company's information needs. |
| Behavior and Control School Human resource (HR) stream | The HR stream does not directly relate the 'lessons learned in progressive general management' to how people use information to achieve organizational goals. In addition, HR's prevailing 'people' functional focus has separated it | The IO model relates HR principles learned from organizational behavior research more explicitly to information usage behavior and management practice. It explicitly relates people's information usage |

| Management school | Major weaknesses | How IO resolves problem |
| --- | --- | --- |
| | from the 'technical' IT function. Hence, the HR stream places little emphasis on the role and impact of IT use on human behavior. In essence using information effectively has been a side issue and not developed as a formal management activity within this school of thought. | behavior to IT support and thereby helps eliminate the schism between the IT and HR disciplines. Incorporating this people-centric view into the evaluation of information usage helps move measurement and management issues away from a purely IT functional perspective and closer to the more holistic view held by senior managers. |
| Management control (MC) stream | Optimizing a company's control mechanisms is extremely difficult when controls on personal behaviors are not integrated with the ways information is managed. This is particularly a problem in that the MC stream fails to consider numerous key dimensions of organizational behavior that contribute to personal motivation in using information for the company's benefit, such as integrity, formality, and transparency. Like the HR stream, formalized management practice related to effective information use has been tangential to this school of thought. | The IO model enforces a more deliberate consideration of the relationship between performance measurement and information management practice at both the personal and company level. By incorporating constructs from both HR and the MC stream, and refocusing them on information usage behavior and values, a better recognition of the role people play in a company's success in information usage is obtained. And, by making the dimensions of information usage behaviors and values more explicit, efforts can be undertaken to formalize and improve this underdeveloped IBV discipline area. |

concept in the minds of senior managers called Information Orientation. We define Information Orientation as the extent to which senior managers perceive that their companies possess the capabilities and behaviors associated with effective information use to achieve superior business performance.

Most importantly, we have demonstrated that information orientation is predictive of business performance in the minds of senior managers. With the principal study survey results based on 1,009 senior managers, we conclude that the link between IT investments and sustained business performance improvement is not direct, but through the interactions of the three information capabilities of the Information Orientation, and through the Information Orientation of the company to business performance.

In interpreting our results, it is important for the reader to remember three major points:

First, we have proven that senior managers possess a high-level strategic concept of effective information use we call their Information Orientation that integrates three key capabilities—information behaviors and values, information management practices, and IT practices.

Second, we know that IO predicts business performance. That is, when an IO score of a company is high, business performance will be high as well.

Third, being good in an information capability (i.e. good IT practices, good information management practices, and good information behaviors and values) is necessary, but not sufficient to improve performance. We conclude that to achieve superior business performance, a company must score high on all capabilities of IO.

In the next chapter, we examine the power of information orientation as a new metric of information effectiveness to improve business performance.

# 7

# Information Orientation: The New Metric of Effective Information Use

If industries are becoming increasingly information intensive, and knowledge is perceived as the new basis for competing in the e-economy, then how do senior managers know whether their companies are effectively using information to achieve better business performance? The answer is that while they may intuitively have some feel for the relationship, their companies are probably not getting an accurate measure because they are addressing the problem with the wrong tools.

Of the three schools of management thinking presented in Chapter 2—the IT School, the Information Management School, and the Behavior and Control School—both the IT and Behavior schools have partially explored how to provide management metrics or tools to improve business performance. However, no school has provided an integrated theory, and empirical validation, of a metric directly linking effective information use to overall business performance. We view this as a major deficiency in the research literature, and a significant practical problem for managers.

In this chapter, we examine, in section 1, what the three schools of management thinking have done in the past to develop and refine performance metrics associated with IT, information management, and information behavior. We assess the strengths and weaknesses of these three schools in developing metrics to gauge the contribution of effective information use to business performance.

Next, we focus on IO as a measure of effective information use in business organizations. Information Orientation (IO), as we have shown in Chapter 6, is an important new metric of effective information use, since our study has shown a causal link between IO and overall business performance. In other words, if a company is good at IO, we know its business performance will improve. While IO is not a final measure of *overall* business performance such as profitability or market share, it is an important measure of how senior managers perceive their companies possess the capabilities associated with effective information use to achieve superior business performance. We will suggest that the leading attempts to develop overall measures of business performance, such as economic value added, balanced scorecard, value-based management, and activity-based costing, have ignored a measure of effectiveness of information use and, as a consequence, have an incomplete view of the capability requirements necessary to achieve sustained business performance improvements.

In section 2, we introduce the 'IO Dashboard' as a diagnostic tool to measure and evaluate each information capability of IO and its link to business performance. We will explain how IO as a metric can be employed inside and across industries, as well as within and among the multiple business units of global companies. We will provide examples of management intervention strategies based on IO measures within companies over time.

## 1. EVALUATING PERFORMANCE METRICS CONCERNING THE IT, INFORMATION MANAGEMENT, AND BEHAVIOR AND CONTROL SCHOOLS

Each of the three schools of management thinking described in Chapter 2 has developed various theoretical and practical approaches to measuring the relationships of IT, information, and people to business performance. In this section, we will assess the strengths and weaknesses of the prevailing approaches to metrics in each school, and discuss how IO as a new business metric can address the weaknesses in previous measurement approaches.

### A. Metrics in the IT School

The Information Technology (IT) School has a rich tradition of building metrics. For more than thirty years IT researchers have focused on developing IT effectiveness measures that examine the relative contribution of IT and support staff at various units of analysis ranging from individual aspects of IT design, to single IT applications, to types or groups of IT, to the overall impact of the IT function, and to assessments of the contribution of the entire corporate IT architecture. In this short section we cannot possibly cover the entire background literature associated with this area. Instead, for discussion purposes we have summarized these IT research efforts into three major foci. The first group of IT academics and practitioners have sought to measure how users of computer-based information systems perceive these systems and employ them. The second group can be characterized as those academics and practitioners who have been concerned with measuring the effectiveness of the IT department or function in a company in terms of user satisfaction, service quality, or contribution to the business. The third group can be characterized as those academics and practitioners who, as we discussed in Chapter 6, sought to measure the direct effect that IT architecture investments have on business performance.

*Focus 1:  Highlights of the IT School's measures of the acceptance and use of computer-based information systems*
Many IT academics have focused on developing measures that examine what users of IT think about a new or proposed IT, how involved users have been in the decision to adopt and implement the IT, and how these factors influence their subsequent acceptance and continued use of the new IT. In this research stream, the focus of analysis is on a singular computer-based information system or other type of IT and its relative acceptance and/or payoff (e.g. Sambamurthy and Poole 1992—GDSS design; Ye and Johnson 1995—expert systems; Nault and Dexter 1994—card lock systems; and Mukhopadhyay, Kekre, and Kalathur 1995—EDI impact on costs).

Probably the most widely recognized studies in this stream are efforts to measure how users perceive the usefulness, or ease of use, of a new IT, and how this perception will affect its actual future use. Fred Davis et al., in 1989, argued that a computer-based information system could not improve business performance if it was not being used. An understanding of why people accept or reject a computer-based information system was needed. Thus, he developed a measure of perceived usefulness, and perceived ease of use, from the perspective of a new user's trial evaluation of an IT system, prior to their decision to continue to use it as a normal component of their job.

He and his colleagues found that people's actual sustained use of a new IT system could be predicted based on an evaluative survey of their perceptions after only limited trial use of the new system. They found that perceived usefulness was the major factor in predicting people's intentions to use a new computer system, while perceived ease of use was a significant, but secondary determinant of new computer system use. These researchers argued that users of computer systems needed to be shown early through prototypes how a system would work, rather than late in the design process. In addition, they suggested that systems designers focus more on demonstrating a computer-based information system's usefulness, before they add fancy user interfaces to make it more 'user friendly', if they want to achieve widespread usage of the IT system.

In parallel with these efforts, Barki and Hartwick (1989) focused on developing measures of perceived 'user involvement', which referred to the degree of users' perceived participation in the development of systems that they were to later use. These researchers suggested that user involvement meant, not just executing a set of activities associated with the development of computer systems, but also a psychological state. They found that users perceive that they are involved when they consider a computer system to be both important and personally relevant. Also, the more users perceive they are involved in development, the more likely they are to use the system.

In a recent study, Kettinger and Lee (1999) built on this concept by finding that satisfaction with the implementation of new IT systems will differ depending on user perceptions of the system attributes (e.g. relevance, complexity, cost, trialability, observability) being implemented and the degree to which users believe they have the expertise to drive the adoption and implementation of the system. Generally, they found that the more users perceive they drove the adoption and implementation of an IT system, rather than the IT department or function, the more satisfied they are with the IT's payoff, particularly when it is less complex and more personal.

*Focus 2: Highlights of the IT School's focus on developing measures that evaluate the performance of the IT department in delivering information systems and services*

This stream has focused on developing measures that evaluate users' perceived performance of the Information Services Function (ISF) or Department's ability to deliver high-quality information systems and services. The unit of analysis on this research is the company-wide IS function or department. During the 1990s attention focused on methods to assess the relative contribution of the IS function during outsourcing evaluations (e.g. Lacity and Hirschheim 1993). Another important avenue of investigation was to evaluate the governance structure of the IS functions to determine whether they were suitably structured to deliver high levels of service (Sambamurthy and Zmud 1992).

Perhaps the most widely researched measure of 'user satisfaction' with the IS function was developed in the early 1980s by Ives, Olson, and Baroudi (1983). These IT researchers developed a measure of user satisfaction that focused on three dimensions of user satisfaction:

1. quality of information products (reliability, relevance, accuracy, and precision);

2. level of user knowledge and involvement (degree of training, user understanding, user feeling of participation); and

3. IS services (attitudes of IS staff, communication with IS staff).

In 1994, Kettinger and Lee refined the Ives et al. (1983) measures of user satisfaction with the information services function. They included additional ideas from marketing practice: reliability of the service; responsiveness of the service provider; assurance of service providers' competence; and displayed empathy of service provider.

They found that two of these ideas, 'service reliability' (e.g. services right the first time and at the time promised) and 'service empathy' (e.g. providing personal attention, understanding specific needs, having the user's interest at heart), were particularly important in determining user satisfaction with the company's information services function. They next demonstrated that their new measure, known as the ISF Service Quality Instrument, better predicted overall user satisfaction than the original Ives et al. measure. This ISF Service Quality Instrument has continued to be improved and refined by many researchers and is now the most commonly referenced user satisfaction measure utilized today (e.g. Pitt, Watson, and Kavan 1995). Even with the relatively widespread acceptance of this measure, it offers little insight as to how superior ISF Service Quality impacts overall business performance.

*Focus 3: Highlights of the IT School's focus on developing measures that evaluate the direct contribution of corporate-wide investments in and performance of the IT department in delivering information systems and services*

The third grouping of IT measurement research is the body of work discussed extensively in Chapter 6—namely, those efforts to directly tie levels of IT architecture investments with business performance gains. These IT researchers focused on measuring IT impact through financial measures such as 'optimal levels of IT investment' (Bender 1986; Cron and Sobol 1983). Despite many earnest attempts, as discussed in Chapter 2, these IT researchers had little success in establishing a consistent causal linkage between levels of IT investment and sustained business profitability (Weill 1989; Turner 1985; Hitt and Brynjolfsson 1996). When IT researchers tried to evaluate 'strategic' IT investments with financial measures such as Return on Investment, or Return on Assets or sales growth, their research context was often too narrow to determine definitely whether sustainable IT investment payoff had occurred (Clemons 1991; Clemons and Weber 1990; Alpar and Kim 1990; Weill 1989; Banker and Kaufman 1988). Although considerable efforts were expended, IT researchers could not advance a practical model to measure whether a company's IT investments will definitely contribute to a sustainable competitive advantage (Kettinger et al. 1994).

### Weaknesses of IT School metrics

While there have been many studies and practitioner attempts at improving IT metrics from both the user and IT function's perspective, most of these efforts have suffered from four key weaknesses.

IT metrics have generally lacked a clear business performance focus and criteria. 'User satisfaction', perceived usefulness of computer systems, user involvement, and ISF Service Quality have not been empirically connected directly to measures of overall business performance at the business unit or corporate levels. While it is important for managers to know that their people are using computer systems, are satisfied with their use, and that the IS function is service oriented, knowing this is not enough. Senior managers are typically concerned with strategic impact and bottom-line results. This pushes for metrics that examine the relationship of these indicators with overall business performance, such as profitability, or market share growth.

Second, most of the IT School-generated metrics have generally focused the information use related to systems developed or purchased within the domain of the IS function. These measures tended to disregard personal information use and support, and do little to measure information use related to manual or informal information and communication exchanges. As a consequence, these measures were not only IS function-centric, but were also employed primarily by the IS managers in the company rather than by business managers.

Given the first two weaknesses, the third weakness is not surprising. IT metrics have not been developed from the perspective of senior managers. Rather, they have addressed the perceptions of users of computer systems lower in the business organization, and have not been tied to a strategic perspective.

Finally, IT measures have captured little of the behavioral capability of information use in companies. Evaluating the use of computers and user reactions to computer systems has been more important than understanding how human behaviors and values influence information use in a business or the relationships between information behaviors, information use, and IT practice in a company.

## B.  Metrics in the Information Management School

If the IT School's approach to metrics has primarily centered on users of computer systems and the IS function, the Information Management School's approach to metrics has focused on two principal fronts as well— viewing information as a process, and as a corporate resource.

### Information as a process

As we noted in Chapter 2, for many years the Information Management School was influenced by the information resource management view of the life cycle of information from creation through use in decision making. Horton in 1985 and later Marchand and Horton (1986) identified the stages of the information life cycle as a model for how information could be managed at different stages of use. Unfortunately, they did not develop a way to measure how effective companies were at managing the different stages of the life cycle, nor did they tie the information life cycle to business performance.

About the same time, Robert Taylor (1986) argued that the focus of information management should be to ensure that information is relevant and valuable to decision making. While he advocated a structured view of looking at information's value in decision making, he did not explore the implications for measuring information use by decision makers in organizations.

More recently, David Best (1996) suggested that information be managed as a 'process', and more specifically through information's role in business processes. Best noted that the role of information in business organizations was clouded by managers' poor understanding of the centrality of information to business processes. This lack of understanding leads to 'massive information overload at all business levels, ineffective use of IT with unrealized benefits and cost overruns, poor decision making, lack of corporate learning, and loss of profits' (Best 1996: 7).

Tom Davenport took a similar view in noting the general failure of managers and academics to understand the role of information in business. In 1995, Davenport and a colleague conducted a case-based study to address how leading firms manage information about their business processes. Results indicate that a key aspect of success in business process improvement is effective management of information about process performance. While they suggest this link between information management and business process performance, they offer no specific ways of measuring the connection between effective information use and overall business performance (Davenport 1997).

Generally, the view of information as process has gotten no closer over the last fifteen years to its goal of understanding the role of information at each stage of its life cycle, or to linking information use in business processes and decision making to overall business performance improvements.

## Information as a resource

The second and related view of information is the notion that information is an organizational resource. Information is viewed as a 'resource' like people, capital, and technology and is fundamental to the way organizations pursue their purposes. Orna has suggested that information is a 'diffused resource' that 'enters into all the activities of businesses and forms a component of all products and services that are sold.' Thus, what constitutes information will 'differ according to the purpose of individuals and organizations' (Orna 1996: 20).

Academics and consultants have studied treating information as a resource from many angles. Some economists have attempted to value information using economic theory (Machlup 1979; Repo 1989). Their work has been largely theoretical rather than empirical. Information scientists have tried to value the effects of providing information through information services and libraries (Broadbent and Lofgren 1993; Koenig 1992). Like the IT School, they have tried to evaluate the services provided by libraries and information centers in companies from a user perspective. The most important measures here have been perceived usefulness, relevance, and user satisfaction. Others have focused on evaluation processes for information retrieval systems of documents and records (King and Bryant 1971). Most of these attempts have emphasized technical criteria of use related to acquisition, storage, indexing, presentation, and composition.

In 1993, Marchand and Stanford suggested that there were three types of problems in defining information value in the business.

First, there was no one view of information value. They defined five distinct ways that information could be valued in a business:

1. the transcendent approach (the value of information is absolute and universally recognizable);
2. the user-based approach (information value is a function of how it is actually used by people);
3. the product-based approach (information is valued for its physical characteristics);
4. the production-based approach (information value is an outcome of user specifications); and

5. the value-added approach (information value is a balance of some-times competing criteria such as relevance, reliability, features, cost, validity, and perceived value).

A major challenge for most companies was to agree on what criteria should be used to evaluate information's value and how to reasonably make these valuations on a regular basis.

Second, Marchand and Stanford pointed out that since information, like knowledge, was inherently contextual, evaluating its value might depend on what business context the information was employed. These authors identified six different business contexts in which information could be used to create value: (1) market value; (2) customer value; (3) product value; (4) process value; (5) partner value; and (6) people value. In each case, infor-mation's value could vary by the context in which it was used, by the people involved in its use, and by the criteria applied to its use. These authors noted that information value depended a lot on where you sit in the organization, and thus there was a critical role for managers in defining what information was needed for decision making and how information should be employed by organizational members (Marchand and Stanford 1993).

Third, these authors suggested that information was often not perceived by managers as a resource that could be explicitly managed, but could only be influenced through people, organizational structures, and processes. Thus, information's value in a business depended greatly on managerial perceptions, criteria, and measures that were at best poorly developed (Marchand and Stanford 1993).

In addition, many managers tended to equate information management with IT management—as if managing the tools appropriately would lead to better information use in isolation from the way people used and valued information in a company. Thus, the authors concluded that there would have to be a major shift in managerial attitudes about treating information as an explicit organizational resource *before* significant progress could be made about measuring information's value to the business in most companies.

### Weaknesses of Information Management School metrics

While the IT School has over the years attempted to develop perceptual and functional criteria and measures for evaluating computer systems and IS function, the Information Management School has focused almost exclu-sively on framing the questions and criteria through which to evaluate information's value to the business rather than to apply appropriate met-rics. Thus, the Information Management School has rightly emphasized the centrality of information use to the valuation problem in business; however, the school has largely failed to operationalize its concepts. Moreover, where there have been serious attempts at measuring value from a user perspective, the Information Management School has focused on measuring the usefulness of libraries and information centers to individuals in the business organization, rather than to the performance of the business as a whole.

Thus, the Information Management School has been deficient in clearly indicating the causal link between effective information use and business performance.

## C. The Behavior and Control School

The Behavior and Control School has primarily focused on developing measures of business performance that emphasize control systems—presenting financial and business information to employees to influence working behavior consistent with the improved performance of the overall business. Robert Simons calls these systems 'diagnostic control systems' that are 'used to motivate, monitor, and reward achievement of specified goals' (Simons 1995: 7).

The four major approaches to business performance metrics are: (1) Economic Value Added; (2) Value-Based Management; (3)Activity-Based Management; and (4) the Balanced Scorecard.

*Economic value added (EVA)*
EVA was developed as a measure of financial performance to help managers increase shareholder wealth in a business. The EVA concept was popularized by G. Bennett Stewart's *Quest for Value* in 1990. The measure was based on the idea that all capital has a cost and that earning more than the cost of capital creates value for shareholders.

EVA can be calculated as follows:

Net Sales
–Operating Expenses
=Operating Profit (Earnings Before Interest and Taxes, EBIT)
–Taxes
=Net Operating Profit After Tax (NOPAT)
–Capital Charges (Invested Capital X Cost of Capital)
=EVA

EVA is a measure that can be calculated not only for any company, but also for the business units and operating units within a company, as long as there are common measures and information for operating profits, invested capital, and the cost of capital. Thus, a key feature of EVA is the capability to closely tie the performance of managers and employees to the EVA of their business unit. This connection is important, since, with EVA, managers and employees are expected to act more like owners and improve shareholder value through their decision and actions.

Stewart has noted that:

Making managers into owners is a proven and potent way to create value. To be sure, ownership must go beyond the merely monetary. It is first and foremost a question of attitude. Pride in one's work, sensible risk taking, and, above all, accepting responsibility for the success or failure of the enterprise are among the attitudes that separate owners from hired hands. (Stewart 1990: 223)

Thus, by getting managers and organizational members to act like owners, EVA is an important measure tying individual decisions and actions to business performance. As a metric, EVA depends primarily on financial information in a business. As the metric is applied by managers and organizational members, EVA has only an indirect impact on information use in a business since neither the metric nor its application necessarily guides managers towards what effective information use means in a business. At best, through the use of EVA, managers and organizational members can theoretically focus their attention, time, and resources on using information that contributes to improved performance. However, EVA provides no specific guidance on how people, information, and IT should be deployed to improve business performance.

*Value-based management*
Value-based management (VBM) first gained attention during the late 1970s, but was revived during the 1990s by G. Bennett Stewart, Alfred Rappaport, and others. Similar to EVA, VBM is based on the idea that the central objective for all publicly traded companies is to maximize shareholder wealth. However, VBM goes further than EVA in suggesting that it is the 'management system' that must 'engage, motivate, and reward the people throughout the organization who create shareholder value' (Slater and Olson 1996: 48). As a management system, VBM comes in many flavors and takes a broader view of performance metrics than EVA.

While EVA is calculated by taking net operating profit after taxes minus the capital charges employed to produce that profit, the metrics of value-based management vary with different proponents. For example, Alfred Rappaport, a leading spokesperson for VBM, calculates shareholder wealth based on 'cash flow' discounted by the cost of capital (DCF) (Rappaport

1987: 59). Cash flow is in turn determined by 'value drivers' within a company such as sales growth, operating profit margins, and customer satisfaction. These value drivers will differ by company.

Advocates of VBM criticize EVA as a flawed concept: 'EVA is a short-term measure based on sunken cost—historical investment—which is irrelevant if you are buying 100 shares in a company' (McConville 1994: 58).

Moreover, they also suggest that EVA only speaks to the financial side of the business and not to the people side of the business since people do not show up on the balance sheet. VBM, on the other hand, examines both financial and non-financial drivers of the business including culture, performance measurements, financial information systems, and incentive systems and looks forward to achieving specific improvements in performance tied to the key value drivers of each business unit (McConville 1994: 58).

Value-based management is intended to establish a direct link between performance metrics, financial information management, and incentive plans for managers and employees (Bannister and Jesuthasan 1997). An essential component is 'to provide employees with key operating' information that permits them to understand the link between their decisions and actions and business performance. While value-based management cannot ensure that optimal strategies are chosen, it does seek to tie employee incentives and behaviors to business performance.

As we have seen, the appropriate use of information control is a key enabler of Information Orientation. However, VBM is silent on the other behaviors and values that affect information use and lead to improved business performance. The key weakness of VBM in this context is its primary focus on financial metrics and financial information management, rather than on effective information use by people across the business organization. Unfortunately, good financial information management will not by itself lead to effective information use in the company, although it is a step in the right direction.

### Activity-based costing (ABC) and management

Robert Kaplan, Robin Cooper, and Thomas Johnson introduced activity-based costing (ABC) in the late 1980s. ABC was a financial analysis technique that aimed at better understanding how the cost structure of a company or business unit is related to its business. The theory behind the method was straightforward: 'Virtually all of a company's activities exist to support the production and delivery of today's goods and services. They should, therefore, all be considered product costs' (Cooper and Kaplan 1988: 96). ABC was oriented to providing more accurate information about production and support costs, so that managers could focus their attention on the products and processes that created the most profits.

ABC analysis is intended to help managers slice and evaluate the business in different ways—by product or group of similar products, by individual customer or client group, or by distribution channel.

While ABC is widely used today in many companies and built into enterprise resource planning systems and software, Johnson (1992) has identified key weaknesses in using ABC in companies:

First, doing ABC does not necessarily lead to improvements in business performance. 'No accounting information, not even activity-based accounting information, can help companies achieve competitive excellence' (Johnson 1992: 132). Industry hype surrounding ABC is often based on the belief in the power of innovative breakthroughs or 'quick fix' solutions.

Second, ABC does not necessarily provide the information required to empower employees to improve processes to better satisfy customers.

This is the point—how to discover and adopt competitive ways of organizing work, not how to follow traditional remote-control management. While ABC gives companies a better 'rack and stack' of their overhead costs, it does not drive them to change their fundamental views about how to organize work to efficiently satisfy customers. (Johnson 1992: 153)

In our view, ABC focuses on good information management over largely financial and operational data, but does not address the ways to make information use more effective across the company. Like VBM, ABC purports to offer new metrics and better financial information for management decisions, but largely fails to address *how* a company should use information, people, and IT to achieve improved business performance. At its best, ABC provides better understanding of a company's costs for processes and products that impact revenues. However, the availability of good financial information does not lead to improved business performance without effective IO.

### The balanced scorecard
In 1992, Kaplan and Norton introduced the 'balanced scorecard' as a business unit performance measurement that supplemented more traditional financial measures with criteria that evaluated performance from four perspectives:

1. Financial (generic measures: ROI, EVA);
2. Customers (generic measure: satisfaction, retention, market share);
3. Internal business processes (generic measure: quality, response time, cost, and new product introductions); and

4. Learning and growth (generic measure: employee satisfaction and information system availability) (Kaplan and Norton 1996*c*).

The balanced scorecard and the management processes required to implement it emphasized building the capabilities and acquiring the intangible assets that would lead a company to future growth. Kaplan and Norton believed that:

many of the most popular non-financial measures (of business performance), such as customer satisfaction and employee attitudes, have some of the same limitations as financial measures.

First, they are lagging measures, reporting how well the organization's strategy worked in the last period. Second, the non-financial measures they use are generic and are not related to specific strategic objectives that will provide sustainable competitive advantage. (Kaplan and Norton 1996*a*: 55)

At the center of the balanced scorecard management approach was the development of an information system for performance monitoring and for building the long-term capabilities to compete. Kaplan and Norton acknowledged the need for excellent information: 'If employees are to be effective in today's environment, they need excellent information—on customers, on internal processes, and on the financial consequences of their decisions' (Kaplan and Norton 1996*c*: 134).

More than any other approach to measuring overall business performance, the balanced scorecard approach suggested, but did not indicate, how effective information use in a business was critical to its success. However, the authors never linked effective information use to overall business performance, even though their approach depends on IO to link information behaviors, information use, and IT practices to business performance. Like many of the other advocates of the Behavior and Control School, good information management was important, but never directly measured or linked to business performance.

### Strengths and weaknesses of Behavior and Control School metrics

Each of the four approaches of the Behavior and Control School discussed above is far more direct than either the IT School or the Information Management School was in directly measuring variables that affect overall business performance. This must be considered a strength. And, each of the four approaches deals directly with 'information control' as a key way of linking employee performance to company performance. Moreover, each approach acknowledges the importance of good information management to support its way of measurement.

While these four measurement approaches have made important contributions, they have some serious drawbacks for measuring effectiveness of information use. For example, none of these four approaches explicitly looks at the interactive effects of information behaviors, information management practices, and IT practices in supplying appropriate information to support their metrics or management 'systems'. In fact, these four approaches have been particularly deficient in measuring the impact that strong IT practices have on effective information use.

Only the balanced scorecard approach recognizes the need for 'front-line employees to have accurate and timely information about customers and processes.' For example, Kaplan and Norton note that some companies have developed a 'strategic information coverage ratio' which assesses 'the current availability of information relative to anticipated needs' for front-line, operational workers (Kaplan and Norton 1996c: 136); however, the authors took their discussion no further.

The bottom line: as was the case with the IT School and the Information Management School, none of the four approaches of the Behavior and Control School has developed a metric of effective information use that is linked to overall business performance.

In the next section, we focus on IO as a much-needed validated measure of effective information use that overcomes the problems endemic in the metrics of the three schools of thought. While we recognize that IO is not a measure of *overall* business performance, we contend that it does represent an important performance measure of how senior managers perceive their companies possess the capabilities associated with effective information use necessary to achieve superior business performance.

## 2. APPLYING IO AS A MEASURE OF EFFECTIVE INFORMATION USE

As we noted in Chapter 6, Information Orientation does not focus on an evaluation of IT function specifically, but rather addresses the effectiveness of information use throughout the entire organization.

As a new performance metric, IO can be applied universally across international borders. As we describe in the Appendix in Tables A.7 and A.8, our statistical analysis showed no significant differences between North American and Western European senior managers regarding the three information capabilities of IO or IO itself. These findings strongly suggest that the model is universally applicable to companies operating in a global context. Moreover, our statistical analysis shows no statistical differences in responses across varying job categories of members of senior management teams, indicating that it has validity and reliability in application across multiple job contexts (see Appendix, Tables A.11 and A.12).

In this section, we discuss how IO can be used as an internal benchmark with individual and multiple business units in the same company and as an external benchmark relative to other companies in the same or different industries.

### The 'Information Orientation Dashboard'

The Information Orientation Dashboard (see Fig. 7.1) provides senior managers with a diagnostic tool to evaluate each information capability of IO in their companies. Percentage rankings of each construct relative to an overall study benchmark show companies exactly which capability of IO they need to improve to realize higher IO. And, since we have shown that higher IO results in higher business performance, improvement in IO dimensions and their associated items should ultimately be felt in business performance gains. At a glance, managers can identify areas of strengths, and areas in need of improvement. In this way, the IO Dashboard provides a powerful management tool to be used for either internal or external benchmarking purposes.

Our study has created an external benchmark of 169 business units and companies. These business units represent the responses of 169 senior management teams. Responses of our sample of 1,009 managers are aggregated into their representative team and each team is treated as representing one business unit in our benchmark sample.

To read the IO Dashboard one must first look at the legend in Fig. 7.1. As can be seen, the 169 business units have been broken down in percentiles, based on their scores relative to the average sample scores across all the measures of the study. The legend is shaded from dark (very high) to light (very low) (relative to the benchmark).

At the far left of the benchmark are the dimensions, and to their right are the information capabilities to which they belong. This is followed by the total IO score for a business unit/company. To the right of the IO total score is the corresponding company's (overall) business performance total score. Finally, to the far right of the dashboard are the scores for the measures of business performance.

A senior manager can use the dashboard to scan in either direction for the following purposes:

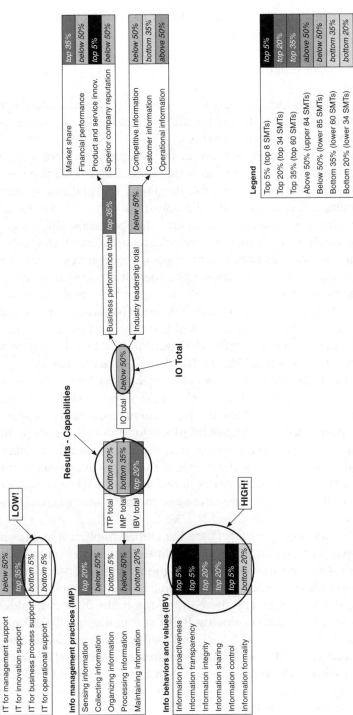

**Fig. 7.1.   The Information Orientation Dashboard: Company X**

*Notes*: This Information Orientation Dashboard depicts the ranking of a Senior Management Team (SMT) within the benchmark sample of the IMD/AC Partnership Project Navigating Business Success. This benchmark sample represents 1,009 survey respondents from a total of 169 international Senior Management Teams from 98 companies.

By using the legend you can identify the relative position of the displayed SMIT within the benchmark sample.

- to gain a snapshot view of where his or her company stands in using information effectively; and
- to understand the relationship of the company's information use to overall business performance.

Once a problem is identified in a dimension, further enquiry can be made regarding the problematic items (specific behavior or practice) that must be improved to raise the company's scores.

This diagnostic tool can be used for intra-industry and cross-industry analysis. In addition, senior managers that need a more effective measure of global IO can use the dashboard as a diagnostic tool in their company for benchmarking and comparing multiple business units and divisions. This metric permits senior managers to identify best practices within a group's portfolio, regardless of product, service, or geographic location.

A Global Financial Services Group employed our survey instrument to develop a profile of 48 of its business units, including two central office senior management teams, covering 336 managers. With these findings, the Group's global IT strategy review team has been able to evaluate the portfolio of business units relative to IO and business performance. This key finding has led the team to redefine their portfolio strategy using IO as a key business metric, rather than employ IT-oriented measures alone.

In meetings with senior managers of several global companies, we have found that the IO benchmark among business units inside their company provides *for the first time* a clear and powerful measure of senior management team perceptions of effective information use and business performance across their company. In addition, it permits senior managers to understand how different teams of senior managers overseeing business units have or have not effectively developed across the IO capabilities relative to other business units inside the *same* company over the past three to five years.

Thus, whether senior managers are benchmarking IO capabilities with other companies or across business units inside the same company, there now exists a tool and diagnostic technique to analyze information use deficiencies in different company situations, and recommend appropriate management actions based on these situations. In the three examples that follow, prescriptions for improving IO in companies are based on the assumption that people behaviors and values are the most difficult to change, followed by information management practices and IT practices. While not scientifically derived, this assumption was derived from extensive conversation with senior executives at IMD as well as in follow-up interviews with study participants.

*Company scenario A: potential high payoff with improved IT practices*
The first case is about a fast growing European retailer of eyeglass lenses and frames. The company focus is on service quality and a store-level style of employee empowerment and responsibility that emphasizes person-to-person relationships and contacts, over formal information practices and IT use.

The acquisition of a European competitor in 1997 doubled the number of employees to 8,000 and increased the number of stores from 200 to 700. The company is now operating in seventeen European countries compared with four before the acquisition.

In the context of this rapid international expansion, the company's CFO was concerned about the sustainability of the company's profits, since no standardized processes or information systems were in place to ensure appropriate day-to-day operational control within and across countries and senior management teams. Moreover, the informal personal style used by senior management was now experiencing breakdowns, as the team now oversaw a geographically diverse company with many different-style stores and modes of operation in each country.

The management style of the CEO, who was one of two founders of the original company, was described as 'management by walking around— based on pure instinct and relying heavily on personal relationships.' This approach had worked well in developing an intense store-level customer focus and service approach, but was not adequate to running a large, diverse retail chain across Europe.

At the time, the CEO was adamant in his opinion about the incompatibility of IT and the company's people culture: 'IT is not in the genes of this company.' In 1998, the company began experiencing supply chain management problems in purchasing and managing eyeglass frame inventories across Europe. Pressures were building to regionalize the supply chain and to define shared processes and systems at the store level across countries.

It was at this time that the company was evaluated with the IO measurement survey. Analysis of results determined that the company scored relatively high on information behaviors and values, but low on information management practices and IT practices, as the dashboard in Fig. 7.2 indicates. Due to its service orientation, people culture, and entrepreneurial growth, this company has the potential for high performance payoffs, if an appropriate IT investment and successful implementation is initiated.

Such a company has already established the importance of information behaviors and values at the store and country levels. People use information proactively in stores, and are willing to constructively respond to problems, mistakes, or errors. Store management is willing to share best

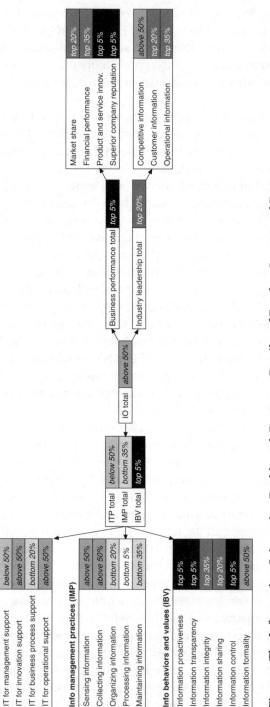

Fig. 7.2. The Information Orientation Dashboard: European Retailer of Eyeglass Lenses and Frames

practices across stores within and across countries. Senior managers share operating results with all employees and across functions and activities.

While information management practices in this retail business are clear and simple for employees and store managers, they tend to be more informal at the store and country levels. However, senior managers recognize the value of achieving regional synergies in supply chain processes and operational systems.

Such a company is ready to address the issues of its regional growth, and the need for establishing shared infrastructure and compatible systems across country operations. As can be seen from its IO Dashboard, this company has the clear potential to reap significant business benefits from investing in the development of its IT capability—particularly in using IT to manage its supply chain, and its financial/managerial reporting across the region. It can also substantially improve the informal information practices across the stores by sharing best practices proactively, and adopting more standard point-of-sales, account management, and customer profiling systems.

*Company scenario B: probable low payoff from more investment into IT until information behavior problems are fixed*

The second case is about the US division of a major financial institution faced with declining market share and customer dissatisfaction. In 1997, the senior managers of this division instituted a major restructuring and business development initiative. As part of this initiative, they approved a multi-year plan to upgrade the IT infrastructure in support of their office communications and document management. In addition, the division instituted a new performance metric for managers, a new rewards and incentive plan, and a more disciplined decision process overseen by the executive committee rather than by the CEO alone. The new IT systems coupled with operational changes for project planning and customer support required organizational members to share information across projects, and to adopt a more open style of managing against performance targets.

While these initiatives improved greatly their capabilities to use IT and manage information across projects and for customers, information behaviors and values remained a major issue. The division's history of information hoarding and manipulation, lack of senior manager integrity in using information, and information secrecy continued with the change in initiatives. One senior manager commented:

There has been a company-wide push to promote information sharing and get people to work together, but trust still does not exist. People continue to use information for their own benefit to position themselves and their department. There is a strong company culture of 'these are my numbers and my information, and I own the customer.'

In this case, the business organization scores relatively high on IT practices, but low on information management practices and behaviors. In such a case, senior managers seem to have somewhat misdiagnosed their problems. While past investments in IT have greatly improved IT practices, they could mistakenly believe that more IT investments and better IT use will improve their information management practices and their behavioral problems with information use.

However, it is clear that business organizations with these information use problems should first address information behaviors and values, and then work on information management practices to improve performance, before any additional major IT investments are undertaken. Based on an analysis of their dashboard, this company determined that the root causes of their performance deficiencies were related to control, transparency, and information sharing, which prevent their managers and employees from using information effectively.

This case is a more difficult situation to change over the short term as compared to the first case, and requires focused attention on improving information behaviors and values over time with a thoughtful IO strategy. More and better IT, in this case, will most likely not show high payoff for improving IO unless they address their weaknesses in information management and behaviors.

*Company scenario C: low on all counts—diligence must prevent it from falling prey to the IT productivity paradox*
The third case involves a European retail bank that over the last five years has gone through repeated restructuring and downsizing efforts as well as one acquisition of a competitor. These initiatives have wreaked havoc on the bank's IT systems and operations as one senior manager commented:

One of the main problems that we have had is that of an old and expensive IT infrastructure. During the last five years, the focus of IT was to integrate systems acquired through our acquisition of a competitor. This was well done, but no one looked forward to future applications and development of our IT systems. We need a major modernization of our IT systems.

At the same time, the information management practices of the bank had deteriorated at the managerial and service delivery levels. Managers and employees experience information overload on one side and information neglect on the other side. Managers continue to receive voluminous reports on day-to-day operations, while employees cannot reconcile customer accounts without the customer identifying the account numbers that the bank has issued.

Information behaviors in the bank have also deteriorated through multiple downsizings and restructuring. No one trusts formal performance reports. People live in fear of redundancies, and do not share information across departments. Information transparency and integrity are very low since no one wants to report customer or operational problems. Managers are reluctant to respond constructively to more 'bad news'.

While the performance of the bank during this period has 'improved', most of the bottom-line improvements have come through cost reductions and elimination of redundancies, rather than growth. The bank's major competitors have merged in the retail market, and have improved their retail services and customer focus significantly. While the bank's performance is OK today, its information capabilities for the future are very low.

In this scenario, the company is low on all three information capabilities of IO. If this company invests in IT, it will see little performance improvement. As the case illustrates, there is a danger that managers may perceive the information problems in their company as IT practice issues which can be corrected over time with better IT systems for operations and business process support. The managers know that IT has been consciously neglected over the last five years, and it is the subject of constant complaints by employees and customers alike. Poor information management may be seen as an outcome of poor IT practices, rather than as an outcome of fundamental weaknesses in behaviors and values among managers and employees.

In this case, the company should first work on information behaviors and values and then address changes in information management and IT practices. However, without a company-wide measure of information use like IO to test for improvements in information behaviors and information management practices over time, senior managers may be tempted to reach for visible improvements in IT—thinking that at least they are removing the most obvious source of business performance deficiencies. This approach addresses the symptoms, but leaves the root causes of their low IO score in place.

### Using IO as a key performance indicator over time

If the senior managers of each of the three companies mentioned above understood the potential for improving and leveraging effective information use, then presumably they could employ the IO measures and, correspondingly, the IO Dashboard as a diagnostic tool, to guide improvements

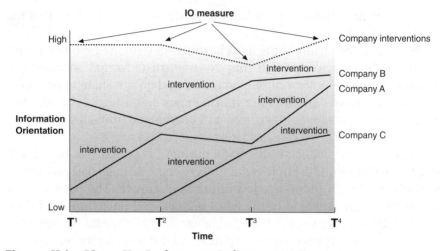

**Fig. 7.3. Using IO as a Key Performance Indicator over Time**

in the appropriate IO capabilities over time. As Fig. 7.3 suggests, companies can use the IO measures and benchmarks as a periodic indicator over time intervals of management actions and initiatives, to improve their effectiveness in using information and, ultimately, business performance.

In the examples in Fig. 7.3, Company A, the retail eyeglass business, scores very low on IO at Time 1. In this case, senior managers in this company may want to take immediate actions to address the causes of low IO. Such an intervention would directly address a recognized deficiency in one of the IO capabilities—IT practices.

A second IO assessment at Time 2 might indicate some improvement, but not at the desired level. Thus, managers could take further steps to implement new IT systems in support of changing information management practices company-wide.

A third assessment at Time 3 may show a slight decline in IO suggesting further focus on improvements to information management practices, as well as a need for faster implementation of IT improvements.

Finally, at Time 4, the marked improvements in IO might indicate that the company is has fully implemented new IT systems company-wide, and can focus on another level of IO improvements to ratchet up business performance even further.

In the case of Company B, the major financial institution, at Time 1 the company shows average IO compared to its competitors. If the company's managers are not proactive in sustaining the current level of IO, IO may decline or drop. An IO assessment at Time 2 indicates a drop in IO that could worsen unless appropriate changes are implemented.

Finally, in case three, Company C, the European retail bank, Time 1 and Time 2 indicate a very low IO. Senior managers in this company will need to dramatically transform the level of IO for future business gains. But again, changes in business conditions, coupled with internal shifts in business strategies and decision making, will require major modifications to company actions and behaviors if the company is to achieve an appropriate level of IO and business performance in the future.

## 3. CONCLUSIONS

In this chapter, we have focused on IO as a measure of effective information use in a business organization and shown how the IO metric can be employed to recommend key strategies for improving information capabilities. While IO is not a measure of overall business performance like EVA, it is a powerful measure of how senior managers perceive their companies possess the capabilities associated with effective information use to achieve superior business performance.

We have examined the measurement criteria and metrics of the three schools of management thinking and practice. Only the IT and the Behavior and Control schools have explored how to provide management metrics or tools to improve performance. The Information Management School has articulated the need for positioning information use at the center of valuing information's link to business performance, but has not developed or tested specific metrics. The IT School focused rather narrowly on developing metrics for assessing the use of computer systems from a user perspective and for evaluating the service levels and quality of the IS department or function in a business. Finally, the Behavior and Control School has been directly concerned with articulating overall business performance metrics such as EVA, VBM, ABC, and the balanced scorecard. However, none of these approaches to assessing overall business performance has focused on a measure of effective information use. We believe that the IO metric is a significant step in addressing the measurement problems of the three schools of thought.

In applying IO as a business measure of effective information use, we have emphasized several key characteristics of IO:

1. IO is a new business metric that is causally linked to business performance;
2. IO is an organization-wide metric, not limited to the IT department or other information management support functions;

3. IO applies universally across international borders. There are no statistically significant differences between the senior manager responses in North America and Western Europe; and
4. IO can be used as a key performance indicator over time to assess the effectiveness of management actions to improve information behaviors and values, information management practices, and IT practices.

We have also presented and explained the use of the Information Orientation Dashboard as a management tool for evaluating and benchmarking IO capabilities and practices within and across industries. Our external benchmark sample of 169 companies and business units permits the assessment of the IO levels of other companies and business units across industries and geographic locations worldwide.

In addition, we have shown, through the collaborative efforts of the Global Financial Services Group and other large international companies, how the IO Dashboard can be employed for benchmarking and comparing multiple business units and divisions globally. Using such IO benchmarking techniques, they can begin to develop portfolio strategies using IO as a common measure of effective information use across business units globally.

Whether senior managers evaluate IO capabilities with other companies or across business units in the same company, we have shown how the IO metric positions companies to assess IO deficiencies and issues and recommend appropriate management actions.

In the next chapter we will determine if there are prescribed paths that companies should follow as they improve their ability to use information to enhance business performance.

# 8

# Developing Information Orientation Maturity in Companies

Attaining high IO does not just happen overnight. A journey typically spans years of developing capabilities to effectively compete with information. It follows from a particular managerial mindset on how to link people, information, and IT to improve business performance and how to put into action prescriptive strategies to affect meaningful change.

Yet, for companies facing a future that demands information-based business models, and especially for those with underdeveloped information capabilities, the task may seem daunting. Given limited time and resources, where should managers start to improve their company's IO? What prescriptive paths can managers embark on to help ensure a successful journey to achieving high IO?

These practical questions raised by senior managers in consulting engagements, or in executive development sessions we have taught over the past several years, drove us to explore a deeper understanding of the relationships between dimensions of each information capability.

Our initial study findings combined with senior managers' inputs and previous research provide us with theories about causal relationships between dimensions of each information capability. Using statistical path analysis, we test these theories for prescriptive paths that a company must follow as it becomes more mature in the development of each information capability. We next statistically examine cross-capability paths that might lead to an 'interaction effect' which increases synergy across information capabilities.

In this chapter, we will present the theoretical path arguments and statistical path analysis conducted to explain these causal links between dimensions in each information capability. From this analysis, we will build prescriptive IO maturity models for each of the three information capabilities. In a fourth model, we will show statistical evidence that linkages across information capabilities exist through key dimensions in each capability.

We conclude by presenting five key characteristics of effective information use that we believe act as catalysts across all three capabilities and help create the conditions in the information culture that drive the causal flows between dimensions. This interpretative explanation will be used to define a mature IO culture and to provide a deeper understanding of the IO maturity models. Finally, we contemplate future research benefits of further validation of an integrated, holistic IO maturity path model.

## 1. DEFINING IO MATURITY

Companies need road maps to show how improvements in one IO dimension affect improvements in other IO dimensions. Once these relationships are clear, companies can prioritize their information practices and behaviors in a causal sequence: in essence, charting the best way to increase the 'maturity' of their information capabilities, and in doing so, raise their overall IO score.

Our findings indicate that more mature IO companies understand the cascading causal paths that connect individual IO dimensions within information capabilities. Thus, more mature IO companies are good at all information capabilities and do four things well:

*IT practices*—more mature IO companies not only use IT systems to support operations, business processes, and product innovation, but also to enhance management-level decision making.

*Information management practices*—more mature IO companies manage information in a consistent and timely way while ensuring that information is accurate and of high quality. In addition to collecting, organizing, and maintaining information well, more mature organizations continue to enhance the sensing and processing practices. These two practices are the two most important points in information valuation judgements and tend to be the most difficult information management dimensions to improve.

*Information behaviors and values*—more mature IO companies instill in their employees precisely those behaviors and values that affect how the company best uses information for customer, supplier, and partner interactions as well as for internal management control. By instilling this requisite set of good information behaviors and values, employees develop strong proactive behavior for information use.

*Cross-capability interaction effect*—more mature IO companies understand the importance of creating greater synergy *across information capabilities*. We call this the 'IO Interaction Effect'. We believe that this effect is greatest when a company has established good behavior for proactive information use; when it is able to sense the right information; and when it has solid processing and IT support of management decision making. To achieve this synergy all three information capabilities need to be developed and maintained at high levels. Importantly, because we believe there is a cross-capability interaction effect, major changes to a dimension in one capability, either positive or negative, will stimulate changes across all capabilities.

## 2. PRESCRIPTIVE MODELS FOR DEVELOPING MORE MATURE IO

Managers of more mature IO companies affect change on two levels. On one level, they carefully build information capabilities over time. On a second level, they make sure their companies exploit these capabilities to compete with information in their industries and markets—making them smarter, faster, and nimbler. This dual strategy suggests that companies are always moving to different levels of IO maturity. The differences between companies come about in two ways:

First, within information capabilities, more mature IO companies systematically work on measuring and improving deficient practices and behaviors.

Second, over time more mature IO companies learn from their experiences and implement improvements to their information practices and behaviors more successfully than do others. In essence, more mature IO companies better recognize the causal paths to improve each information capability and know how to act on this knowledge within their unique business context.

In this section, we will introduce causal path models for each of the three information capabilities (IT practices, information management practices, and information behaviors and values) and one causal path model for cross-capability linkages. These theory-driven path models are based on existing management theories as outlined in Chapters 3, 4, and 5, and on our own discussions with senior managers.

*Model 1: building IT practices maturity*

For many managers and companies, the link between IT investments and practices and improving business performance remains elusive. Companies—and their competitors—spend more and more on IT, but they often gain little competitive advantage from their IT practices. Many companies do achieve cost reductions and improved productivity because of their IT investments; unfortunately, their competitors quickly do the same, passing the benefits on to customers as more and cheaper products and services. In the age of information ubiquity, the pace of IT-enabled competition intensifies in every industry. Unless information asymmetries can be established, companies seem locked into IT spending more out of 'competitive necessity' than for 'competitive advantage'.

Of course, companies with high IO know they must do well in deploying IT to manage operations. But they also target their investments on those uses of IT that can create competitive advantage, namely those that can improve product and service innovation and provide superior management insight into strategic decisions. These more mature IO companies seek innovative ways of using IT to re-engineer their business processes, to encourage innovation in new products and services, and the most difficult task of all—to improve unstructured senior management-level decision making.

As we discussed in Chapter 3, senior managers must ensure that IT is managed to help achieve both intended and emergent strategies. To implement intended strategy, managers seek to formalize and institutionalize decision making and deploy information systems that help ensure predictable results. IT for operational and business process support enables transactional activities and core business processes which should mirror the intended strategies of senior managers. On the other hand, to respond to an ever-changing business environment, emergent strategies must be nurtured to result in novel products, services, and new business concepts or to enable the making of strategic decisions. In mature IO companies, structured decisional information from operations is further refined by IT for innovation support. This information increases the possibility for people-based discovery, creative exploration, openness to new business ideas, new uses of knowledge, and new ways of deploying IT to 'enable' a company to innovate. Using IT for innovation support well means that a company possesses a high level of learning capacity and flexibility. This, combined with well-understood and executed IT-supported business processes, permits managers to further develop their IT support of unstructured decision making, enabling managers to recognize and act on information to better respond to emergent strategic situations. Based on these theoretical relationships between IT practice dimensions, we propose that companies follow a linear causal path in developing IT practices maturity.

Consistent with past literature that has developed a decision-based hierarchical model of IT practices (as discussed in Chapter 3 and highlighted in Fig. 3.1), our linear path theory is based on the premiss that IT practice dimensions cumulatively contribute towards developing better IT support for making unstructured and strategic decisions. Our path theory contends that good IT for operational support of structured decisions contributes to all the other IT practice dimensions by providing the operational foundation for accurate and timely information delivery. Good IT for operational support has the greatest effect on IT support for business processes, as the transactional data is required to successfully complete process activities. IT for operational support and process support improves IT for innovation support by allowing product and customer information on cross-functional and cross-organizational bases to feed into the innovation process. IT for business process support provides consistent information on the efficiency of intended business activities and provides a steady stream of customer feedback: both necessary for developing sophisticated IT applications and models to support strategic decision making. Finally, better IT for innovation support provides an underlying basis for improving IT for management support, enabling recognition and refinement of emergent strategies.

We used statistical path analysis to test this model and determine directionality of causal links between dimensions. Using path analysis it is possible to postulate a causal relationship and determine the direction and strength of these relationships. Both direct and indirect paths can be identified using this type of statistical test. Using this analysis, we can test, for example, whether IT for operational support has a direct influence on IT for business process support or whether this relationship, in fact, goes in the opposite direction with IT for business process support directly influencing IT for operational support (see the Appendix for further discussion of path analysis and our results).

We initially tested the path model theorized above and it surprisingly did not hold up statistically. We ran several very similar path models and found the model with the best fit was the one that dropped two of the initially theorized causal relationships. The first path dropped was the IT for business process support to IT for innovation support path. The second path that was dropped was the direct path from IT for operational support to IT for management support. Fig. 8.1 shows the statistical scores supporting our original theory of directionality of the IT for management support dimensions, but including the two dropped theorized paths.

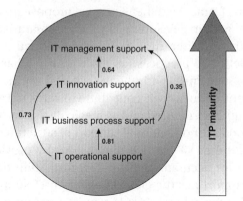

**Fig. 8.1. The ITP Maturity Model: A Path to Mature Information Technology Practices**

*Note*: The arrows indicate a causal relationship between the dimensions.

For example, having good IT for operational support will increase a company's ability to deliver good IT for business process and innovation support.

Path coefficients in the models reflect the amount of direct contribution of a given dimension on another dimension when effects of other related dimensions are taken into account. For example, we can conclude that IT for management support is more strongly influenced by IT for innovation support (0.64) than IT for business process support (0.35). Significance of these coefficients were tested using $t$-tests and all show statistical significance at the $\rho=0.01$ level. The relative magnitude ($0<\rho<1$) of causal linkage can be observed through comparing the path coefficients (see Appendix for further discussion).

From Fig. 8.1, we can see that causal links exist in the direction from IT for operational support to IT for business process support (.81) and to IT for innovation support (.73). Technology supporting innovation, therefore, is influenced by the quality of systems for operations, rather than those focusing on process issues. These results suggest, for example, that IT supporting innovation, such as virtual reality modeling of genetic cell make-up in a pharmaceutical laboratory, is better supported by basic transactional applications providing information on patient morbidity rates than from data originating in the ERP system focusing on the order fulfillment business process between the company and pharmacies. In essence, IT for innovation support is improved when a company can use and interpret large data sets from operational systems to distill new trends or business opportunities.

Our results do indicate that IT for operational support provides a baseline for other IT levels, and manifests itself through linear paths to IT for business process and innovation support, rather than through a direct causal link to IT for management support. IT for business process support, however, did not show a direct causal path to IT for innovation support, but did show a direct causal link with IT for management support (.35) as theorized. Finally, there exists a strong causal path from IT for innovation to IT for management support (.64), which supports our initial theory.

In addition to these direct influence paths, this model also provides us with evidence of an indirect but cumulative path influence. For example, IT for operational support influences both IT for business process support and IT for innovation support factors, which in turn influence IT for management support. Thus, IT for management support is affected indirectly by IT for operational support, in addition to the two direct effects from IT for innovation and IT for business process support. As a result, IT for management support is the dimension that is most influenced and dependent on the other dimensions within the IT practices capability. As a consequence, the requirement to have strong performance across the other dimensions as a prerequisite for high IT management support helps explain why it has been so difficult to achieve complete success in applying IT to support unstructured decision making. As a consequence, IT management support remains the most difficult dimension to control due to its dependence on the effective development and deployment of the other IT dimensions.

What this model suggests is that to reach IO maturity, a company must not only focus on the operational and business process IT support needs of the company, but must focus on improving its IT to support innovation. This will allow it to adequately develop and use IT for management support for the more difficult tasks associated with less structured decision making. Conversely, we can say that senior managers wanting to improve their IT for management support will have to do a good job at all the IT support dimensions first.

The causal path in Fig. 8.1 reflects the maturity track of the IT practice capability, providing us a basis to show how a successful IO company builds more mature IT practices. More mature IO companies have been able to leverage all four IT practice dimensions, and are able to build strong IT for management support. While they know they must focus on doing well what is competitively necessary—deploying IT to manage business operations and processes effectively—they also target their investments on those uses of IT that:

1. help them to be more innovative in developing new products and services in their industry; and

2. prepare their managers and employees for tomorrow's information-based competition.

All too often, companies focus IT investments on increasing output and productivity rather than supporting innovation and new knowledge producing activities. Indeed, the well-known IT productivity paradox suggests that if managers *believe* that IT investments can only make the company more efficient and reduce costs, then that is what they will do with IT. In one sense, the IT productivity paradox is a self-fulfilling prophecy.

Thus, we can conclude that companies with high IT investment and lower IT practices maturity may be spending too much on IT to support the basic operations; failing to evolve into the stage of business and innovation support that could provide them with IT for more competitive advantage. In contrast, companies with higher IT maturity aim to invest enough in IT to operate basic systems and to use IT in business process support to compete with other leading companies in their industry. However, senior managers in these companies push IT development into the realm of innovation and foster the building of systems to support IT for management support. Mature IO companies understand that this allows them to build distinctive information capabilities and achieve higher returns on effective information use—possibly establishing information asymmetric competitive advantages.

When reflecting on this IT practices maturity model, we begin to recognize important organizational characteristics underlying the causal linkages of the IT practice maturity model. Examining the model from a more interpretative perspective indicates that mature IO companies exhibit several more developed cultural characteristics. Absence of one or more of these characteristics may affect a company's ability to fully leverage the paths existing within the IT practices maturity model. For example, the ability of people to focus on relevant information for their decision context can result in information overload and decisional paralysis. The ability of a company's people to quickly learn and act flexibly is an important underlying characteristic of effective IT practices. The role this underlying characteristic plays in establishing a more mature IO culture will be discussed below.

Imagine the situation where a company is not able to focus on what information it needs to make good business decisions. What results is information overload. IT for operational support fails to provide the needed structured information for routine decisions. Managers and employees, frustrated with the existing system, may begin to develop IT solutions independently, which disrupts the ability of the company to carry on business process activities to innovate or address less structured decisions.

More *focus on relevant information* can be used to improve decision making on the operational and process levels, which helps improve task and process efficiency. Likewise, focused use of information affects other levels of decision making, especially at the management level. Companies that use IT for business process support well can develop IT practices for management support more effectively because they know who needs the information and the type of information that can be supported by technology. These companies leverage focused information across their business processes and with customers and suppliers to gain better knowledge for spotting emergent customer needs, forming strategy, and analyzing risk.

The ability of a company's people to learn also has a catalyzing effect on its ability to create mature IT practices. For example, using IT for operational support within an environment that stresses learning facilitates the sharing and use of information company-wide, thus improving product development and creativity. Knowledge creation resulting through IT for innovation will also improve the creativity, exploration, and knowledge exchange of highly skilled people for future strategic decisions prompting improvements to IT for management support. This *learning capacity* enables better decision making concerning more unstructured management thinking, providing opportunities to reposition competitive strategies.

Finally, more *flexibility* as a cultural characteristic provides the basis for developing IT solutions above and beyond the operational and business process levels. IT support on the innovation and management levels is what allows a company to improve the way it manages information for unstructured decision making processes that may deal either with innovation and creativity, or unstructured management decisions not based on past trends but on future strategic direction. Flexibility to change one's assumptions and act on what has been learned allows companies to create an outward-looking environment that not only tries to 'do things better' but also to 'do better things', driving appropriate changes and development of IT to respond to this dual need. A company environment where flexibility is discouraged by not rewarding or acknowledging actions that challenge existing ways of doing things may put a damper on the development of systems that do not conform to standardized processes and systems.

*Model 2: leveraging information management practices*
In our discussions throughout this book, we have argued that high IO companies create information asymmetries that offer competitive advantage within their industries. As we have seen in the previous section, more mature IO companies understand the path that improves IT support at each

level of decision making and, in doing so, have made important strides to address the challenge of supporting unstructured decision making for product innovation and charting strategic direction. High IO companies know that to create information asymmetry there must exist a fundamental link between well-developed IT capabilities, positive information behaviors and values, and the effective management of the dynamic information life cycle. In this section we will discuss the prescriptive path that firms follow to improve information management practices within their company.

As we saw in Chapter 4, managers recognize the dimensions of the information life cycle—sensing, collecting, organizing, processing, and maintaining. Their understanding of each of these phases suggests that a life cycle path exists where improvements in one dimension of the life cycle will sequentially have a positive affect on the next. This effect works in a circular fashion among the four traditional phases on the life cycle—collecting, organizing, processing, and maintaining.

To manage information well companies must take into account both the personal and situational contexts of their employees' work. They must recognize that information value judgements are determined within a broader business context that defines information usage norms, and practices. To manage information well managers must understand that tacit knowledge resides in people and, therefore, they must find ways to encourage their people to translate implicit knowledge into explicit information through more formal channels. Finally, companies must recognize that information use is a dynamic process, involving repeated and recursive cycles of information sensing, collecting, organizing, processing, and maintaining. Thus, understanding how the five information management practices interact as an information life cycle is important to understanding how to improve and formalize the management of information at both the individual and organizational level.

In Chapter 4, we argued that the traditional view of the information life cycle included a continuous and circuitous set of phases including collecting, organizing, processing, and maintaining. More recently, scholars have identified an additional and newer information management practice dimension—sensing. This phase provides the life cycle with a cognitive bridge to usage behaviors whereby external informational stimuli help define new information needs and ultimately help determine what information will be collected. Unlike the other four information management dimensions, sensing has been depicted outside the traditional closed circle of the life cycle, feeding into it at the collection phase by helping to define information needs, and therefore driving changes to what information would be collected within an organization.

With the exception of sensing, our model assumed that these five phases were associated in a continuous circular relationship, each dependent on the last (see Fig. 4.1). Sensing information from outside the company on market shifts, customer needs, and new technology changes influences what information is collected by establishing information needs. Collecting relevant information not only prevents information overload, but also directly determines how a company organizes it (i.e. how well a company indexes and classifies information and links databases to promote access and use by its people). Organizing information properly enables managers and their employees to process information for different decisional contexts. Finally, companies that know what information to process and how to maintain it save time and resources by effectively avoiding retaining and collecting irrelevant information, or re-collecting the same information.

To test this model, we ran the same statistical path analysis as on the first IT practices model. As Fig. 8.2 shows, our statistical analysis supported the general directionality of the information life cycle, from sensing to collecting (.62), collecting to organizing (.96), organizing to processing (.94), and processing to maintaining (.86). The data supports our contention that sensing remains a critical link to the effective management of information. As we had theorized, the data also showed a negative score for maintaining to collecting (–.28), supporting our initial theory that better maintaining practices would lead to a decrease in the collecting phase.

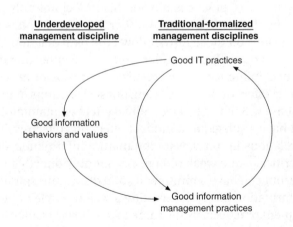

**Fig. 8.2. The IMP Maturity Model: A Path to Mature Information Management Practices**

*Note*: The arrows indicate a causal relationship between the dimensions.

For example, being good at collecting information leads to better-organized information.

The existence of both positive (sensing) and negative (maintaining) path values suggests that optimal levels of development of information collection will be determined by decisions stemming from both sensing and maintaining practices within a company. Our findings indicate more intertwined relationships between our information management practices exist than with either of our other path models.

The unique circular path among dimensions of this model also raises several issues concerning the maturity of the information management practices. First, due to its circular nature, the model does not give us a clear indication of where the path begins, or ends. Both tacit and explicit information exists within organizations that are constantly being evaluated at both the individual and company level at each phase of the life cycle. This evaluation determines how far the information goes within the cycle. For example, during the sensing phase people will use cognitive responses to evaluate the usefulness of new information to address new or future problems or decisions. During the collecting phase, people will determine whether the benefits of information collection are worth its costs. At the organizing phase, decisions concerning data structures, standards, and routines will determine whether information is organized for company use. During the processing phase, information is evaluated for its impact and appropriateness for decisions. During the maintenance phase, people will determine whether information should be refreshed and updated for future use.

Second, as in our IT practices model, this model not only shows direct influence of one dimension upon another, but also implies the indirect effect of dimensions on those further down the path diagram. This indirect effect is enhanced through the circular model. Collecting, therefore, will not only have a direct influence on the organizing phase of the life cycle, but will have an indirect effect on the processing phase. Decisions made during the processing phase will not only have a direct effect on maintaining information, but will have a subsequent indirect effect on collecting. The implication of this relationship on developing mature information management practices is critical—one weak dimension not only directly influences the next practice, but can have a multiplying and downward spiraling effect on the entire information life cycle, creating a vicious circle of poor information management practices. By the same token, however, identification and improvement in one weak link can have a greater influence on even weaker dimensions through the circular effect. Thus, the revolving nature of causal linkages can be a two-edged sword for establishing effective mechanisms for sensing, collecting, organizing, processing, and maintaining information.

The circularity of the model, and the combined positive and negative effects on collecting from maintaining and sensing, demands necessarily that to achieve information management practices maturity, as shown in Fig. 8.2, companies must develop *simultaneously* all five information practice dimensions. Unlike the approach that can be taken with our IT practices model, linear development of the information life cycle dimensions over time will not necessarily lead to greater maturity. Because of the circularity of the model, all other phases need to be fine tuned holistically to manage this optimal level of data collection.

This model does suggest that two key dimensions of the information life cycle demand special interest given their importance to information valuation—processing and sensing. Within the closed causal circle, processing is possibly the most critical valuation point since it determines whether the information sensed, collected, and organized meets the problem solving needs of the business context. As we have seen from our data in Chapter 4, sensing, based on more cognitive responses, is the least formalized and consistent information management practice in companies today, suggesting the need to better understand and develop this phase of the life cycle. Although it lies outside of the closed circular path, sensing has a direct causal effect on defining new information needs for collecting relevant information and thus does have a critical influence on strengthening the life cycle. Ultimately, filtering information at the sensing phase determines whether or not a company can create new emergent competitive strategies to address changing business realities.

What enables and disables the development of these causal paths? We again turn to more interpretative discussion of what might underlie these paths within a company. What cultural characteristics of effective information use will improve the information life cycle? First, in this volatile and dynamic business environment, managers and organizational members must *focus* their attention, time, and resources on the decisions that lead to improved performance. Focus not only improves the type of information sensed and collected, but enables a company to make better processing decisions and evaluation of which information to maintain and what new information is needed. A company with little focus on what decisions, both operational and strategic, will improve business value may sense, collect, and organize a lot of information, but the information will be too much to process in any effective way or not relevant to the actual needs.

Being *more explicit* with personal information and knowledge is another cultural characteristic that might drive a mature information life cycle. For information to be managed as a corporate resource, information and knowledge within people's heads must be recorded in a usable format, collected, and incorporated into the knowledge base of the organization. Similarly, information that is sensed by organizational members also needs to be made explicit for others to be able to use it. A company that does not create a culture for the transfer of this knowledge has many repetitive information tasks occurring simultaneously throughout the organization. In addition, such a company may suffer from 'brain drain' once people leave the organization.

In a culture that fosters the transfer of this knowledge, people are *more selfless* and ready to contribute to organizational goals. For example, people who are willing to sense information, not only for their own decision contexts, but also for those of other people and functions within the organization, will improve the quality and scope of information available through the collection and organizing practices. They must be willing to share the information they have sensed and collected to improve decision making, improve the maintaining dimension, and reduce the need to re-collect the same information in other areas of the company.

Finally, to ensure that accurate information is being sensed people must be *ready to learn* to interpret changes or errors within their working environment and *have the flexibility* to act on what they are learning. This is important to allow for changes in information that might affect future business decisions and strategic direction.

### Model 3: influencing people's information behaviors and values

Of our three information capabilities, the information behaviors and values capability probably demands the greatest understanding of how its dimensions interact with each other. Given the complexity and difficulty of changing people's behaviors, this information capability has the longest learning curve to reach a satisfactory maturity level. A deeper understanding of the causal relationships between dimensions can help accelerate a company's development of this information capability.

As we argued in Chapter 5, there have been few formalized management activities focusing on the development of appropriate behaviors and values for effective information use. Our research model is based on the idea that to improve information use at the organizational level, more deliberate management activities need to be identified and formalized to increase effective information use. Based on this premiss, we recognize that people's disposition and willingness to think about and use information will help define these management activities. We believe that in companies where people are proactive in their willingness to think about, use, and improve the management of information, these management activities are more clearly defined and information is used most effectively.

Our model also assumes that developing proactive information behavior does not occur in a vacuum, but is instead dependent on a set of other information behaviors and values that influence the degree to which it is manifested in an organization (as seen in Fig. 5.1). Drawing on literature from two research streams, we identified five behavioral dimensions that we believed had either a direct or indirect impact on creating proactive information use. These dimensions, drawn from both human resources and management control literature streams, included integrity, formality, control, transparency, and sharing.

We believed these dimensions would directly and indirectly influence the degree to which proactiveness, the most dependent dimension, would be manifested within an organization. This literature and these discussions suggested that there exists a linear relationship between integrity, formality, control, transparency, sharing, and proactiveness. We suspected that a company that attempts to teach its organizational members to be proactive would not succeed unless the other information behaviors were also present.

As seen in Fig. 8.3, we suspected that the causal direction would therefore begin with information integrity facilitating the formal use of information. Integrity establishes shared boundaries and values—honesty, candor, and openness—establishing trust in formal information sources inside the company. The trust in and subsequent use of formal information is also necessary for information control. The willingness of people to trust the performance-based information given by their senior managers relates directly to the amount of trust they have in the integrity of the managers and the quality of the shared performance information. In addition, we believe that integrity and a positive view of sharing performance-based information create a climate for transparency where people willingly expose failures, mistakes, and errors for remedy. A company that treats mistakes and failures as opportunities to learn creates the atmosphere of openness necessary for employees to share *all* information willingly. A company that provides performance-based information to employees at all levels also encourages the sharing of other types of information as well. Only when employees understand their impact on company performance and are willing to share personal and corporate performance information will conditions be right for them to seek information inside and outside the company proactively. These 'enlightened, proactive information seekers' demonstrate positive affective behavior towards accelerating the capability of a company to make decisions rapidly and effectively in the face of continuous change. Based on these theoretical relationships between information behaviors and values dimensions, we propose that companies follow a

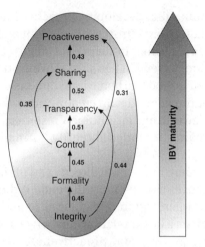

**Fig. 8.3. The IBV Maturity Model: A Path to Mature Information Behaviors and Values**

*Note*: The arrows indicate a causal relationship between the dimensions.

For example, high information integrity leads to higher information formality and transparency.

linear causal path in developing information behaviors and values maturity.

Using statistical path analysis we tested for causal directionality of the information behaviors and values model. In Fig. 8.3, statistical path analysis shows direct causal paths from integrity to formality (.45), formality to control (.45), control to transparency (.51), integrity to transparency (.44), transparency to sharing (.52), control to sharing (.35), sharing to proactiveness (.43), and control to proactiveness (.31). As we suspected, the causal direction of the information behaviors and values dimensions is confirmed with high model fit (for further discussion see Appendix).

This model also supports our theory concerning the need for integrity, formality, control, transparency, and sharing to create proactive information use through direct paths, as through control and sharing, as well as through indirect paths of all information behaviors and values. The path model shows that proactiveness is not only the end point, or goal, of our third maturity path model, but is also the behavior most dependent on other behavioral dimensions, supporting our initial theory.

This causal path in Fig. 8.3, therefore, reflects the maturity of the information behaviors and values capability, providing us a basis to see how a successful IO company progresses through the proper path toward more mature information behaviors and values. Mature IO consists of the development of all six information behaviors and values that allows companies to leverage the causal relationships to build a more proactive organization. In companies with less IO maturity, senior managers may talk to their employees about the importance of information sharing, for example, but not deal openly about mistakes and errors to encourage the sharing behavior, and may not have control mechanisms in place that link individual to organizational performance to provide incentives for information sharing.

As in our other two maturity models, the question remains as to what enables or hinders a company from leveraging these causal paths. Turning again to an interpretative discussion, effective information use may be enabled through similar cultural characteristics discussed within the context of our first two models.

First, a company culture that encourages its people to be *more explicit* with personal information and knowledge may enable the causal paths between integrity, formality, control, and transparency. Explicitness facilitates the integrity to formality path through the conversion of truthful information from informal to formal channels within the organization. This improves availability and access to information for everyone within the organization, and creates an environment of belief and credibility for formal information use. A company culture that encourages explicitness also improves its ability to control information so it is not scattered throughout the company or kept within the heads of individuals. This enables clearer communication of performance-based information. Explicitness also improves the ability of a company to be transparent, improving the visibility of both 'negative' (errors and mistakes) and 'positive' information and providing a way to share information. A company that does not encourage a culture that expects this kind of conversion will not be able to leverage the power of more formal information use that transcends personal relationships. This will also affect the ability of managers to link individual performance to company performance. Finally, a company that does not make information explicit will not deal as effectively with mistakes and errors since this information will be kept within the knowledge of only a few people.

In a company culture where people are encouraged to be *more selfless*, people will be willing to contribute to organizational interests, not just to their own interests. Selflessness as a key characteristic of a mature IO culture helps to improve integrity transparency, sharing, and proactiveness causal paths. Selflessness helps to encourage boundaries of organizational integrity to discourage information selfishness and distortion. This improves the transparency of the organization by ensuring that the information available to members is accurate, honest, and not distorted for personal gain. Organizational transparency about failures, errors, and mistakes can be more easily shared between members in an organizational environment that stresses contribution to organizational interests.

Selflessness also encourages senior managers to share valid, credible, and useful information about the performance of the company at every level. The outcome is the creation of more proactive employees who understand the idea of 'enlightened self-interest' where information is used to improve not only their own performance, but also the performance of the organization as a whole. This creates energized and enlightened proactive information seekers, accelerating decision making ability in the face of change. Companies that do not create a more selfless working environment will have more problems with information used for political and power struggles, serious issues that undermine integrity, transparency, and sharing paths.

Finally, the *ability to learn* and the *flexibility to act* on what is learned are important cultural characteristics that encourage the view that errors, mistakes, and failures are opportunities for organizational learning and growth. This will have an important effect on the proactiveness of a company's workforce—improved ability to share both good and bad information will improve employees' ability to respond quickly to changes in competitive environments, and think more actively about how to create or enhance products and services. People in companies with a culture that prefers to follow the status quo and discourages disagreement will have problems learning from errors and mistakes and become more static in proactively looking for ways to enhance or create new products and services.

*Model 4: the IO interaction effect: linking dimensions to achieve high IO*
As we have discussed in this chapter, managers recognize that certain dimensions of an information capability such as 'control' cause other dimensions such as 'transparency' to be higher which in turn causes sharing to increase. We have argued that the causal path within an information capability explains how a successful IO company gains maturity.

In addition to the causal relationships within each capability, we also believed that companies with high IO maturity were able to increase maturity levels among the three information capabilities through cross-capability relationships. Thus, companies with more IO maturity can leverage capability synergies more fully than companies with less IO maturity. We believed that cross-capability causal linkages created a spiraling effect of mutual interaction between key dimensions of the three information capabilities. Thus the maturity of each information capability would not only be affected by inter-capability dimensions, but also by positive or negative stimulus between capabilities.

Which cross-capability dimensions held the strongest relationships and how could this be interpreted in a prescriptive model? When addressing this important question, where possible we relied on the theory we had developed and demonstrated earlier to suggest the key cross-capability dimensions. Based on our previous findings, we identified 'proactiveness' from information behaviors and values capability and 'IT management support' from IT practices capability as end points in their respective linear causal chains. As the last dependent dimensions in each model, these two dimensions were the most significantly affected by the maturity levels of those dimensions that preceded them within these two capabilities. Thus, proactiveness and IT for management support framed two key dimensions of the cross-capability model.

However, due to the circular nature of the information management practice life cycle causal pattern, we could not easily pinpoint the key end point dimension(s) likely to be most representative of the maturity of the information management capability. To resolve this dilemma, we decided to examine statistical correlations to interpret the broad triangular patterns of relationships across the five information management practices (sensing, collecting, organizing, processing, and maintaining) with proactiveness and IT for management support. This triangular correlation analysis allowed us to determine which dimension(s) of the information management practice capability had the strongest relationship to the key dimension of the information behavior capability and IT practices capability.

As Fig. 8.4 illustrates, the strongest triangular correlations occur between proactiveness and *sensing* (.56), proactiveness and *processing* (.54), *processing* and IT for management support (.57), and *sensing* and IT for management support (.47). Interesting, these were the two information management practice dimensions that were discussed in Chapter 4 as being the most important information valuation points in the information management life cycle. As the reader will recall, these are the points where key value judgements are made determining whether information from the external environments has the potential to best satisfy a new information need (sensing) or whether existing information really satisfies a particular decisional context (processing). These two key information management dimensions formed the remaining two dimensions to be included in our cross-capability path analysis.

As the model in Fig. 8.5 indicates, proactive information use is the critical information behavior for cross-capability relationships; which people in companies must possess to actively seek out information about changes in the company's business environment, and to respond quickly to them as these changes become competitively meaningful. Sensing and processing,

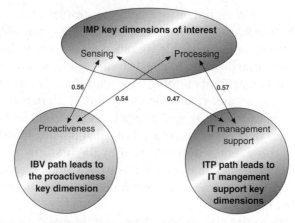
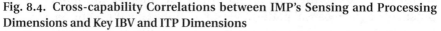

Fig. 8.4. Cross-capability Correlations between IMP's Sensing and Processing Dimensions and Key IBV and ITP Dimensions

not as highly correlated with each other as with the other information capability dimensions, are the critical information management practices dimensions for valuation and a focus of cross-capability interaction. IT for management support is the critical information technology practice that allows for cross-capability relationships supporting management decision making and increases the affinity to be proactive. These paths are especially meaningful in that they support the three maturity models presented earlier in this chapter. They also suggest that when a company has developed IO

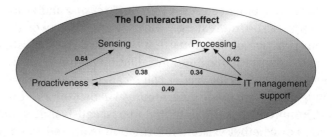

Fig. 8.5. Cross-capability Statistical Path Analysis

*Note*: The arrows indicate a causal relationship between the dimensions.

For example: High proactiveness leads to an increased ability to sense and process information. Higher sensing facilitates the better design and use of IT management support systems, which further increases the ability to process information in support of decision making, which in turn heightens proactive information usage behavior. More mature IO organizations possess this energized information culture, enjoying the benefits of the IO interaction effect.

maturity in all three information capabilities, there is greater synergy, creating more interaction between the three information capabilities which, in turn, influences business performance.

We believe this synergy is manifested through directional causal linkages across these three dimensions. The ability of a company to create affective responses through proactive information behaviors would create the willingness and recognition of the need to seek out information and sense information in the external environment to identify new information requirements. If people have the proactive disposition to sense, they begin to identify patterns and decision needs. Heightened awareness of the need for a larger sensing capability demands new tools to meet changing decision needs, driving improvements to IT for management support. Following a recursive circle, better IT for management support improves the ability of the organization's people to be proactive information users.

The cumulative effect of this reinforcing spiral is to create an energized environment of information use. Within this energized environment, proactive information users who are constantly thinking about, seeking out, and responding to information are in a better position to evaluate new information. IT for management support ensures that highly skilled employees are equipped with tools to access information, share knowledge, and evaluate the usefulness of the information, further improving the organization's ability to better process information for unstructured decisions such as those concerning future strategy.

Statistical path analysis confirmed our belief in a cross-capability IO interaction effect and its directionality that creates synergies across all three information capabilities. As seen in Fig. 8.5, data results show causal directionality from proactiveness to sensing (.64), sensing to IT for management support (.34), IT for management support to proactiveness (.49), proactiveness to processing (.38), and IT for management support to processing (.42). The scores also showed high model fit (for further discussion, refer to Appendix).

We can now see how companies with mature IO create business results. The data has identified proactive information behavior, sensing information, information processing, and using IT for management support as the four critical cross-capability relationships displayed in companies with IO maturity. This cross-capability interaction we call the 'IO Interaction Effect'.

It is through this IO interaction effect that companies with mature IO across all three information capabilities can achieve synergy and benefit from these causal influences: proactive information behavior provides the affective response and sets the environmental preconditions for the more cognitive practice of sensing to occur. On an aggregate level, people in an organization with a propensity to actively use cognitive skills to sense for information will also make better evaluative judgements about the importance and applicability of certain information to decision contexts. Such proactive information behavior would also seem to drive more effective information processing practices as well as lead to better deployment of IT to support decision making.

We can see from the data that this IO interaction effect explains the 'spiral of information effectiveness' described in Fig. 6.7 whereby good information behaviors and values act as a precondition to drive better information definition and management, which improves the capability to use IT to support decision making and problem solving, which in turn reinforces good information usage behaviors and values. When one of these links is derailed, the recursive aspects of the spiral are disabled and a company is less effective in using information. When all of these links reach maturity, the recursive circle creates energized information use that leads to high IO and improved business performance.

*What is the essence of an energized and mature information culture?* An interpretative discussion of cultural characteristics of effective information is warranted here. A cultural context, for example, that stresses *learning* will encourage proactive employees to sense and acquire new knowledge. A learning environment will also allow the proactive employee to test existing competitive assumptions and make better processing choices.

Within a working environment where proactive people are *more selfless*, people are more apt to sense for information that will benefit others within the organization, as well as themselves, improving synergy across the behavioral and information management capabilities of proactiveness and sensing.

People in more mature IO companies that accept continuous change and *flexibility* as a natural feature of modern organizational life will be willing to respond quickly to new challenges. This flexibility allows people to leverage what they have learned and sensed to permit emergent situations and strategies to be addressed. Flexibility will also allow the people in the organization to respond to these changes through improved IT support for management decisions, which will further encourage proactive behavior.

People in more mature IO companies who are able to *focus* their scarce attention and time on the 'right' or 'relevant' information, and not spend their time on sensing, collecting, or processing information that is not used in decision making and executing organizational tasks, will be able to improve decisions concerning business value and performance. A cultural orientation towards more focused information use will allow people to allocate scarce time and attention on the relevant information for decision making, thus improving the proactiveness to processing link. More focus also improves the efficacy of IT tools that help with more unstructured decision processes on the management level to improve processing abilities throughout the organization.

In short, the causal paths of our cross-capability model are enabled by a culture that directs the attention and focus of the people on the right or relevant information for decision making. This culture also encourages people to acquire and use knowledge to learn, is flexible enough to allow change on a continuous basis, and creates a working atmosphere where people are willing to contribute to organizational interests

To leverage the interaction effects of IO, companies do not just have to put the necessary building blocks of each information capability in place. They also have to use these as a base on which to build capabilities in four key areas: proactiveness, sensing, processing, and IT for management support. Mature IO companies manage *each* information capability to reach the highest levels of IO. They understand that they can use the resulting cross-IC interactions to pace the growth of each capability. Thus, more mature IO companies work on improving the three capabilities simultaneously and create powerful cross-capability interaction effects that lead to higher IO, and, ultimately, higher business performance.

### The mature IO culture

Within our three capability path models we have tried to make an interpretative analysis of what situations help these paths materialize. Upon reflection, we believe we have learned that IO maturity is not attained by information systems and processes alone, but through people. The general context of effective information use in business organizations is people-centric and influenced by more general cultural characteristics that, when present, help to increase IO maturity. As we have discussed throughout this chapter, we see more mature IO cultures as having:

- *More selflessness*. People in more mature IO companies use information to support the organization's interests and do not act solely on their own self-interest. They are motivated to proactively share and use information that not only benefits their own needs in the company, but others' needs as well. People in less mature IO companies act primarily to further their own personal interests over those of the organization as a whole.

- *More explicitness*. People in more mature IO companies make their tacit knowledge more explicit by articulating and communicating their knowledge and ideas in a way that can be used and developed to attain organizational goals. Less mature IO companies may block their members from making their tacit knowledge explicit, by not creating the contexts in which conversion can occur, by not rewarding a person when they do so, or by penalizing individuals for articulating their tacit knowledge.

- *Clearer focus.* People in more mature IO companies are able to focus their scarce attention and time on the right or relevant information, and not spend their time on sensing, collecting, or processing information that is not used in decision making and executing organizational tasks. They understand what information seeking is relevant to improve their own performance as well as that of the organization. People in less mature IO companies feel overwhelmed by information, and do not necessarily know what is relevant to their own or the organization's business decision objectives.
- *Greater learning capacity.* People in more mature IO companies are willing to proactively acquire new knowledge, question existing ways of solving problems, and learn from this information to change. They are willing to openly share and discuss errors and failures and find ways to fix them. People in less mature IO companies do not discover, share, or learn from mistakes. Moreover, they are less likely to challenge assumptions.
- *Greater flexibility.* People in less mature IO companies are resistant to change. They do not like to change their mode of thinking and working, and prefer the status quo. People in more mature IO companies accept continuous change as a natural feature of modern organizational life and are willing to respond quickly to new challenges. Their flexibility leverages learning capacity to permit emergent situations and strategies to be addressed.

When an organization reflects these five cultural characteristics (see Fig. 8.6), we believe that its people will use and manage the links within each information capability more effectively and they will create a powerful interaction effect across IT practices, information management practices, and information behaviors and values that leads to higher business performance.

## 3. CONCLUSION

In this chapter, we have introduced new research that builds four prescriptive models for building IO maturity over time. We have seen how IO matur-

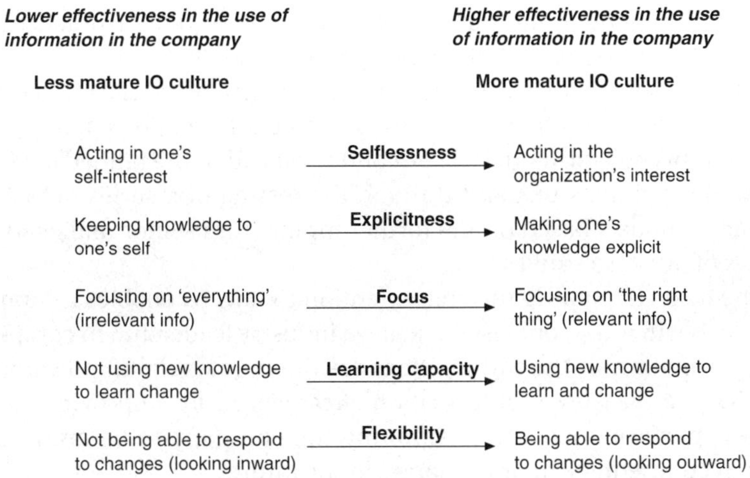

| Lower effectiveness in the use of information in the company | | Higher effectiveness in the use of information in the company |
|---|---|---|
| Less mature IO culture | | More mature IO culture |

| | | |
|---|---|---|
| Acting in one's self-interest | **Selflessness** → | Acting in the organization's interest |
| Keeping knowledge to one's self | **Explicitness** → | Making one's knowledge explicit |
| Focusing on 'everything' (irrelevant info) | **Focus** → | Focusing on 'the right thing' (relevant info) |
| Not using new knowledge to learn change | **Learning capacity** → | Using new knowledge to learn and change |
| Not being able to respond to changes (looking inward) | **Flexibility** → | Being able to respond to changes (looking outward) |

**Fig. 8.6. Key Characteristics of Effective Information Use in a Mature IO Culture**

ity is achieved through the improvements to all dimensions of our IO model. We have also seen that IO maturity is achieved through development of proactive information behavior, sensing and processing information practices and IT for management support, and the interaction effect that companies can leverage to produce synergy across the three information capabilities.

Our four causal models for IO maturity are an important new area for future research. We believe that a program to improve IO requires a systematic approach to organizational improvement. With the research presented in this chapter, we have begun to draw a road map that will specifically lay out a plan to improve effectiveness in information use. Using the IO maturity models created, we can show companies how to begin to institute changes within their companies to best leverage the causal relationships between dimensions of IO.

To date, our research has led us from confirmatory factor analysis of a high-level idea—IO—to an understanding about how individual information capability dimensions of this idea relate. In this chapter we have explored causal relationships through four separate IO maturity models. In future research, we will build upon these maturity models, applying company case studies to gain more knowledge about these causal relationships among and across dimensions. We will explore these in-depth case studies and look at what real companies actually do in their journeys to improve IO. We hope to further clarify and formalize prescriptive managerial actions that can be taken to improve behavioral aspects of information use and raise this discipline to the same level of recognition that IT practices and information management hold in companies today.

In future research, we will test for more sophisticated causal models of an overall holistic theory that integrates our three information capabilities. A search for this holistic model will be conducted with more refined measures of capability dimensions and through the testing of a series of possible alternative models based on the further inputs from senior managers and analysis of our case studies.

In the next chapter, we turn our attention to how IO enables a company not only to win today, but also to achieve industry leadership in competing with information in the future. What are the managerial implications of using IO as a measure of information effectiveness for improving current business performance and positioning the company to be an industry leader in competing with information in the future?

# 9

# Competing for the Future : Industry Leadership Using Information

Senior managers know that sustaining a competitive advantage is dependent on balancing the intended strategies of today with the emergent opportunities in the future. As we discussed in Chapter 1, we have entered an era that will require senior executives to think in entirely new ways about leveraging their competitive, customer, and operational information to both support existing strategy but, even more importantly, enable the firm to leapfrog into new competitive positions of industry leadership. Industry leaders in the information age look beyond performance today and assess the expectations of the firm to handle challenges in information use that loom in the future.

Senior managers are heeding the call and are developing information-oriented action strategies that direct their companies down a path that places information at the center stage of their market and organizational behavior. This path will lead managers to attempt:

1. to create information asymmetries in the competitive marketplace;
2. to redesign organizational structures to be centrally controlled but physically diverse; and
3. to establish the capability to seamlessly exploit ever accelerating IT opportunities in a smarter and faster way than competitors.

We contend that, in the e-economy, a perquisite of future industry leadership will be the plans that senior managers put in place today concerning how their companies will compete in using information. Accordingly, a literature review was conducted to establish important aspects of 'Industry Leadership in Competing with Information'. The result of this review suggested that three dimensions are important in depicting future industry leadership in competing with information:

1. *Leadership in the use of competitive information*—using information to better compete in the marketplace. These leaders can acquire and use competitive information better than their rivals to define a niche in the industry where others have tried and failed.

2. *Leadership in the use of customer information*—using information about customers, as well as interacting with customers, to provide better products and services and retain their business. These leaders can gain and employ customer information to provide targeted knowledge about their products to meet the customers' emerging needs; and

3. *Leadership in the use of operational information*—using information that will boost operational effectiveness. These leaders can outpace competitors and satisfy customers with customized, faster, and smarter ways of using operational information to respond to customer orders and deliveries. Let's look at three cases of companies that compete and lead their industries with information.

*SkandiaBanken—leveraging competitive information to exploit a market niche*

Direct banking emerged in Sweden during the 1980s. Most of the major Swedish banks operated direct banking services as a means of supplementing their traditional branch services. These efforts during the early 1990s had met with mixed success, especially after the near collapse of the Swedish banking system during 1992, due to depressed real estate prices that created huge operating losses for the banks. Also, direct banking was viewed as a threat by the traditional banks to their own branch networks and established customers.

In 1993, the well-known Swedish insurer Skandia Insurance created SkandiaBanken. During October 1994, SkandiaBanken opened for doing direct business with one branch office (required by Swedish bank regulators) in its home office building in downtown Stockholm. Skandia Insurance funded the bank's start-up by building the bank's initial business on a former finance company that worked with car dealers to purchase/lease vehicles.

The new bank leveraged the consumer distrust of established banks, and also took advantage of a new tax rate on individual retirement accounts that had just been approved by the Swedish government. Its customer offering was based on product simplicity, on 'truthfulness' in relating to customers, and on high interest rates. The bank offered one basic account through which all of a customer's business would be managed. It played on customer distrust of traditional banks by portraying itself as the 'good guy' in the marketplace—always candid and open with customers. Finally, it offered substantially higher interest rates than competitors on savings accounts—8.4 per cent as compared to 5–6 per cent.

SkandiaBanken could be competitive on interest rates and loans, since its direct business model was based on three key principles: low cost operations, pragmatism—doing what works—and adding value where possible and outsourcing the rest.

First, as a branchless bank, SkandiaBanken replaced the brick and mortar of branches with IT systems that were easy to use for its employees and customers alike.

Second, it implemented new products, systems, and databases in modular projects that could be easily understood, were as simple in design as possible, and were implemented in steps rather than all at once.

Finally, SkandiaBanken integrated all its customer and product information in one internal database that all employees could access on-line.

However, the secret to the bank's low-cost model depended upon leveraging the IT infrastructures of all the other Swedish banks. So, Skandia-Banken employed the national ATM network, the national bill clearing and payment system, the credit card charging and payment systems, the telecommunications network for telephone and Internet banking, and the stock trading system for clearing equity trades directly, rather than through brokers, for its customers.

Thus, by leveraging its niche position and competitive information better than more traditional banks, SkandiaBanken has experienced rapid and profitable growth as Sweden's most successful direct bank. Moreover, by accessing the established financial service infrastructures of its competitors, SkandiaBanken has been able to operate at the lowest cost possible and still offer attractive interest rates to customers.

*Hilti AG—surrounding products with information and services in the construction industry*

Founded in 1941 in the principality of Liechtenstein by two brothers, Hilti is one of the world's leading companies specializing in drills, fasteners, and demolition systems for the construction industry. With their distinctive red protective hats and toolboxes, Hilti's 7,000-person direct sales force not only sells Hilti products, but also provides extensive hands-on advice and training in the use of Hilti tools to solve fastening, anchoring, and demolition problems for customers. Every Hilti sales person is not only extensively trained in the use of their products, but is backed up by call centers and customer service units where more in-depth training and human expertise is accessible to customers and sales persons alike.

All Hilti sales persons are trained in accessing and using product and customer profiling information provided through the Hilti Sales Force Automation (HSFA) that delivers to each sales person recommended schedules for customer visits and identifies product cross-selling opportunities by type of customer. Each sales person at Hilti is responsible for direct marketing, sales, and service with each customer account, so accountability and information use are highly focused. Hilti sales people are rewarded for understanding the customer and sensing new business and product development opportunities on a continuous basis and sharing their knowledge with product developers and service centers.

Continuously visiting customers at their work sites, understanding how Hilti tools and fasteners are used, and learning about new customer needs for solutions are the ways that Hilti achieves superior customer service, significant growth, and retains its significant price advantage in the construction industry. Hilti senior managers understand that customer bonding is a direct result of using information effectively to respond to customer needs, to provide superior service, and to learn about new product opportunities before their competitors do.

### Cemex—delivering cement your way by managing order and delivery information better than competitors

Cemex SA is the world's third largest cement producer. In the early morning, a typical urban construction site may have five to ten cement trucks parked at the entrance and ready to be unloaded during the course of the morning. Trucks and drivers may have to sit idly until given the signal for their truck to advance onto the site for pouring. This is not the case for Cemex. They promise delivery of concrete within twenty minutes of an agreed-upon time and offer discounts of 5 per cent for late deliveries. How is this possible? Cemex trucks are equipped with dashboard computer terminals that allow them to be monitored and tracked by a Global Positioning System (GPS) using satellites. CemexNet, operated out of the company headquarters in Monterrey, Mexico, provides real-time tracking of all customer orders, manufacturing plans, order delivery schedules, truck usage, location, and availability, and order fulfillment at the site.

CemexNet customers can check, through their laptops, the daily production, kiln condition, crushing, loading, and shipping output of any of Cemex's production sites. Truck and driver productivity has increased 35 per cent. Since its implementation in 1995, the GPS system allows the company to do 'dynamic synchronization of operations' by managing all aspects of supply chain management from the customer order to delivery. Cemex now employs the GPS system in all major cities around the world in which it operates. With global sales in 1997 of $3.7 billion and a cash flow margin of 31 per cent—10 percentage points higher than its two leading international competitors—Cemex has successfully adapted the Burger King motto, 'have it your way', to the use of operational information in the cement business.

What lessons can we learn from these three cases? Each of these high-performing companies successfully competes with information beyond the capabilities of their competitors in their industries. In Chapter 6, we discovered that the Information Orientation of a company predicts business performance. In turn, we noted that low IO also predicts low business performance. We suspect that high IO companies generally get better, and low IO companies do more poorly, unless they can break out of their current IO mindset and build IO capabilities over time. Decision making in business organizations is not just about reducing today's uncertainty, but about deciding what ideas and information are needed for learning and changing in the future. As we discussed in Chapter 8, proactive information use shapes the sensing and processing of information that, in turn, should define the enabling role of IT for management and innovation support for a business. When integrated with strong information behaviors and information management practices, information technologies can have important impacts on markets and industries in addition to individual firms.

First, as IT use intensifies in industries, IT can make companies more efficient in terms of outputs by reducing coordination costs in firms as well as with suppliers, partners, and customers (Varian and Shapiro 1998). As firms get more efficient with IT, so do industries where price competition intensifies and market prices are driven lower and lower (Hagel and Armstrong 1997).

Second, as IT use intensifies in markets, IT also makes information more accessible, which lowers barriers to entry for competitors and provides more leverage to customers. The increase in customer information, in turn, provides more bargaining power for customers and intensifies the demand for firms to provide customers with richer and deeper information than they have previously.

Finally, as 'hyper competition' heats up in most industries, companies are compelled to compete on price unless they can shift the competitive battleground to creating superior value and growth (D'Aveni and Gunther 1994: 1–16).

The results of these shifts in IT use in industries, and in information use between companies and customers, means that it is getting harder and harder for companies to compete successfully for two reasons, as we will explain in this chapter.

First, companies must gain information advantages and establish information asymmetries faster than their competitors. Information asymmetries exist whenever a company leverages information about customers, competitors, and operations that is unusable or unavailable to its competitors (Evans and Wurster 1997; Desiraju and Moorthy 1997; Nault 1998). A somewhat overly popularized but valid illustration of this point was Dell Computers' ability to distinguish itself as the premier direct PC retailer to the corporate community worldwide. Michael Dell's initial strategy was not to maintain physical storefronts, and focus primarily on corporate purchasing through a direct sales force as well as telephone and Internet channels. Dell recognized early that exploiting an e-commerce model that mass customizes products built on unique customer information, followed by superior customer service, would permit a solid lock-in whereby the same corporate customers would reorder when the next generation of PC chips were released, typically every eighteen months. Over five years, this strategy permitted Dell to better project capacity, control cost, and satisfy customers. Dell won the industry leadership spot.

However, industry leadership in competing with information is a 'temporary' state, and must be continuously won as Fig. 9.1 suggests (Kettinger and Hackbarth 1999). Today's information advantage may become tomorrow's strategic necessity. For example, the information asymmetry that Dell had established in its industry was at first scarcely recognized by the likes of Compaq and IBM. But eventually, recognition grew until today e-commerce-based direct sales are the primary business model for corporate PC marketing. IBM, Gateway, and Compaq have put in place similar IT-enabled direct sales capabilities and the competitive advantage that Dell once possessed is now threatened. Dell is attempting to renew its industry leadership position by establishing a second information asymmetry by selling peripheral products and service through partners.

So, we define industry leadership in competing with information as belonging to those companies that can create information asymmetries in their markets in the future. We have categorized leadership in competing with information in three ways:

- using competitive information;
- using customer information; and
- using operational information.

Industry leadership in competing with information is critical today since all companies in a market economy compete in markets where information plays a significant role (Varian and Shapiro 1998).

Second, Internet and electronic markets are beginning to drive industry

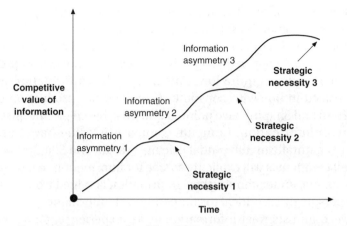

Fig. 9.1. Future Industry Leadership with Information: Renew or Lose over Time

shifts in financial services, retailing, and other industries where past information advantages enjoyed by companies with their customers, suppliers, and partners are dwindling away. As these changes have accelerated across services and manufacturing industries, every business has become an 'information business' (Earl 1999). Future industry leadership depends on using information to create and sustain customer relationships, to detect competitive trends before other players do, and to achieve operational efficiencies in time, cost, and control.

In this chapter, we define, in section 1, precisely what we mean by information leadership in using competitive, customer, and operational information. In section 2, we focus on how senior managers think about future industry leadership in competing with information. We also discuss how Information Orientation is linked to senior manager expectations about future industry leadership in competing with information. In section 3, we discuss how IO can be used as a metric of future industry leadership to assess and manage future expectations. We will suggest three alternative action strategies for pursuing IO improvements into the future.

# 1. LEVERAGING COMPETITIVE, CUSTOMER, AND OPERATIONAL INFORMATION IN YOUR INDUSTRY

In this section, we explain how a company competes with three major types of information: competitive, customer, and operational information.

However, before we begin, it is important to recognize what type of 'economic good' information is (Varian and Shapiro 1998: 3).

First, information is costly to produce, but cheap to reproduce. The cost of producing the first copy of this book is very high, but the cost of producing additional copies is quite low. This means that information goods should be priced in line with consumer value and not production costs. Thus, as Varian and Shapiro have pointed out, 'cost-based pricing' just does not work with information. Companies must use 'value-based pricing (which) leads naturally to differential pricing' (Varian and Shapiro 1998: 3). While not all companies will explicitly charge for information that they provide to customers, understanding how information is valued from a user or consumer perspective is critical to competing with information.

Second, economists treat information as an 'experience good': that is, users or consumers must experience information to value it (Varian and Shapiro 1998: 5). Information companies use brand image, reputation, and browsing as ways of getting people to sample or purchase information before they know exactly what they are getting. Thus, image and reputation count in the information business, since people must trust the information source before they experience the information good.

Third, an abundance of 'potential information' or data is available to businesses and consumers today, especially over the Internet. So the real value of information management is in appropriately identifying and targeting just the information that the customer or organizational member needs. Thus, 'infomediaries' play a critical role in linking information users to the relevant sources of information as efficiently as possible or providing the filtering aids so they can locate and use information directly (Hagel and Singer 1999). This explains the popularity, high usage, and economic value of 'portals' on the Internet, such as Yahoo, which offer attention management aids, and receive advertiser revenue, because they serve as critical infomediaries on the web.

Fourth, the ubiquitous use of IT infrastructure today has increased exponentially the capabilities to 'manipulate data' or potential information and to leverage 'network effects' (Varian and Shapiro 1998: 13–17). Network effects exist, since, as the base of users on the Internet or IT networks in general grows, the potential value of networks to all users grows as well. Moreover, as the technology for manipulating potential information increases with new capabilities such as intelligent agents, push tools, and expert search engines, the diffusion or spread of these IT capabilities means that all industries and companies will be affected by these new ways of using and managing information over time. So, identifying and creating the right information asymmetries is critical to industry leadership in the future.

Recognizing the competitive value of information as outlined above, our literature review and consulting experience lead us to believe that there are three major ways that companies can compete with information in their industries in the future. We will define the information practices associated with each, before we examine in section 2 how senior managers actually expect to compete with information in their industries in the future.

## A. Using information for competitive advantage

An industry leader in the use of information for competitive advantage is a company that:

- senses competitive information to shape its business strategies,
- leverages information to ensure partner loyalty,
- maintains control of its suppliers through extensive information exchange,
- exploits information received from customers and partners to win new markets or operate more efficiently, and
- eliminates information 'middle men' who do not add value in their industry.

### Sensing competitive information to shape business strategy

An industry leader must continuously sense and anticipate the competitive information that it needs to shape its business strategies. There are two ways that companies seek competitively meaningful information about the future.

The first way is where companies collect lots of formal and informal information about the future to try and 'predict' what the future will be for their company. This approach is heavily influenced by traditional notions of 'planning', where senior managers have staff who go out and collect various views and data internally and externally about what their industry or business environment will 'look like' in the years ahead. Usually, these inputs are filtered and interpreted by staff and senior managers, and developed into a prediction of future plans, performance expectations, and implementation actions. Typically, information is collected informally from customers, suppliers, and partners, as well as obtained through publicly available information in the press. In addition, today the company may commission special industry and technology reviews, as well as access the web for information on competitors and business trends. From all these sources, senior managers try to 'forecast' the future and predict what actions they must take to respond. This approach can work well in stable industries and times. However, these are turbulent times with disruptive changes occurring in most industries almost on a daily basis, so predicting the future is hazardous at best (de Geus 1997: 35).

The second way that companies develop better 'industry foresight' to shape strategy is to develop a 'memory for the future' among managers and organizational members. The memory for the future serves two functions:

1. it gets people and the business organization ready for action once a 'view of the future materializes'; and
2. it acts as a filter to deal with the overload of data and signals that humans continuously experience.

Arie de Geus describes the memory for the future as the capability of people to continuously imagine future events and states towards which they can act. Information about the business environment must 'fit' one of these imagined states if managers and organizational members are to act in a particular future direction. Thus, managers must continuously 'visit the future' by exposing their perceptions of signals about change that offer alternative paths for their company to pursue. The challenge for managers is to get their companies to build up sufficient 'memories for the future' among their members and to be ready to act when perceived signals or early intelligence trigger one path to the future versus others. Anticipating the future using this second approach requires proactive information use and continuous sensing of the business environment by managers and organizational members to develop the right path toward shaping business strategy (de Geus 1997: 36).

### Leveraging information to ensure partner loyalty

An industry leader is seldom in a position to act alone. Alliances play an increasingly important role in winning new markets or leading in existing markets. A future industry leader must collect and use information to ensure that its partners are loyal by creating win/win relationships wherever feasible (Desiraju and Moorthy 1997). Potential allies can be identified not only among suppliers, customers, and companies from complementary industries, but also among competitors. Networks of banks, insurers, and even suppliers to automobile companies could not be created without partnerships among competitors. 'Co-opetition' means that companies must create relationships where leveraging information to prevent partner loss is critical to future success in an industry (Kettinger and Hackbarth 1999).

Solectron, a company based in Milpitas, California, is the world's number one provider of contract manufacturing services to original equipment manufacturers of electronic systems and subsystems. Providing leading edge production capabilities, and consistent quality, permits Solectron to develop close and continuous information exchanges with OEM producers. The company builds electronic systems in several industries, including avionics, computers, communications, industrial, and medical instrumentation. Its services range from product design, assembly of systems, packaging, to warehousing. Its partners included Bay Networks, Hewlett-Packard, Honeywell, Cisco Systems, Dell, IBM, Intel, and Sun Microsystems. Solectron is among a new breed of companies that play a critical role in the supply chains of their partners and where their processes are intertwined with the processes of their partners.

### *Maintain control of suppliers through extensive information exchange*

Supplier management has been one of the major concerns of companies to compete efficiently in industries. Just-in-time delivery, zero inventory, and total quality management have led to close collaboration between suppliers and manufacturers over the last fifteen years. IT enables a tighter collaboration between suppliers and producers through business to business networks such as Extranets and the use of the Internet (Tapscott and Caston 1993: 90; 1996: 85). Future industry leadership in competing with information requires companies to maintain control of its suppliers through extensive two-way information exchange (Desiraju and Moorthy 1997).

An example of this is the Automobile Network Exchange (ANX) (www.anxo.com) by the Automotive Industry Action Group (www.aiag. org) (GM, Ford, Daimler-Chrysler, TRW, Bosch, Caterpillar, DANA, and United Technology). ANX is focused on moving most of the electronic interactions among thousands of automotive suppliers from private networks to a public, data exchange infrastructure. The ANX is letting as many as 40,000 parts suppliers, dealerships, and financial service companies share everything from CAD files and e-mail to order processing on the same network. The participants in ANX, who are competing in the same industry, recognize that, through collaboration, they could leverage the commonality of parts and designs and reduce costs. ANX is intended to enable 'coordination' in the auto industry as well as increase the commitment and loyalty of auto industry players to each other. The intent is to drive cost down and improve margins throughout the industry; however, those players that will gain the most will probably be a few large customers that can leverage secondary suppliers and coordinate purchasing across the net.

*Exploiting information from customers and partners to win new markets or operate more efficiently*

A company has to manage growth by winning new markets or growing in existing markets. At the same time, companies have to ensure that their operations and processes remain efficient. Customers and partners are important sources of new market, product, and operational information. A leader in future information practices must understand how to capture and exploit information from customers and markets to ensure future growth and efficiency of operations.

For example, since the late 1980s, American Izuzu Motors Company has employed Geographical Information Systems (GIS) to locate new dealerships near potential customers based on actual customer profiles rather than in response to decisions to locate dealerships made by competitors. In addition, GIS has been used to launch new models in specific markets and help dealer representatives assist Izuzu dealers in building sales in their local areas, as well as in collecting better information from dealers about product needs, market characteristics, and promotional effectiveness (Nolan and Bradley 1998).

On the Internet, personalization software companies such as Netperceptions (www.netperceptions.com) and E-piphany.com develop software to operate intelligent agents to build profiles of customers and to filter information intended for their use. Software products can be used to teach an intelligent agent to find similar agents on the Internet for building customer relationships, as well as to track the habits of Internet users that are using targeted web sites. Microsoft uses intelligent agents in its electronic wallet application called Passport. Passport acts as a repository for a consumer's personal information such as credit card numbers, shipping information, and on-line cash. The electronic wallet can reside on the consumer's PC, or on a network server to facilitate identification and one-click ordering. Using the intelligent agent software, Microsoft can monitor the use of electronic wallets by consumers, and learn about consumer shopping and buying patterns, as well as screen product offers to consumers based on their unique customer profiles.

*Eliminating information 'middle men' who do not add value in an industry*

Traditional middlemen functions such as wholesalers, brokers, and buyers are being increasingly eliminated through digital networks and direct approaches to selling and buying. The elimination of middle men follows another development in the digital world: customers have access to more and better product information and want to be serviced where and when they want. Customers no longer want to wait until middle men are ready to service their needs, or are ready to update information (Tapscott 1996: 56; McKenna 1997: 36). Clearly, the popular business press has focused on the potential of disintermediation in many industries. And one only needs to look at the skyrocketing stock prices for many of the Internet-based companies that would assist in eliminating middle men, to recognize the value that the financial markets place on this trend. Companies like Priceline.com, e-Bay, and Amazon all intend to cut out physical retailers, and auctioneers, with IT supported networks. And, many experts see fundamental changes in the automobile retail industry, as car dealers are just now beginning to feel the effects of Internet-based auto pricing, location, and purchasing services such as AutoWeb, Auto-buy-tel, and CarPoint.

As businesses and industries become more 'disintermediated', information leaders need to be proactive in adapting their value chains to this new reality. Increasingly, whole sectors of industries are moving to direct digital relationships between buyers and sellers to reduce costs, increase choice, and create more value. Ironically, as old intermediaries are eliminated, new intermediaries develop to offer better services to customers. For example, the Internet Travel Network brings travel reservations to more than 150 companies such as United Airlines, Proctor&Gamble, CNN Interactive, and the World Bank. ITN's corporate, consumer, and leisure booking services for airline, hotels, restaurants, and vacation tours are widely used on the Internet in the USA as well as internationally. ITN represents a real threat to travel agent networks, as well as eliminating the need for internal company travel offices that were, in the past, simply intermediaries for internal travel purchases with airlines, hotel chains, and rental car companies.

## B.  Using information to increase customer satisfaction

An industry leader in the use of information to increase customer satisfaction is a company that:

- details customer needs so that it can offer customized products and services;
- engages in two-way information exchanges with its customers to better understand why they buy its products and services;
- embeds high-quality information in its products and services to differentiate them from those of its competitors;

- pushes information on its customers to encourage consumption of its products/services and to offer incentives for moving them to new offerings; and
- links customers in after-sales exchanges to help increase customer loyalty.

### Detailing customer needs to offer customized services and products

Customers today seek products and services that not only offer high quality, but also have the precise features that they want at no additional cost. In the past, customized products and services were either not available at all, or available only at a premium price, since they were provided by companies operating as craft shops. Developments in IT practices, coupled with improved ways of managing information and physical production processes, have enabled companies to offer customized products at little or no additional cost, or to charge a premium for services that other companies in their industry can only mass produce (Victor and Boynton 1998: 12–18).

Increasingly traditional clothing manufacturers and retailers have been under pressure to rethink their strategy in an effort to cut costs and retain their fleeting customer base. In response, some retailers, such as Levi's have equipped their stores with a capability that allows customers to design customized jeans to their own individual specifications. The measures of a customer are entered into a computer by a 'fit specialist', and then e-mailed over a data network to a distant factory. Some retailers are even attempting to charge more for providing this customized value to the customer.

Similarly, CDNow (www.cdnow.com), which claims to be the world's most popular online music store, helps a customer build a personalized interface called 'My CDNow'. While signing in, customers provide demographic information as well as their music preferences. Through the customer's personalized site, CDNow observes and registers the customer's queries, purchases, clicking paths, and adapts the interface and the service offered to the customer's actual search behavior and music preferences. When a customer shifts his or her music tastes, CDNow adjusts to the individual's new music preferences with special discounts and purchase offers as well.

Increasingly, customers expect tailored products and services. Companies that want to be industry leaders in competing with information will track the details of customer information and modify their products and services to personalize their offerings on a one-to-one basis.

*Engaging in two-way information exchanges with customers to understand why they buy the company's goods and services*

As customers look for increasingly personalized products and services, companies must anticipate changing customer needs down to a unit of one. Traditional advertising and retailing approaches focus on broadcasting information to customers. Customer focus groups and surveys provide only group or category indicators of customer preferences.

However, if companies can engage their customers in continuous two-way dialogue, then companies have the opportunity to better understand why customers are doing business with them, and what the company can do to bond with the customers by anticipating their changing needs. Although Internet technology is greatly enhancing the opportunities for establishing two-way dialogue with customers, some companies are supplementing the direct web interfaces with personal contacts as well.

For example, one of Spain's leading retail banks trains its employees in maintaining ongoing dialogue with individual customers. While the bank is using direct banking channels such as ATMs, telephone banking, and Internet banking, nonetheless, the bank's branch employees engage in direct telephone follow-ups with customers that use the new direct channels. Branch employees are assigned a certain number of customers and schedule regular phone conversations with customers regardless of which direct ways of banking they use. In this way, the bank is able to monitor the effectiveness of its direct services, discover new ways of offering value through these services, and promote or cross-sell banking products and services that the customer may not be using yet.

By engaging customers in two-way dialogue about why they buy, not just what they buy, companies can both personalize their products and services to these customers, and they can personalize prices as well. On the Internet, companies can fine tune their product and service offers to customers to differentiate them from generic products and services. Economists call charging a customer just what he or she is willing to pay 'perfect price discrimination' and it comes in three varieties. A company can offer personalized prices by selling to each user at a different price. It can offer group pricing by setting different prices for different groups of customers, as in discounts for retired people. Finally, a company can engage in 'versioning' by offering a product line and letting customers choose the version of the product most appropriate to them—de luxe, premium, or standard (Varian and Shapiro 1998: 39).

While companies have employed differential pricing and personalized their products to a degree in the past, the use of Internet 'point-to-point' technology provides companies with the opportunities to fine tune two-way dialogue with customers and respond to them on a one-to-one basis.

### Embedding high-quality information in products and services to differentiate them from those of competitors

Providing a service or selling a product is no longer considered a discrete event, as marketer Regis McKenna observes, in the lives of customers or companies, but a 'process of creating a customer environment of information, assurance and comfort' (McKenna 1997: 53). Many companies are using call centers, kiosks, 800 numbers, and Internet services to provide the right mix of information and response to customers in all phases of the 'customer activity cycle': before, during, and after sales (Vandermerwe 1993). Indeed, the cycle of customer contact today is no longer viewed as a set of functions in the company, but as a seamless set of experiences that can be offered to the customer surrounding the product or service.

Embedding high-quality information in and around a company's products and services helps a company achieve future advantage over competitors in several ways (Varian and Shapiro 1998: 128).

First, products are perceived from the experience of the consumer rather than the company. How can we best inform the consumer about the appropriate use of our product?

Second, surrounding the products with call center or Internet services provides the customer with alternative channels to interact easily with the company.

Third, good after-sales information about maintaining the product, disposing of the product, or returning the product provides the customer with the assurance that the company will support the customer throughout the product's life cycle.

Thus, the company provides a seamless process of attracting, engaging and, most importantly, retaining the customer over time—a sustainable advantage over competitors.

For example, Dell would like you to feel that buying a computer from the company is not just an event, but also an 'experience' that Dell uses to differentiate its approach from other direct sellers as well as from in-store retailers. Dell provides the customer information about its products and order-to-delivery services as well as friendly and personal call center support to 'talk' customers through the specification and purchasing process before, during, and after sales are made. The company is able to differentiate the customer experience by learning from thousands of customer experiences in purchasing PCs direct through the Internet or by phone and using that information to make the Dell 'PC experience' both rewarding, pleasurable, and secure.

### Pushing information to customers encourages consumption and offers incentives to move customers to new products/services

Traditional advertising uses mass media and sends messages to broad groups in a population. The information provided is widely disseminated and rather shallow in content. Broadcast media decide in favor of what Evans and Wurster call broad 'reach' and narrow 'richness'. They define 'reach' as 'the number of people at home, or at work, exchanging information,' while 'richness' is defined by three aspects of the information itself:

The first is *band width*, or the amount of information that can be moved from sender to receiver in a given time. Stock quotes are narrowband; a film is broadband. The second aspect is the degree to which information can be *customized*. For example, an advertisement on television is far less customized than a personal sales pitch but reaches far more people. The third aspect is *interactivity*. Dialogue is possible for a small group, but to reach millions of people the message must be a monologue.

Evans and Wurster (1997: 73–4) note that the trade-off between high reach and low richness characterizes the 'old economics of information'. A sales force, or branch offices, or chain of stores, could be formidable barriers to entry in markets in the past, since they represented the channels by which rich information about products and services were delivered to customers.

Using Internet technology, a company can eliminate the traditional trade-off between richness and reach by providing both to large numbers of people on an individual basis. Competing with information today means being able to 'push' rich information to the PCs of millions of people. Thus customers can 'choose' from all of the information available what information they would like to receive on a regular basis (Evans and Wurster 1997: 73).

For example, specialized financial Internet portals such as ragingbull.com or theStreet.com push e-mail to millions of subscribers' e-mail accounts and continually entice them back to their web sites on a daily basis. Their view is that information value is only 'one click away'. Increasingly, companies like these will move away from simple e-mail push techniques, and will use more sophisticated multicasting technologies to actually push personalized information out over the Internet to your desktop.

### Linking customers in after-sales information exchanges to increase customer loyalty

As we discussed earlier, after-sales information about products and services are critical to building customer bonding and loyalty. Good information is critical to the after-sales customer experience as we noted earlier. Traditional techniques such as customer reward and loyalty programs can increase customer satisfaction and bonding as well as provide excellent and rich information about future customer needs and profiles of product or service use. Charge card companies such as American Express traditionally retain customers for many years. Over this period, the company builds a rich database of customer purchasing patterns through which it can discover new purchasing trends among its customers prior to competitors, and target its customers with new or enhanced services.

However, it is on the Internet that the possibilities for engaging customers in after-sales information exchanges are most interesting. Companies such as Amazon are focused on building customer loyalty by engaging their customers in virtual communities around their products and services. Companies seek to develop virtual communities around shared interests such as book lovers with Amazon, or around shared fantasies with ESPN Sports, or transactions such as auctions with e-Bay.

The company intent in each of these cases is to build a community on the Internet that enjoys communicating and sharing information about its products and services and to which other companies will be attracted. The distinctive feature of virtual communities is the need to grow membership on two fronts at the same time. There must be a critical mass of members of the community and there must be a critical mass of business transactions that members and companies can do together. Since a virtual community exists to conduct business, the primary challenge that the community faces is to build critical mass on both sides to capture 'the increasing returns' that are possible from the community's electronic commerce and membership interests at the same time (Hagel and Armstrong 1997).

## C.  Using information to achieve operational excellence

An industry leader in the use of operational information is a company that:

- monitors information about its business processes to eliminate unnecessary activities, cut costs, and reduce cycle times;
- delegates decision making to the lowest levels possible in the company by delivering the right information to the right place at the right time;
- allows its people to work more effectively in groups by using information to coordinate activities and people; and
- reduces the need for the physical movement of people, projects, and facilities by delivering the right information at the right time.

*Monitoring information about processes*

The focus on process management through total quality, continuous improvement, and re-engineering, has, over the last two decades, placed more and more emphasis on monitoring processes in day-to-day management. However, the role of information in monitoring processes has rarely been addressed. Typically, companies have measured and monitored their performance through predominantly financial indicators. But these measures have generally been viewed as incomplete and sometimes ineffective in monitoring business processes and operational performance.

In one of the few studies of managing information about processes in the USA, Davenport and Beers discovered that 'even some of the most process-oriented firms in the United States have not fully developed infrastructures for providing process performance information to managers and workers' (Davenport and Beers 1995: 58). These authors also noted that the role of process information is better understood in quality improvement programs than in process re-engineering programs. Most of the twenty companies that they studied still had not developed effective and comprehensive approaches to generating, sharing, and using process information to monitor business processes day to day.

Davenport and Beers suggested that several difficulties stood in the way of developing effective process information programs in companies:

First, process quality and effectiveness could be measured in several different ways. A company could focus on cost measures such as outputs or waste; on time measures such as cycle time to customer; on product quality measures such as reliability, performance, or serviceability; on service quality measures such as responsiveness and empathy; and on customer satisfaction measures such as complaints or use. Thus, in developing process information, there was a clear need for deciding on the right measures (Davenport and Beers 1995).

A second difficulty in developing process information focused on its use in learning about how processes perform. On one side, companies needed to concentrate on day-to-day performance monitoring. On the other side, they needed to make sure that their processes were aligned with changing business needs. Davenport and Beers compared these two ways of learning about processes as equivalent to 'single loop' and 'double loop' learning suggested by Argyris and Schön (1978) and discussed earlier in this book. Companies needed to develop appropriate information to perform both types of learning in process management (Davenport and Beers 1995).

However, this is difficult to achieve. For example, in a study that looked at efforts to institutionalize process improvement at the Bose Corporation over a ten-year period, Harkness, Kettinger, and Segars (1996) found that the development of such 'process thinking' evolves in a bottom-up fashion over time, and that top-down efforts to standardize process quality were not immediately accepted into practice. It was double looped learning that enabled people to act proactively in their personal behavior related to improving processes, and in sharing process-based information with their co-workers.

Finally, the third difficulty in developing process information concerned the uneven state of best practices associated with identifying, collecting, distributing, and using process information in companies. Davenport and Beers found that the company's culture would often constrain how process information would be used by organizational members. In some companies, people were very proactive with process information, while in other companies people had neither incentives, training, nor real motivation to make process performance information transparent or to share it with others (Davenport and Beers 1995).

Thus, it appears that firms that effectively monitor their processes and use appropriate process measures and practices to improve performance, can achieve significant paybacks (Grover and Kettinger 2000). Companies need to have full control of their processes to adapt flexibly to changing market needs, as well as deliver products and services of superior value at the lowest cost possible. The challenge of continuously monitoring processes for day-to-day performance, and for fit with changing business needs, increases in importance and urgency.

### *Delegating decisions to the lowest levels possible by effectively delivering information at the right time and place*

Decentralizing decision making and redefining the business around customers are moving companies in two directions simultaneously.

First, managers desire to empower workers with full responsibilities to make decisions related to customers, process management, and operational performance day to day. This requires companies to engage in 'connected, but localized' decision making (Nault 1998). Here, decisions are delegated to local decision making units. However, people in these units are connected together through networks where they can share and use information that, in the past, was not readily available to local decision makers. For example, global or regional customers of many companies require their suppliers to provide 'one face to the customer', even though the supplier's operations are localized in many countries and markets. Thus, the supplier to the global customer must be able to solve the paradox of acting locally and globally at the same time. The suppliers that can do so must link all their local operations together through IT infrastructures and systems, while at the same time they must permit their people to be fully informed about the status of the company's global interactions with the customer, when organizational members act locally.

The second response is either to use IT to fully automate routine and well-defined decisions, or to employ automation to assist lower-skilled workers in making decisions that affect operational performance or customer satisfaction. For example, companies such as Northrop Corporation that manufacture jet fighters use 'expert systems' to plan and assemble the over 20,000 parts that go into an aircraft for their customers. These systems assist engineers to evaluate the sequence of manufacturing processes, and the required materials and expertise for each phase. In addition, the same systems are accessed during the assembly process to facilitate day-to-day decisions by workers about correct installation of parts and components. Here IT systems are used both to capture and structure a complex series of decisions and related information necessary to coordinate the design, planning, and manufacture of jet fighters, and secondly, to assist assembly workers in executing their daily responsibilities in a highly disciplined manufacturing process.

Companies that expect to be industry leaders in using operational information in the future will head in both directions at once; empowering local workers to make operational decisions, but connecting them to company-wide networks, so that they can coordinate their decisions with other organizational members in various locations (Dewan and Min 1997). In addition, these companies seek to use IT to either automate routine decisions involving transactions to improve output, or to assist lower-skilled workers in making appropriate decisions with customers each time.

### Improving the ways people work in groups effectively by using information to coordinate people and activities

During the last ten years, many companies have employed collaborative software products such as Lotus Notes, or used centralized databases, to make sure that teams and groups whose members were separated by time and location could effectively use and share common documents and files. Travel agents and airlines have long employed networks and sophisticated databases to coordinate reservations and seat assignments. Companies have used 'replication' technology to automatically update all versions of databases, files, and documents that teams are employing as changes occur.

Information in operational processes is synchronized continuously to assure that all members of the organization are using the most up-to-date information about the status of activities and people.

For example, beginning in 1996, Norwich Union Direct began serving the general insurance needs of its customers in the UK over the phone. Shortly after its launch, Norwich Union Direct Financial Services added its life and pension products to the general insurance products previously offered. The call center operation was now supplemented by a remote sales team that provided face-to-face financial planning advice to customers who required customized solutions to meet their needs. Since each sales person uses a portable computer, the customer files between the call center database and the sales representatives are continuously updated or replicated every time the sales rep dials into the network, so that customer interactions, appointments, and product sales information are kept as up to date as possible.

Thus, companies that want to be industry leaders in the future will increasingly be using replication technology to synchronize the actions and activities of their people working in teams. Collaborative work through teams and projects is a key aspect of the virtual office, and can only be effectively implemented with real-time information refreshment, reuse, and updating.

### Reducing the need for physical movement of people, projects, and facilities by delivering the right information at the right time

In his 1995 book called *Being Digital*, Nicholas Negroponte introduced the idea that 'moving bits' is much quicker and more cost effective than 'moving atoms':

As one industry after another looks at itself in the mirror and asks about its future in a digital world, the future is driven almost 100 percent by the ability of that company's product and services to be rendered in digital form. (Negroponte 1995: 12)

While there will still be a need for goods, people, and physical facilities in the future, the capability of a company to manage information about its products, services, people, and facilities will change the way the physical resources are employed. Goods will be manufactured just in time, as orders are received, so that inventories can be reduced substantially. People will learn and work remotely through digital technologies and global communications, instead of continuously traveling to routine meetings. Services will increasingly be offered through a combination of personal, telephone, and Internet channels. Even physical facilities will be redefined as offices move from dedicated spaces for individuals to office 'hoteling' whereby companies maintain offices for their employees on an as-needed basis, much like renting a hotel room. Also, manufacturing plants and warehouses will be reconfigured to reduce both the number and types of these facilities in use through better coordination of their capacities on a regional and global basis, rather than on a local basis alone.

Increasingly, industry leaders in the use of operational information will seek to digitally move information about goods, services, people, and facilities to improve the management of these resources for the company, and to reduce ineffective movements and wasteful uses of physical resources as well. The 'virtual value chain' will enhance, and in some cases replace, the physical value chain as companies leverage the power of digital information to manage services, interactions, and information exchange to improve business performance (Rayport and Sviokla 1995).

## 2. WHAT SENIOR MANAGERS REALLY THINK ABOUT INDUSTRY LEADERSHIP IN COMPETING WITH INFORMATION

We have explained and defined the three ways companies can use competitive, customer, and operational information to seek industry leadership by competing with information. Next, we look at how senior managers actually think about these uses of information through our confirmatory factor model presented in Fig. 9.2. We will also examine how the three information capabilities of IO predict future industry leadership in using competitive, customer, and operational information as presented in Fig. 9.3. In Fig. 9.4, we will explain the relationships between IT practices, information management practices, and information behaviors and values and the expectations of senior managers for future industry leadership in Figs. 9.5 and 9.6.

### A. Future industry leadership with information—a measurable construct

Based on the literature review and relationships outlined in section 1 we analyzed each of the three dimensions of future industry leadership with information using the same confirmatory factor analysis techniques as presented in Chapter 6. As we suspected, the results of this analysis, presented in Fig. 9.2, show that senior managers perceive that a comprehensive high-level idea measuring the extent to which their company will be a leader in

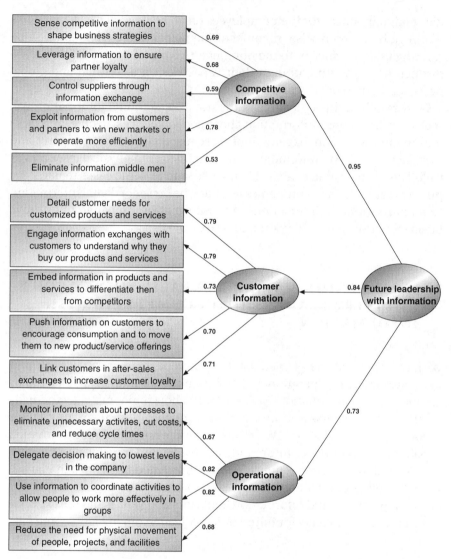

**Fig. 9.2. Confirmatory Factor Model of Future Industry Leadership with Information**

use of information in the future exists in their minds. We call this second-order factor 'Future Industry Leadership with Information'. This validated high-level construct represents a new and integrated view of how senior managers think about achieving future industry leadership in competing with information. The three dimensions of industry leadership in using competitive, customer, and operational information were shown to be distinct, yet clearly related.

Moreover, if we look at the individual items in Fig. 9.2 that comprise each of the three dimensions, we find that the individual items under each dimension reflect the ideas discussed earlier in this chapter. In general, most items loaded strongly on their corresponding dimension with the exception of two items:

First, 'controlling suppliers through information exchange' appears not to be as well reflected in senior managers' idea of competing with information in the future. Perhaps senior managers view information exchanges with suppliers as a 'competitive necessity' in most industries today. Most manufacturing and service companies must be competent at influencing suppliers to their advantage in their industry, but must also recognize that suppliers are able to move from one business customer to another. The challenge of influencing suppliers may be nothing new for managers and may be perceived as a basic condition of playing in the industry, but not as a basis for competitive advantage.

Second, 'eliminating information "middle men" ' is not as clearly perceived by senior managers as contributing to the competitive information measure for perhaps two reasons:

- the idea of eliminating middle men may not be perceived as a way of gaining competitive advantage in some industries that have depended on intermediaries in the past such as wholesalers, distributors, and retailers; and
- for senior managers, the elimination of middle men using Internet technology and direct models of doing business is a new concept and may not be as well understood or accepted in some industries versus others.

Except for these two items associated with competitive information, all the other items linked to competitive, customer, and operational information dimensions loaded strongly and resulted in a strong model fit. This confirmed our proposition that senior managers were actively considering these three ideas as core dimensions in their strategy to achieve future industry leadership with information.

## B. Information Orientation as a predictor of future industry leadership in competing with information

As we suggested earlier, it is our belief that effective information use today will predict industry leadership in the use of information in the future. What this means in measurement terms is that the newly identified Information Orientation (IO) factor will predict future industry leadership with information. Furthermore, because we found that IO is a comprehensive representation of a company's competence and synergy in effectively using information across its three capabilities (IT practices, information management practices, information behavior and values), we conclude that it will better predict a direct causal link to future industry leadership with information than would any single dimension or subset of dimensions.

Just as we had conducted a 'two competing model test' for determining the predictive link between IO and business performance, we performed a similar two competing model test for the link between IO and future industry leadership with information.

The first approach tested a direct effects model and attempted to causally link each information capability (IT practices, information management practices, and information behaviors and values) to the criterion variable (industry leadership). This model displayed poorer fit, and we concluded that these individual capabilities did not adequately predict future industry information leadership.

The second test examined the association of the three information capabilities of IT practices, information management practices, and information behaviors and values as measured through a causal link between the second-order factor IO and future industry information leadership. As Fig. 9.3 indicates, the paths between the three information capabilities of IO and future industry leadership in competing with information are high, with solid indicators of overall model fit. Thus, we conclude that IO is not only a strong predictor of business performance, but also of future industry leadership in competing with information.

What is important for the reader to remember in interpreting our results is the following two key points:

First, we now have a high-level validated measure of senior managers' expectations of future industry leadership with information.

Second, high IO predicts future industry leadership. In other words, if the IO score of a company is high, then its expectations about future industry leadership in competing with information will also be high.

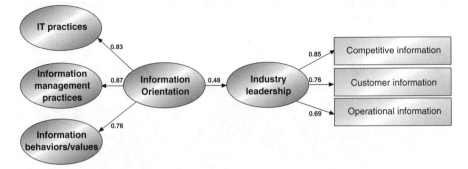

**Fig. 9.3.** Coalignment Model: Information Orientation Predicting Future Industry Leadership with Information

## C. Probing for deeper understanding of the relationships between the dimensions of future industry leadership with information

Given the existence of the future industry leadership with information factor, as a powerful high-level idea in the minds of senior managers, how do we propose that the three dimensions of future industry leadership with information factor interrelate? Based on what we have learned from our path analyses in Chapter 8, we next present several key ways we propose that the leadership practices and dimensions interact to increase a company's ability to use information to compete in the future (see Fig. 9.4). In future research, we hope to confirm these relationships through path analysis or other types of causal modeling.

First we believe that senior managers clearly view the importance of sensing and using competitive information to shape business strategies, leverage partner loyalty, influence suppliers, win new markets, and eliminate middle men as central to industry leadership in the future. We believe there are important relationships in the minds of senior managers between using competitive information to achieve industry leadership and sensing and being proactive with information as well as using IT for management support.

As we noted in the previous chapter, proactive information use seems to be an important driver of a company's Information Orientation and is linked with sensing information and using IT for management support. Senior managers realize that to achieve future industry leadership in competing with information, their company must sense and be proactive with information not just for today, but for tomorrow as well. In addition, they also emphasize the importance of sensing market, customer, and partner

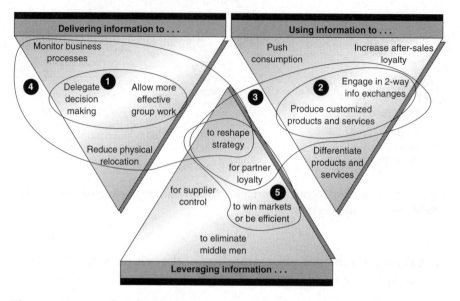

**Fig. 9.4. Proposed Relationships between Dimensions of Future Industry Leadership with Information**

*Notes*:

1. Operational decision making and group work go hand in hand.
2. Interacting with customers and customizing products are directly linked.
3. Reshaping strategy and promoting partner loyalty precede detailing customer needs and customizing products.
4. Sensing information to reshape strategy also redefines operational information needs.
5. Reshaping strategy, ensuring partner loyalty, and winning new markets are closely linked.

trends as triggers to appropriately act on the information that they perceive may be relevant to the future.

Therefore, a key responsibility of senior managers is to develop 'memories for the future' in themselves, and in organizational members, so that faint or ill-defined signals about market trends can be detected and addressed appropriately. Companies that develop 'industry foresight' earlier than their competitors and shape future business strategies to act on their foresight will achieve future industry leadership with information. Moreover, senior managers believe that IT should be used to enable the use of competitive information in the future and not just be aligned to today's business strategies and market trends as we noted in Chapter 3. IT for management analysis and decision making should support the evolution of the company's emergent strategy by fostering new ideas, sensing information better, and permitting a company to be more proactive with competitive information.

If we turn to Fig. 9.4, we can see some other important proposed relationships.

*Operational decision making and group work.* First, we believe there is a strong relationship between using operational information to delegate decision making to the lowest possible levels in a company and allowing people to work more effectively in teams. Senior managers clearly emphasize the need for teamwork and information sharing within teams as necessary conditions for delegating information to the lowest possible levels in the company.

*Interacting with customers and customizing products.* Second, we see a strong relationship between using customer information to detail customer needs to offer customized products and to engage in two-way information exchange with customers. Senior managers understand that in order to effectively customize products and services, they must be in continuous two-way information exchanges with customers.

*Reshaping strategy and promoting partner loyalty.* Third, we feel that industry leadership in sensing information to reshape business strategy and to leverage partner loyalty will be shown to be strongly related with detailing customer needs to offer customized products and engaging in two-way information exchanges with customers to better understand why they buy products and services. While senior managers understand the value of sensing customer needs and interacting with customers, they also believe that sensing competitive information to change strategy and maintain partner loyalty must be done at the same time. It is not good enough to simply understand your customers and why they buy today's goods and services. Senior managers and organizational members must always keep a watchful eye on unexpected shifts in competitive conditions in their markets as well as among their 'partners', since today's partner may become tomorrow's competitor!

*Sensing information to reshape strategy.* Fourth, sensing information to reshape business strategies would seem to be strongly associated with all four ways of using operational information to monitor business processes, delegate decisions to lower levels, permit people to work in groups effectively, and reduce the need for physical movements of goods, people, and facilities. Senior managers clearly perceive that operational information and processes as well as IT support must reflect not only today's way of doing business, but also tomorrow's view of changing business operations and needs. As we noted earlier in this chapter, the use of operational information for achieving future industry leadership requires companies to evaluate their processes and operations not only for meeting today's business needs, but also for changing these processes and operations to flexibly adapt to business conditions in the future. Senior managers perceive the need to follow what Derek Abell calls a 'dual strategy' of running the business with information on the one side and changing the business with information on the other (Abell 1993).

*Leveraging information to reshape strategy.* Finally, in using competitive information, we propose that senior managers perceive that sensing and exploiting competitive information to reshape strategy, ensure partner loyalty, win new markets, or become more efficient are more closely related than maintaining control of suppliers and eliminating middle men. Maintaining control of suppliers may be a strategic necessity, while eliminating middle men may be either too new in some industries or less feasible for senior managers to consider as important than the other three competitive information practices.

## 3. IO AS A METRIC OF FUTURE INDUSTRY LEADERSHIP: ASSESSING AND MANAGING EXPECTATIONS

As we have discussed in this chapter, our study has developed an additional business metric—future industry leadership in competing with information. This measurement can be combined with the IO metric to set future managerial expectations. Since our study has established that IO predicts future industry leadership (i.e., companies with high IO will be industry leaders), a plot of a company's IO to future industry leadership can be used by managers to assess current IO capabilities relative to future industry leadership in competing with information.

As Fig. 9.5 illustrates, companies or business units can fall into one of four assessment categories:

*Tunnel Vision.* In the first case, companies have low IO today and low expectations about future industry leadership in competing with information. These companies possess tunnel vision today, because they have low IO and also low business performance. Their senior managers do not perceive that they have the capabilities to respond to changing business conditions. Moreover, their expectations for future industry leadership are low, so that we can expect these companies to be low performers in the future.

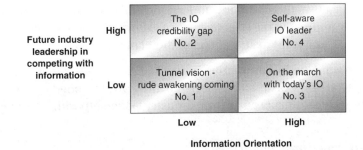

Fig. 9.5.  Industry Leadership and IO: Implications for General Managers

Apparently, their senior managers have set low expectations for themselves into the future—a prospect that may be 'realistic', but could be dangerous to the future health of this company or business unit. We believe that these companies or business units exist on very fragile ground in their industry and may be in for a rude awakening if they do not take drastic and significant action to change their mindsets first and their IO second.

*Credibility Gap.* In the second case, companies have low IO scores today, but have high expectations of future industry leadership in competing with information. These companies have an IO credibility gap. They have low effectiveness of information use today, but for some reason, they believe they can move to industry leadership in the future. Thus, they will have to really invest heavily in their efforts to improve problematic IO capabilities if they are to meet their high expectations to be a future industry leader.

*On the March.* In the third case, companies have high IO today, but low expectations for being an industry leader in competing with information in the future. These companies are 'on the march with today's IO.' We believe that this case occurs less frequently. It may occur in industries where companies already compete very intensively with information; and self-doubt, or industry uncertainties, translates into fears that information-based competitive advantages cannot be sustained. For example, as the equity trading industry moves to Internet-based on-line trading, it may be very difficult for companies that already have high IO as equity traders to lead their industry with information asymmetries against other on-line traders. While these companies expect to enjoy advantages over more traditional, agent-based equity traders in the future, their expectations against major on-line traders may be lower in this turbulent financial industry sector.

*Self-Aware Leader.* Finally, in the fourth case, there are the smart companies that have achieved high IO today and have high expectations regarding future industry leadership. We call these companies 'self-aware IO leaders'.

Senior managers in this company understand and continuously emphasize the need for improving the effective use of information to impact business performance, and want to stay ahead of their competitors.

Senior managers in companies in each of these four categories have different strategic options to exercise if they are to achieve or change expectations regarding IO and future industry leadership with information.

*Strategic option 1: breakout to high IO*
The first strategic option is for the most vulnerable of companies that have low IO today and low expectations about future industry leadership in competing with information. Not only do managers in these companies exhibit a form of tunnel vision since they have been low performers in the past, but they also are susceptible to rude shocks and competitive moves by other companies in their industry. Low IO has, in the past, not only contributed to low performance, but it has made these companies more vulnerable to disruptive competitive shifts in their own industry. Unless they are 'protected' by regulation, or geographic or national advantage, these companies will be in for a rude awakening when artificial barriers to competition are lowered in their industry.

What should such a company do?

We believe that such a company needs a 'breakout' strategy in two steps. First, managers in this company need to break out of their existing mindset concerning low performance, low IO, and low future industry leadership expectations In Fig. 9.6, the vertical dotted line signifies the shift in senior management mindset or 'mental breakout' that is required before managers in the company can take the next step—implementing an IO strategy that targets IO capabilities improvement as a key strategic priority of the firm.

A strategic breakout in such a company is only possible if the senior managers have the will, courage, awareness, and sense of urgency to support both steps in the process to improve information behaviors and values, information management practices, and IT practices in an integrated way. Often, these improvements will have to start with the senior managers themselves if they are to take hold quickly with organizational members. Since information behaviors are the most difficult aspects of IO to change, senior managers will have to display changes in information behaviors and values themselves, before they can expect similar changes among organizational members.

For example, as we mentioned in Chapter 7, at the European retail bank that has experienced numerous bouts of restructuring, downsizing, and

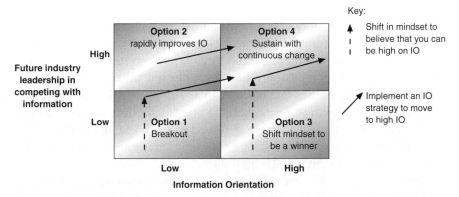

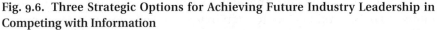

Fig. 9.6. **Three Strategic Options for Achieving Future Industry Leadership in Competing with Information**

one major acquisition over the last five years, these changes have resulted in low performance and low IO across each information capability. IT practices have not been developed to keep up with industry practices. The bank suffers from poor information behaviors and values. People are not transparent with information, do not share information, do not trust managers with information, and do not act proactively with information. Finally, information practices related to customer accounts and products are 'in a state of chaos' according to one senior manager.

While the existing senior management team are aware of these deficiencies in IO capabilities, they tend to be resigned to not being capable of achieving future industry leadership with information any time soon. This is dangerous in a market that is quickly being deregulated and where over-capacity in retail banks is a serious problem. Unless this bank's senior managers accelerate the build-up of IO capabilities, its prospects for the future are not good.

Thus, companies with low IO today and low expectations about future industry leadership with information will require transformational initiatives to improve IO capabilities rapidly. The good news is that the first 'breakout step' rests with senior managers—if they are willing to change their mindsets, there is hope that they can change the behaviors, values, and mindsets of organizational members. If they are unable or unwilling to change their mindsets and break out to higher IO, they may be betting their careers and those of organizational members and placing the company at serious risk.

*Option 2: rapidly improve IO*

The second strategic option is for companies with low IO today, but with expectations to be future industry leaders in competing with information in the future. These are companies that have aspired to industry leadership with information in the past, but have experienced substantial difficulties in building IO capabilities due to deficiencies in information behaviors, IT practices, or information management practices. Since future industry leadership is only achieved and maintained through the integration of the three information capabilities of IO, a company cannot sustain high expectations in the future with low IO capabilities today.

This is especially the case with companies that have built up over time high expectations with customers and partners that they have the IO capabilities to deliver value—the IO credibility gap. The gap can appear in two ways: by promising IO capabilities to customers and partners externally, and by expecting more IO delivery internally than the company is ready, or is able, to sustain. When this gap develops, managers must build IO capabilities and improve behaviors rapidly, or suffer loss of face with customers, partners, and employees.

For example, a leading European freight forwarding company has to build IO to sustain industry leadership in providing complete freight forwarding solutions worldwide for its large customers. However, over the last ten years, the company has been unable to build the IT systems to implement its 'next generation' freight forwarding concepts with global customers. Instead, it has provided end-to-end tracking of freight shipments and account management through a series of incompatible IT systems dating back over a decade. What it has lacked in computer integration, it has made up for so far with PC and spreadsheet solutions, lots of human communication, and direct customer interfaces on the Internet that look good, but require enormous human effort and time to support. The company's greatest IO credibility gap rests with its inability to successfully implement an integrated freight forwarding system even though the company promotes this capability to its customers.

In addition, the company also suffers from uneven information management practices that are now being corrected by its new CEO: 'You have to understand a forwarder: he makes an invoice and thinks that this is his profit.' In the past, many information management practices were informal and poorly executed. Today, the level of professionalism expected of freight forwarders by customers requires close attention to institutionalized processes and information management practices.

Finally, the company's information behaviors have also been uneven historically not only in the company, but also in the industry: 'The players in the forwarding industry are still seen as highway robbers. You use to give your shipment to a forwarder and hoped that it got to its destination!'

Information integrity, control, and sharing have been key concerns within and among freight forwarding companies.

As the company has improved its industry image in recent years, it has done so by promoting its IO capabilities to deliver up-to-the-minute information to customers about their shipments and accounts worldwide. Thus, the company must build its IO capabilities quickly before customers realize the credibility gap. Otherwise, it will lose its future industry leadership position in competing with information.

*Options 3 and 4: sustain IO leadership*
Industry leadership with information does not continue indefinitely. Clearly companies that are high in IO and are industry leaders in the use of information will have a privileged position to win in the marketplace. But these companies will not remain as leaders by just continuing past behaviors and practices. As we showed in Fig. 9.1, the competitive value of information declines with time. Companies that seek to maintain their leadership with information must constantly challenge their progress and redefine their information practices, to either meet new information needs for competitive, customer, and operational information, or respond appropriately to new IT advances. They must constantly move their capabilities to their next 'S-curve' in Fig. 9.1. The difference between Option 3 and Option 4 is in the confidence and commitment to maintain an industry leadership position.

For example, a leading Spanish retail bank is achieving industry leadership and superior performance with the successful integration of information management practices, information behaviors and values, and IT practices leading to increased employee, customer, and shareholder value. The bank's managers are intensely interested in using information effectively in adding value with customers and cross-selling banking, insurance and other financial products.

Information on customer needs is collected by all employees at the branch level in databases that can be used wherever and whenever a customer accesses a branch or direct channel such as phone banking, Internet banking, or ATMs. Product information is well segmented by types of customers and product profiles of customers appear on screens with customer account information as well. All branch employees must proactively cross-sell financial products to customers during the execution of transactions as the head of retail banking notes:

When branch representatives interact with customers during the execution of transactions, they have the obligation to cross-sell one product. The bank's systems provide the information about the best cross-selling opportunity for each customer and we reward cross-selling activities.

Thus, the bank's IT infrastructure supports the bank's information practices and appropriate information behaviors. The head of IT believes that the 'integration of business with technology is the best way to create barriers and gain competitive advantage.'

Although the bank has achieved an enviable position of high IO, high performance, and high expectation for future industry leadership, nonetheless, it has no intention of 'marching with today's IO' even in an information intensive industry, and in a very dense and competitive retail banking market. As soon as it completed a major bank-wide, four-year improvement program in 1998, the senior managers of the bank agreed to launch another four-year improvement program to sustain its leadership as one of Spain's premier retail banks.

## 4. CONCLUSIONS

In this chapter, we have discussed how companies can be industry leaders in competing with information in the future. We have defined 'future industry leadership in competing with information' as belonging to companies that will be able to create information asymmetries in their markets and sustain them over time. Information asymmetries exist whenever a company leverages information about markets, customers, or its operations that is unusable or unavailable to its competitors. We have categorized the information practices for attaining leadership in competing with information in three ways: using competitive information, using customer information, and using operational information. Within each category or dimension, we have identified emerging practices and trends that we believe senior managers expect to exploit to attain future industry leadership in competing with information.

We have also noted that competing with information is critical today for several key reasons:

First, all companies in market economies compete in markets where information plays a significant role.

Second, Internet and electronic markets are driving industry shifts in financial services, retailing, and many other industries where past information advantages enjoyed by dominant companies with customers, suppliers, partners, and competitors are dwindling away or radically shifting.

Third, every business is becoming an information business since companies must not just compete on the basis of their physical resources and value chain, but must also leverage their information resources and 'digital' value chain as well.

Finally, we believe that industry leadership in competing with information is temporary and must be continuously won or sustained over time. There is a constant movement of one company's competitive advantage to the industry's competitive necessity as innovations in information practices and capabilities are replicated over time within and across industries.

In this chapter, we revealed a high-level idea held in the minds of managers that comprehensively captures three dimensions of using competitive, customer, and operational information. We call this new factor 'future industry leadership with information'. Our confirmatory factor model also indicates that we have successfully represented the individual information practices supporting each dimension of future industry leadership in competing with information. Thus, our study has identified a new and integrated view of how senior managers think about achieving future industry leadership in competing with information.

A major conclusion of our study is that the Information Orientation of a company not only predicts business performance, but also predicts senior manager expectations regarding future industry leadership in competing with information. If the IO score of a company is high, then its expectations about future industry leadership in competing with information will also be high.

Finally, since our study has shown that IO predicts future industry leadership in competing with information, a plot of IO to future industry leadership can be used by managers to help assess their current IO capabilities relative to their expectations about future industry leadership with information.

In the last section, we identified four situations that companies and business units could find themselves in today, and we offer four strategic options they might undertake in moving from their current IO position to meeting their expectations about future industry leadership with information. In particular, we noted that companies that are low on IO today and have low expectations about future industry leadership face a precarious position in two ways:

First, if they do not change their future expectations or IO capabilities, they face further decline or disruption in their business performance.

Second, if they seek to change their future expectations and IO capabilities, they must first transform their mindsets and information behaviors and values if the rest of their employees are to engage in the IO transformation that is required.

We call this the 'breakout strategy' since it requires managers and employees to break out of their mindsets about IO and business performance before they can take effective action to improve information behaviors and values, information management practice, and IT practice capabilities. Developing and implementing an IO strategy requires a new set of tools, discipline, and a rededication of senior management's strategic attention. Breakout will be a tall order for highly challenged companies to undertake, but they may be left with little choice if they wish to survive in the e-economy.

# 10

# Epilogue: Transforming Management Practice and Metrics in the Age of Information Capitalism

In his prescient manner, Peter Drucker sensed, as early as 1993, that

while the world economy will remain a market and retain the market institutions, its substance has been radically transformed. If it is still 'capitalist', it is now dominated by 'information capitalism.' The industries that have moved into the center of the economy in the last forty years, have as their business, the production and distribution of knowledge and information, rather than the production and distribution of things. (Drucker 1993: 181–2)

In posing this transformation in the early 1990s, we believe that Drucker fully captured the transformation of both economic theory and management practice that we are experiencing.

For economic theory, he observed, 'we do not fully understand . . . how knowledge behaves as an *economic* resource' (Drucker 1993: 183). He suggested, 'we need an economic theory that puts knowledge in the center of the wealth-producing process.' However, it was only in the late 1990s that economists began to fully appreciate and measure how information contributes to economic productivity. We are still a long way from fully understanding how knowledge residing in the minds of people creates growth, innovation, and new types of wealth beyond labor, land, and (money) capital. Despite the rapid pace at which information technology advances, we are still a long way from understanding how knowledge and information are 'the main producers of wealth'. Like the new breed of 'Internet millionaires and billionaires', we want to believe that we understand how sustainable success is around the corner even though we are still in the early, formative years of the age of 'info capitalism'.

Drucker was among the first to recognize that the essence of the modern 'management revolution' involves 'knowledge being applied to knowledge'

(Drucker 1993: 42). The responsibility of management is to create the organizational conditions where people with different levels and types of knowledge and information can create, apply, and use their knowledge and information to achieve organizational purposes. He coined the term 'information-based organization' for describing more broadly the new ways for organizing people, information, and IT to achieve business success in the new era (Drucker 1989: 207).

However, with all the debate and media attention to the 'knowledge economy', 'e-commerce', and 'the role of IT in the new economy', if one cannot measure the impact of IT on economic productivity, or the role of information use in business organizations, then discussions of the 'knowledge economy' or 'information-based organization' are interesting, but not compelling. Moreover, while it appears that the economic measures for IT's impact on economic productivity are improving, there has been no significant progress, until now, for establishing a practical business metric of effective information use that was causally linked to business performance improvement.

When we began to plan the research study reported in this book almost three years ago, we noted that senior managers of companies in industries that produced both 'things' and 'services' were facing a significant dilemma. From all sides, they were being admonished to recognize the 'new realities' of the market economy and the new 'information-based organization'.

However, in practical terms, management thinking and practice concerning how to achieve significant business results with information, people, and IT was, as we noted in Chapter 2, functionally driven and fragmented. Senior managers are being asked to manage differently in the new era with no clear signposts or measures of what 'success' or 'progress' is. The situation became more cloudy as management gurus, consultants, and business school professors offered diverse prescriptions for what senior managers should do to better manage knowledge workers, the information resources that these workers used to convey, communicate, and express their knowledge, and the IT practices required to support their tasks.

Without a business-oriented measure of effective information use in companies, senior managers were left adrift—knowing that they needed to launch their company on a new transformational journey, but without a clear measure for assessing progress and success along the way.

The good news, as we have discovered in our survey research and case study work, is that managers in many companies have learned how to integrate people, information, and IT to achieve superior business performance. The bad news is that they have had no clear metric for evaluating the interactive effects of people, information, and IT on business performance in their business units or companies. Thus, they have acted like skippers of many sailboats. Senior managers have developed a good feel for success, but find it difficult to say precisely what decisions or actions actually led to their success in winning the race with their crew.

We believe that we have just begun to explore in this book the management implications of using Information Orientation as a new business metric for enabling business transformations and success. However, since we have now presented and validated a new, comprehensive theory of how people, information, and technology can be managed to improve business performance, and have advanced a new business metric to assess progress along the way, we are prepared to systematically evaluate and share winning strategies and practices of successful senior managers in navigating their companies to business success.

In the future, we will turn our attention to how companies can use IO as a business metric to improve business performance. We will refine our techniques for measuring IO among managers and organizational members over time. We will also focus on how senior managers can improve their leadership approaches and personal management styles for influencing the ways information can be effectively used in their companies.

In addition, we will assess the journeys undertaken by companies to improve IO, and the managerial lessons from these journeys. We will also explore how IO can create new business opportunities and increased use of knowledge in companies. We will specifically examine how senior managers use IO to implement business strategies, and what initiatives can be implemented to transform the information behaviors of people—the most challenging of the IO capabilities to rapidly change.

Finally, we will explore how IO can be linked to other measures of overall business performance. We will look at how a management process for fully utilizing IO as a business metric can help organizational managers and members position their companies for business leadership in competing with information and knowledge in the new era of 'information capitalism'.

# APPENDIX: THE STUDY'S RESEARCH APPROACH AND STATISTICAL RESULTS

This Appendix outlines the research methodology of the 'Navigating Business Success' study, and includes important statistical outputs from the analyses. It should be noted that the literature reviews, research arguments, statistical analyses, and reported results presented here in this Appendix and throughout the chapters of this book represent a synopsis of more detailed enquiry prepared initially in several unpublished IMD working papers that are currently being reviewed and refined for further scholarly publication.

The purpose of this Appendix is to provide interested readers with more background on how the research was conducted, and why we are confident in making the claims presented in the main body of this book. It is organized in the following subsections: (1) research objective; (2) literature review and theory development; (3) survey development; (4) data collection and sample description; (5) survey data analysis; and (6) follow-up interviews.

Our major research findings are based on empirical data analysis using sophisticated statistical techniques. The main statistical techniques used are Confirmatory Factor Analysis (CFA) and Structural Equation Modeling (SEM). While research methods and statistical output will be presented in this appendix, the reader is directed to Chapters 3 through 9 for theoretical and managerial interpretation of our research findings.

## 1. RESEARCH OBJECTIVE

The research objective of this study is to demonstrate that an enterprise must achieve competence and synergy in three vital dimensions of effective information use to achieve superior business performance. Specifically, we determine the extent to which the dimensions of effective information technology practices, effective information management practices, and effective information usage behaviors form a nexus of effective information use that is a necessary precondition for superior business performance.

The major research question of the study is: *does effective information use lead to better business performance?* Sub-questions of the major research question are:

- Is there a comprehensive measure of overall effectiveness of information use?
- What are the dimensions of this measure?
- How do these dimensions relate in forming a comprehensive measure of effective information use?
- Is this measure reliable and valid enough for practical use?
- Does a comprehensive measure better predict business performance than the single dimensions?
- Is there a relationship between a comprehensive measure of effective information use and industry leadership in competing with information?
- Do different industries, job positions, and regions share the same view of effective information use?
- How can a comprehensive measure be used within a company to direct its information use strategy?
- Are there prescriptive paths that companies follow in improving their effectiveness in using information?

Several important challenges had to be successfully addressed to achieve the research objective, including:

- Linkage of the research premiss to prior academic literature and leading business practices to establish the theoretical justification for our research approach;
- Involvement of the highest-level international executives from a representative sample including a wide variety of company types, sizes, and industry sectors;
- Utilization of methodologies designed to provide empirical, quantitative analyses of perceptual data across a variety of complex business issues; and
- Utilization of qualitative techniques to gain additional understanding of the context surrounding the ideas discussed in this research.

Table A.1 sets forth the research study phases and implementation schedule.

## 2. LITERATURE REVIEW AND THEORY DEVELOPMENT

### A. Framing the research perspective

Following in a long tradition of academic and managerial research investigating the proposed positive effect that information technology has on business

**Table A.1.** *Research Study Phases and Schedule*

| Study phases | Implementation schedule |
| --- | --- |
| 1. Literature review and theory development | September 1997–January 1998 |
| 2. Survey development | January–March 1998 |
| 3. Data collection and sample description | April–November 1998 |
| 4. Survey data analysis and on-site interviews | November 1998–July 1999 |

performance, we carefully examined the literature on this topic dating back more than twenty years. This literature review determined that little hard evidence has surfaced directly linking IT investments to increases in business performance. As discussed in Chapter 6, the contributions of scholars such as Clemons (1986), as well as Brynjolfsson and Hitt (Brynjolfsson 1993; Brynjolfsson and Hitt 1996; Hitt and Brynjolfsson 1996), point to the difficulty in establishing the direct link between IT investment and sustained superior business performance. Researchers such as Kettinger et al. (1994) found that this link was far more complex than many earlier IT researchers had surmised and required a broader research perspective. As discussed in Chapter 6, their research indicated that a company's IT practices were but one dimension in a set of important 'foundation factors' that interact with management's 'action strategies' to determine higher business performance.

Our study team initially targeted the foundation factors Kettinger et al. (1994) identified as being related to effective information use. These included the *organizational base* (people's competence to exploit IT opportunity), *learning curve* (ability of the people in an organization to acquire and manage knowledge), *technological resources* (IT infrastructure, IT applications, and competence of the IT function to build and implement information systems), and *information resources* (the richness and content of an organization's knowledge base and information management practices).

As discussed in Chapter 6, these four foundation factors shaped our thinking related to the presence of: (1) a people-related behavioral information usage dimension; (2) an information technology practices-related dimension; and (3) an information management practices-related dimension—all of which come together in the minds of managers to form an even higher-level information usage competence factor that, in turn, predicts a positive effect on business performance. While attributes of these three dimensions had been touched upon in previous research, past studies failed to recognize the importance of this higher-level and more comprehensive construct of effective information use.

A detailed literature review of three different schools of thought related to the use of information in organizations only fortified our belief that these three distinct dimensions of effective information use existed, and that their higher presence would predict superior business performance. Our next task was to extract, from these three schools of thought, key ideas related to the way managers perceive effectiveness in information use in their companies. These ideas would later be formalized and validated as the empirically derived constructs that provided the basis for subsequent testing of our research questions.

## B. Theory development and construct identification

In examining the literature streams related to effective information use and business performance, three distinct 'schools of thought' emerged, which we term the IT School, the Information Management School, and the Behavior and Control School.

*Technological resources* such as IT architecture and models of IT design were the primary focus of authors in the IT School. Interestingly, while the IT School mentioned the importance of information to the firm, this school did not devote much attention to the assessments of people's behaviors surrounding effective information use, or its management. Instead the IT School focused considerable research energy toward finding the direct link between IT and business performance. In some part, this focus was a direct response to the often-cited 'IT productivity paradox' debate questioning the bottom-line payoff of IT investments.

Ideas surrounding *information resources management*, or the stewardship of an organization's knowledge, were developed through an Information Management School where authors concentrated on the effective management of the information life cycle and to a lesser extent on information valuation. While this literature stream offers insight into how to effectively manage information as a resource, it never focused on testing an empirical link between effective information use and business performance.

The importance of people's behavior and values, their capability to learn and contribute to the organization, as well as their ability to establish effective controls were the primary focus of authors of the Behavior and Control School. However, while past research in the Behavior and Control School linked personal behaviors to performance, they did not directly measure how people's information usage behaviors affected business performance, nor did they give much attention to the interrelated roles of good IT practices or information management practices on performance.

Detailed literature review within each school did identify key concepts, issues, and problems related to the effective information use within the context of each school itself. And, in limited instances, researchers within one school refer to relationships of ideas shared between schools. However, our literature review did not uncover an existing unifying theory of effective information use that tightly tied together all ideas shared by each of the three schools.

The lack of previous development of a comprehensive construct integrating ideas of each of the three schools into a higher-level information usage competence factor seemed to contradict what we had been hearing from senior managers in classroom case discussions and in focus groups over the past several years at IMD, the University of South Carolina, and at Andersen Consulting. These conversations suggested that senior managers saw competency in key aspects of each of the schools as being closely coupled with business performance success. This observation led the research team to postulate that the viewpoints of senior managers concerning the effective use of information were not completely captured within the theories of each individual school of thought, and that senior managers had a more complex and comprehensive view of effective information use that integrated dimensions from each of the three schools.

In addition to identifying key concepts and potential variables from each of the schools of thought, we examined the literature related to measures of business performance. Business strategy literature has suggested that multiple measures should be used to measure business performance given the different perceptions of key stakeholders such as employees, customers, shareholders, and, particularly, senior managers. Based on the recommendations of Venkatraman (1985), Kettinger et al. (1994) had included two indicators of business performance—financial performance and market share growth. Further suggestions in the more recent strategy research article by Chan et al. (1997) led us to add two additional indicators to the performance measure—improvements in reputation and in product/service innovations—rounding out our overall measure of business performance. In their study, Chan et al. (1997) tested these same four business performance indicators and determined that they generally showed strong reliability and validity.

The concepts of the three schools of thought and the multidimensional concept of business performance formed the basis for subsequent survey development.

The high-level conceptual model that drove our investigation was formalized to show the hypothesized relationships between a proposed higher-order measure of effective information use, as viewed by senior managers, and its underlying three capabilities (dimensions): IT practices, information management practices, and information behaviors and values. As outlined in Fig. A.1, the model implies our belief that this higher-order measure of effective information use is theoretically parsimonious enough to be used as a representation of these three dimensions. We later coined this hypothesized higher-order effectiveness measure as the Information Orientation of a company. Lastly, but most importantly, Information Orientation's direct positive effect on business performance was hypothesized in our conceptual model. This conceptual model formed the basis for the development of validated constructs within

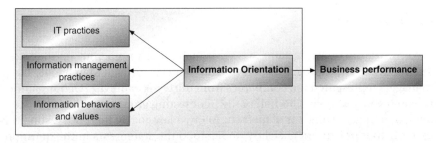

**Fig. A.1. Study's Conceptual Model**

each of the capabilities (IT practices, information management practices, information behaviors and values), and for the testing of the research questions.

## 3. SURVEY DEVELOPMENT

### A. Instrument development

An absence of empirical work in the area, and a need to gather many observations to ensure stable model solutions, suggested the use of survey data collection. All the survey measures were developed from the literature review integrating existing and previously tested constructs and variables. When literature did not provide a complete picture of a specific sub-dimension, additional questions were added. The questionnaire contained seventy-four questions (items). Multiple items were used to measure all proposed dimensions including: IT practices and its four proposed sub-dimensions; information management practices and its five proposed sub-dimensions; information behaviors and values and its proposed six sub-dimensions; business performance; and future industry leadership and its three proposed sub-dimensions.

### B. Questionnaire pre-test

At the draft stage, the questionnaire was reviewed and tested by numerous faculty members and research associates at IMD in Lausanne, Switzerland, as well as by faculty members and Ph.D. candidates at the University of South Carolina. The focus of this activity was two fold: (1) to review the substance of the instruments and ensure content validity, and (2) to address presentation issues. This pre-test effort resulted in feedback and observation regarding language interpretation, duration of completion, and unclear meaning and references by the very same types of executives who would be participating in the project. This was invaluable in improving the clarity, format, and length of the final survey instrument.

## C.  Pilot testing

Next, the study questionnaire was rigorously pilot-tested with 151 managers attending executive programs at IMD from January through March 1998. These managers represented 100 companies from thirty-six countries. Of our planned research study sample, one-half of the pilot testing group were the CEO, president, or managing director of their company. A key goal of this pilot testing was to verify that practitioners clearly understood the statements in the questionnaire, and whether there was enough variation in the responses to detect relationships between variables. Again, the questionnaire was improved according to the respondents' feedback. In addition, the confirmatory factor models later described in the analysis section of this Appendix were first tested with the pilot test sample and the models showed acceptable model fit and factor loadings. This provided strong positive news to proceed with our study approach.

## D.  Final survey instrument

As we wanted to use a full set of parametric statistical techniques to analyze the data, with the intent of producing the most robust and meaningful inferences, we made use of continuous scales. These scales are anchored to produce a judgement on a continuous basis. Based on the rigorous multi-phased development process described above, a final survey instrument was honed to measure the conceptual model's constructs and sub-dimensions.

## 4.  DATA COLLECTION AND SAMPLE DESCRIPTION

While national and cultural differences exist, managers of international companies are challenged to address a common global competitive environment while facing a barrage of new information technologies. To better understand their common perceptions, a representative international sample of senior managers was used in this study. This section outlines the overall strategy for data collection. In the first two parts of this section, issues pertaining to the 'organizational informant' of the study and the data collection procedure are discussed. The third part details the profile of respondents and characteristics of participating firms. The final part outlines procedures for assessing the underlying distributional assumptions of the data and the identification of the structural models tested in earlier chapters.

## A. Role of an 'organizational informant' in data collection

In many empirical studies, the measurement of organizational characteristics has typically utilized 'key informants'. In essence, this method of data collection relies on a selected set of members for providing information about a social setting. Such informants are not chosen at random; rather, they are chosen because they possess special qualifications, such as a particular status, level of experience, or specialized knowledge. In survey research, targeted respondents assume the role of a key informant, and provide information on an aggregated unit of analysis, by reporting on organizational properties rather than personal attitudes and behaviors (Venkatraman 1989). We followed this approach by selecting senior executives as our key informants concerning the effective use of information within their companies.

In focusing on senior managers, we adopted Hambrick and Mason's (1984) upper-echelons perspective that the organization becomes a reflection of its top executives. They argue that top management characteristics and functions have a far greater potential for predicting business performance and strategic choices. This view was based on the premiss that top managers structure decision situations to fit their view of the world. Other studies that adopt this perspective including Child's (1972) strategic choice perspective of organizational adaptation, as well as Thompson's (1967) 'dominant coalition'. Studies by Bourgeois (1984), Hrebiniak and Joyce (1985), and Stubbart (1989) also suggest that choices made by top managers influence organizational design outcomes and firm performance.

## B. Sampling frame and sampling procedure

For this study, potential participant companies were randomly selected from IMD's international database of partners, business associates, and other companies which had participated in executive program activities over the past five years. The selected study sample of 376 companies represented multiple industries, with varying company sizes, levels of business performance, and years of existence. Of the companies invited by direct mail, 103 or 27 per cent signed a Corporate Participation Agreement. These companies were then requested to identify one or more senior management teams at the corporate, division, or business unit level whose members would complete the study questionnaire. Of the 103 participating companies, the total of 1,009 senior managers had fully completed study questionnaires by November 14 1998, at which time data analysis activities commenced. Senior managers' responses received after that date were used for subsequent data validation purposes.

## C.  Sample profile

Of the total 1,009 senior managers in the study sample, chief executive officers (CEOs) represented the highest concentration of responses within an individual management position category. The majority of study responses (58 per cent) came from chief executive officers, executive and senior vice-presidents, and general managers/directors.

The 1,009 senior managers represented twenty-six countries and twenty-five industry sectors (see Tables A.2 and A.3). They worked for companies that ranged in size from small to very large (250,000+) employees.

**Table A.2.**  *Countries Represented by Individual Respondents in Study Sample*

| Country | # of respondents |
| --- | --- |
| United States | 215 |
| Switzerland | 135 |
| United Kingdom | 120 |
| The Netherlands | 99 |
| France | 57 |
| Germany | 55 |
| Sweden | 49 |
| Australia | 42 |
| Denmark | 42 |
| Norway | 38 |
| Spain | 26 |
| Austria | 19 |
| Finland | 18 |
| Belgium | 16 |
| Singapore | 11 |
| Italy | 11 |
| Malaysia | 11 |
| Liechtenstein | 10 |
| Canada | 9 |
| Thailand | 6 |
| Mexico | 6 |
| Luxembourg | 5 |
| Portugal | 4 |
| Chile | 3 |
| Poland | 1 |
| Russia | 1 |
| Total countries | 26 |

*Note*: The 169 senior management teams (SMTs) included in the core sample represent 22 countries, since regional SMTs were comprised of individual respondents from multiple country locations.

Table A.3. *Industries Represented by Individual Respondents in Study Sample*

| Industry | # of respondents |
|---|---|
| Insurance companies and brokers | 167 |
| Fast-moving consumer goods | 162 |
| Banking and financial services | 106 |
| Electric and electronic equipment | 85 |
| Industrial machinery and equipment | 80 |
| Chemicals | 73 |
| Motor vehicles aftermarket | 60 |
| Metal and mineral mining, except coal | 43 |
| Building and construction | 41 |
| Metal products | 26 |
| Motor vehicles | 26 |
| Air transportation | 22 |
| Crude petroleum, gas, and oil extract, coal mining | 20 |
| Water, sewage, and sanitary services | 15 |
| Instruments, medical, optical | 13 |
| Power generation (nuclear/atomic, electric, gas, steam) | 11 |
| Shipping | 11 |
| Textile, clothing, leather | 9 |
| Tyres and other rubber products | 9 |
| Printing and publishing | 6 |
| Lumber and wood products | 5 |
| Freight transportation | 5 |
| Building maintenance services | 5 |
| Miscellaneous manufacturing | 5 |
| Management and other consultants | 4 |
| Total industries | 25 |

The study sample included respondents who had held their existing position from less than one year to over sixteen years, of which the majority (58 per cent) have been in their positions from one to five years. In addition, respondents have been employed by their company for less than one year to over sixteen years, the majority of which (51 per cent) have been associated with their companies for over eleven years.

Of the total sample of respondents, 94 per cent were male and 6 per cent were female. The sample captured respondents from ages under 35 to over 56. The majority of the respondents (62 per cent) were between the ages of 41 and 55.

## D. Checks for statistical assumptions and model identification

In building and testing covariance models, it is important to formally assess: (1) the congruence of the data's distributional properties with the distributional assumptions of the technique; and (2) the identification of estimated models. The main analysis technique used in this study, structural equation modeling (SEM), is generally more sensitive than other multivariate techniques to departures in multivariate normality and kurtosis (Jöreskog and Sörbom 1989). A lack of multivariate normality substantially inflates the $\chi^2$ statistic creating an upward bias in critical values for determining significance. Model identification, on the other hand, guarantees that the proposed model has a unique solution. That is, a separate and unique equation exists for the estimation of each path coefficient (Bollen 1989). Models which are not identified are 'indeterminate'; therefore, resulting estimates are only one of an infinite number of feasible solutions.

Multivariate normality (the combination of two or more variables) implies that the individual variables are normal in a univariate sense and that their combinations are also normal. Therefore, if a variate is multivariate normal it is also univariate normal. However, the reverse may not always be true. Because multivariate normality is difficult to test, it is recommended that univariate normality among variables be initially tested. In essence, establishing univariate normality among a collection of variates helps gain, though not guarantee, multivariate normality (Hair et al. 1992). Such testing can be accomplished through examination of the moments around the mean of each variate's distribution. If a distribution is normal, its standardized third moment is 0 and its standardized fourth moment is 3 (Bollen 1989). These statistics are available in the PRELIS program that accompanies LISREL (Jöreskog and Sörbom 1989) and were examined for each of the study's variables. In general, no serious departures in univariate normality were detected.

As a further test of statistical assumptions, PRELIS reports several of Mardia's (1970) multivariate tests of skewness and kurtosis. This statistic is based on the fact that if observed variables have a multinormal distribution, then the marginal distributions of each observed variable should have the kurtosis and skew of a normal variable. If any fail to, then the multivariate distribution cannot be multinormal. Checks of these statistics for the variables of this study revealed no serious departures from multivariate normality or excessive kurtosis.

## 5. SURVEY DATA ANALYSIS

The purpose of this section is to describe the rationale for the methodological design for operationalizing factors and testing the relationships of the measurement models. The analysis of this study follows a two-step approach in establishing the logical linkage of the central construct Information Orientation with business performance. First, the content and measurement of this complex construct is established using confirmatory factor analysis. Second, to address our ultimate research question, 'Does effective information use lead to better business performance?', we adopted a data analysis approach that has been shown to be successful in determining whether the presence of first- and second-order factors predicts an increase in a performance criterion. In general, each of the performance-based models is tested within the perspective of 'coalignment'. This perspective is used to assess the ability of a group of factors in predicting a performance criterion. If coalignment is inferred, then the shared variation, 'common meaning', among a set of factors is more powerful in predicting performance than any of the individual factors.

As stated, to establish the validity and reliability of our pre-specified factors within each of the three dimensions, Confirmatory Factor Analysis (CFA) was used. CFA was also used to test the presence of higher order factors (Jöreskog and Sörbom 1989). Unlike Exploratory Factor Analysis approaches, CFA directly tests the viability of a pre-developed measurement model's structure (theory) against the observed data. Within this frame, a unique solution can be obtained and statistical metrics can be employed to determine the adequacy of the model in capturing the observed covariances.

To conduct the CFA of the first-order factors, and later test for coalignment, the statistical framework of structural equation modeling (SEM) was employed. In general, SEM assesses the ability of item measures to distinguish unique constructs (convergent validity), and the tendency of those constructs to be significantly different from each other (discriminant validity). In our research, SEM is implemented through confirmatory factor analytic techniques associated with the covariation perspective. The logic behind this modeling is that the pattern of covariations among first-order constructs can be captured as separate unobservable constructs that have no directly observable indicators (Venkatraman 1990). Typically, the statistical frameworks utilized for such modeling are Jöreskog and Sörbom's (1989) LInear Structural RELationships (LISREL) model and EQS from Multivariate Software Inc. (Bentler 1995). These technique are widely used within the social sciences to uncover the existence and properties of latent constructs as well as determining the causal nature between them (Bagozzi, Yi, and Phillips 1991; Venkatraman 1990; Breckler 1990; Marsh and Hocevar 1985; Bentler 1986; Bagozzi and Phillips 1982; Segars and Grover 1998).

## A. Developing and testing the dimensions of information orientation

### IT practices

Literature review and expert opinion were relied upon for the development of a content and operational domain for IT practices. The result of this analysis seems to suggest that four dimensions are useful in describing IT practices. These dimensions are:

1. *Operational Support*—IT's support for operations;
2. *Business Process Support*—IT's support of business processes;
3. *Management Support*—IT's support of decision making; and
4. *Innovation Support*—IT's support of business innovation.

Item measures were developed to provide an operational framework for assessing these unique dimensions. Scale reliability was calculated using Cronbach's alpha values. Acceptable alpha values indicating reliability obtained for the factors IT for operational support, IT for management support, and IT for innovation support were 0.76, 0.86, and 0.74 respectively. The slightly lower alpha score (0.62) for business process support can most likely be attributed to the fact that only two items make up this factor.

Fig. A.2 illustrates the results of SEM modeling. As shown, reliabilities of items to the first-order constructs of process support, operational support, management support, and innovation support are very strong, suggesting good measurement properties. Reliabilities between first-order constructs and the second-order construct of IT practices are extremely strong, providing compelling evidence of a second-order factor structure. While no definitive metric exists for assessing the absolute strength of model fit, the Comparative Fit Index (CFI) is a very strong 0.93, and the Root Mean Squared Error of Approximation (RMSEA) is 0.08, also providing evidence of model fit. In addition, highly significant $t$-values ($t > |2.00|$) can be observed for each indicator, giving evidence of convergent validity (Bollen 1989; Jöreskog and Sörbom 1989).

To assess discriminant validity, each pairwise correlation between the first-order constructs is fixed at 1.0. Then the measurement model is re-estimated. In total, six separate constrained models are established and compared to the estimated unconstrained model (Segars and Grover 1993). If the chi-square value for the constrained models is significantly higher than the unconstrained models, then evidence of construct unidimensionality is realized (Bagozzi and Phillips 1982).

Table A.4 depicts the test results. In each of the comparisons, the chi-square values were highly significant, indicating properties of discriminant validity. In sum, these findings suggest that IT practices is a complex concept (construct) that can be accurately measured through the items representing the unique first-order dimensions.

### Information management practices

Literature review and executive interviews were conducted to identify dimensions and associated indicators that may provide a definitional context for the information management construct. The outcome of this analysis suggests that

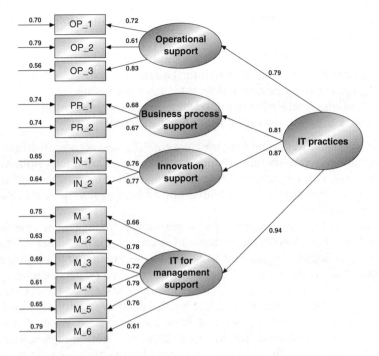

**Fig. A.2.   Factor Model of IT Practices**

*Note*: CFI=0.93; RMSEA=0.08.

**Table A.4.** *Results of Discriminant Validity Tests: IT Practices*

| Test | Model chi-square | d.f. | Chi-square difference | Significance |
|------|------------------|------|------------------------|--------------|
| *Unconstrained model* | 465.439 | 59 | | |
| *Constrained models* | | | | |
| Operational support with | | | | |
|   Business process support | 499.134 | 60 | 33.695 | $p<0.001$ |
|   Innovation support | 502.604 | 60 | 37.165 | $p<0.001$ |
|   Management support | 515.497 | 60 | 50.058 | $p<0.001$ |
| Business process support with | | | | |
|   Innovation support | 479.234 | 60 | 13.795 | $p<0.001$ |
|   Management support | 503.886 | 60 | 38.447 | $p<0.001$ |
| Innovation support with | | | | |
|   Management support | 477.717 | 60 | 12.278 | $p<0.001$ |

five dimensions may represent a useful domain for defining information management practices. These dimensions are:

1. *Sensing*—scanning the environment for relevant information;
2. *Collecting*—acquiring relevant information;
3. *Organizing*—reconciling and synthesizing information;
4. *Processing*—conversion of information into more useful forms;
5. *Maintaining*—removing information obsolescence.

Based on literature review, item measures of these respective constructs were developed and iteratively refined during pilot testing. Cronbach's alpha values for this construct were 0.70 for sensing, 0.78 for collecting, 0.80 for organizing, 0.81 for processing, and 0.87 for maintaining, indicating that the scale reliabilities are satisfactory.

As shown in Fig. A.3, the construct for information management practices is modeled as a second-order factor that is measured by the first-order constructs of sensing, collecting, organizing, processing, and maintaining. In turn, these first-order constructs are modeled as a function of their respective items.

Observed reliabilities of item measures to their associated factors seem to suggest that relatively strong fit exists for the five-factor solution. The Comparative Fit Index (CFI) of 0.90 and Root Mean Squared Error of Approximation (RMSEA) of 0.08 are within suggested cutoff ranges and factor loadings between the first- and second-order factors are very strong. Highly significant *t*-values for all indicators show that convergent validity is achieved.

Similar to the IT practices construct, discriminant validity was assessed through comparisons of pairwise constrained models to an unconstrained one. Since the chi-square values are very significant, we can conclude that each of the hypothesized factors is different from the others in Table A.5. Thus, reasonable evidence exists for acceptance of this model as an accurate operational and definitional lens for measuring information management practices.

### Information behaviors and values

Similar to building a definitional domain for information management practices, literature review and expert opinion were utilized to form a definitional and operational context for information behaviors and values. The result of this exercise was a construct space of six distinct dimensions including:

1. *Proactiveness*—the active concern to obtain information and the desire to put useful information into action;
2. *Transparency*—openness in reporting and presentation of information on errors, failures, and mistakes;
3. *Integrity*—use of information in a trustful and principled manner;
4. *Sharing*—willingness to provide others with information in an appropriate collaborative fashion;

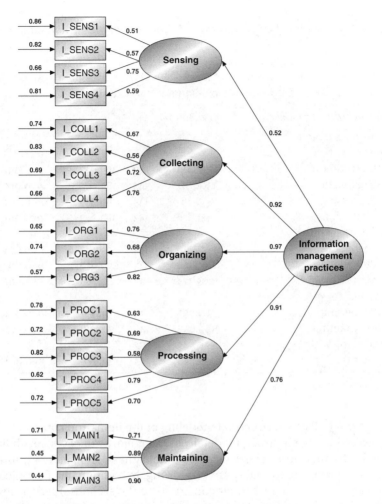

**Fig. A.3. Factor Model of Information Management Practices**

*Note*: CFI=0.90; RMSEA=0.08.

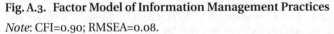

5. *Control*—extent to which information about performance is continuously presented to people to help manage and monitor performance; and

6. *Formality*—the willingness to trust and use institutionalized information.

Consistent with the constructs of information management practices, the operational content of these constructs was developed through item measures. Again Cronbach's alphas were calculated and showed reliable scales (0.80 for awareness, 0.87 for transparency, 0.76 for integrity, 0.71 for sharing, 0.74 for control, and 0.77 for formality).

**Table A.5.** *Results of Discriminant Validity Tests: Information Management Practices*

| Test | Model chi-square | d.f. | Chi-square difference | Significance |
|---|---|---|---|---|
| *Unconstrained model* | 1137.806 | 142 | | |
| *Constrained models* | | | | |
| Sensing with | | | | |
|    Collecting | 1327.429 | 143 | 189.623 | *p*<0.001 |
|    Organizing | 1300.711 | 143 | 162.905 | *p*<0.001 |
|    Processing | 1328.361 | 143 | 190.555 | *p*<0.001 |
|    Maintaining | 1321.778 | 143 | 183.972 | *p*<0.001 |
| Collecting with | | | | |
|    Organizing | 1157.908 | 143 | 20.102 | *p*<0.001 |
|    Processing | 1209.028 | 143 | 71.222 | *p*<0.001 |
|    Maintaining | 1209.174 | 143 | 71.368 | *p*<0.001 |
| Organizing with | | | | |
|    Processing | 1171.727 | 143 | 33.921 | *p*<0.001 |
|    Maintaining | 1169.656 | 143 | 31.850 | *p*<0.001 |
| Processing with | | | | |
|    Maintaining | 1199.294 | 143 | 61.488 | *p*<0.001 |

As shown in Fig. A.4, structural modeling of the items and constructs seems to suggest a relatively strong model fit. In the majority of cases, reliabilities of items to the first-order constructs of proactiveness, transparency, integrity, sharing, control, and formality are very strong. In addition, the factor loadings (or reliabilities) of the first-order constructs to the second-order construct of information behaviors and values are also very strong. Similar to information management practices, the CFI of 0.90 and RMSEA of 0.07 suggest good model fit, particularly given the complexity of the model. Given the highly significant $t$-values for each of the indicators, the construct seems to possess the qualities of convergent validity. Tests of discriminant validity show that, in 14 out of 15 cases, the chi-square statistic is statistically significant at $p$-levels better than 0.001 and one remaining case was also significant at $p = 0.05$ level. One can conclude that the measures achieve discriminant validity, and that these six dimensions of information behaviors and values can, indeed, be treated as distinct dimensions. Based on this analysis, it seems reasonable to conclude that information behaviors and values is a complex construct consisting of six distinct first-order factors (See Table A.6).

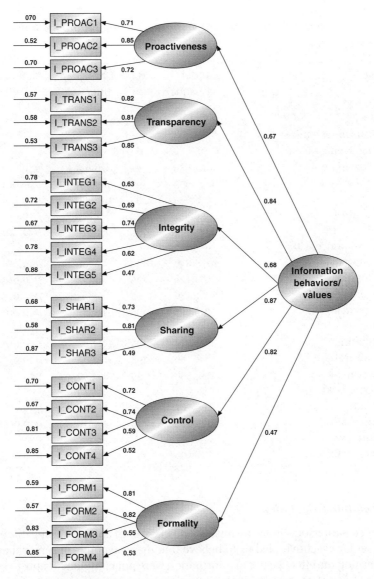

**Fig. A.4.  Factor Model of Information Behaviors and Values**

*Note*: CFI=0.90; RMSEA=0.07.

**Table A.6.** *Results of Discriminant Validity Tests: Information Behaviors and Values*

| Test | Model chi-square | d.f. | Chi-square difference | Significance |
|------|------------------|------|-----------------------|--------------|
| *Unconstrained model* | 1057.008 | 194 | | |
| *Constrained models* | | | | |
| Proactiveness with | | | | |
|   Transparency | 1095.849 | 195 | 38.841 | $p<0.001$ |
|   Integrity | 1247.659 | 195 | 190.651 | $p<0.001$ |
|   Sharing | 1158.094 | 195 | 101.086 | $p<0.001$ |
|   Control | 1126.457 | 195 | 69.449 | $p<0.001$ |
|   Formality | 1221.886 | 195 | 164.878 | $p<0.001$ |
| Transparency with | | | | |
|   Integrity | 1078.846 | 195 | 21.838 | $p<0.001$ |
|   Sharing | 1071.226 | 195 | 14.218 | $p<0.001$ |
|   Control | 1062.891 | 195 | 5.883 | $p<0.025$ |
|   Formality | 1103.595 | 195 | 46.587 | $p<0.001$ |
| Integrity with | | | | |
|   Sharing | 1158.774 | 195 | 101.766 | $p<0.001$ |
|   Control | 1146.216 | 195 | 89.208 | $p<0.001$ |
|   Formality | 1139.558 | 195 | 82.550 | $p<0.001$ |
| Sharing with | | | | |
|   Control | 1109.782 | 195 | 52.774 | $p<0.001$ |
|   Formality | 1177.483 | 195 | 120.475 | $p<0.001$ |
| Control with | | | | |
|   Formality | 1116.016 | 195 | 59.008 | $p<0.001$ |

### Information Orientation

As stated earlier, our literature review, and classroom and consulting discussions with senior executives, led us to believe that the viewpoints of senior managers concerning the effective use of information were not completely captured within the theories of each individual dimension (originating from one of the three schools of thought), and that senior managers had a more complex and comprehensive view of effective information use that integrated dimensions from each of the three schools. Our conceptual model indicated that IT practices, information management practices, and information behaviors and values must all be significantly present (or coaligned) in order to achieve superior business performance. From a practical perspective, this suggests that these dimensions are distinct and yet significantly related. This relationship or 'common core' of the three dimensions is the concept or construct of 'Information Orientation'.

Therefore, similar to our previously defined models, a set of first-order factors (IT practices, information management practices, and information behaviors and values) should be governed by the second-order construct of Information Orientation. However, different from the previous analyses, the first-order factors of this analysis have been established as being second-order factors across other sets of first-order factors. Within the framework of SEM, the estimation of such models, without collapsing item scales, is not possible. To estimate a model of this type, item measures must be collapsed, and then treated as an indicator.

Using the factor loadings obtained through SEM (see Fig. A.2 Fig. A.3, and Fig. A.4), the multiple items for each construct of IT practices, information management practices, and information behaviors and values were collapsed into a composite factor score. Factor scores represent measurement that is free from random error (Hair et al. 1992). They can also be viewed as the degree to which a respondent scores high on a group of items that, in turn, load high on a factor. Therefore, a respondent that scores high on several items that have heavy loadings for a factor will most certainly obtain a high score on that factor (Hair et al. 1992). The formula for computing the factor score of a respondent for a particular construct is as follows:

$$\sum_{i=1}^{n} (\lambda i * Si)$$

Where . . .
$n$=the number of items associated with the construct
$\lambda i$=the loading of item $i$ on the construct
$Si$=The observed score of item $i$

These calculations reduced the item set from 54 to 15. These 15 items were then used to assess the efficacy of capturing Information Orientation through the shared relationship (or shared variation) between IT practices, information management practices, and information behaviors and values.

Fig. 5 illustrates the result of the structural equation modeling (SEM). As shown, each of the item measures (factor scores) loads very highly in its respective first-order construct. In turn, the loadings between the first-order factors and the second-order factor of Information Orientation are very strong. This result, along with the favorable CFI of 0.90 and RMSEA of 0.09, suggest that this model is a good representation of the collected data. Highly significant $t$-values of the factor score items further suggest evidence for convergent validity.

In sum, it seems reasonable to conclude that Information Orientation is a distinct construct that is accurately measured by IT practices, information management practices, and information behaviors and values. This confirms our view that suggests that IT practices, information management practices, and information behaviors and values are important complementary components to a more complete measure of information use effectiveness. Given the

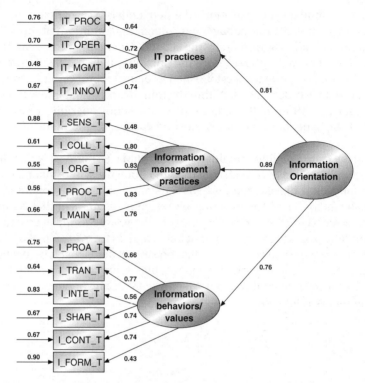

**Fig. A.5.  Factor Model of Information Orientation**

*Note*: CFI=0.90; RMSEA=0.09.

validation of a meaningful high-level Information Orientation second-order factor, it is now possible to assess its relationship with business performance.

## B.  Measurement of 'coalignment'

As briefly introduced above, this relationship between Information Orientation and business performance is tied to the notion of coalignment. Coalignment is a central concept within the field of strategic management and information systems research (Das, Zahra, and Warkentin 1991; Venkatraman 1989; Venkatraman and Camillus 1984). The basic theme of the concept has been widely and consistently articulated within the literature of both fields; however, derivation of a precise conceptualization in terms of empirical operationalization has proven rather complex (Venkatraman and Grant 1986). A number of statistical techniques are available for modeling coalignment; however, choosing the appropriate method depends on the degree of specificity of the theoretical relationship(s), and whether the concept of 'fit' is anchored to a particular criterion (e.g. effectiveness) (Venkatraman 1989). In some contexts, a precise functional form of the relationship can be specified. In others, certain variables are said to fit together without description of a precise form. Additionally, some researchers specify fit that is intrinsically related to a criterion variable; in others, a criterion-free specification is adopted.

Within the perspective of covariation, coalignment is a pattern of covariation or internal consistency among a set of theoretically related constructs. Operationalizing fit as covariation is based on the principle of factor analysis, the analysis technique also applied to test and establish the Information Orientation concept. Such analyses seek to explain covariation among a set of indicators (items) in terms of a smaller set of first-order factors. The covariation among first-order factors is explained by a still smaller set of second-order factors. Fit, as measured within this perspective, is specified as a second-order factor that explains the covariation in the first-order factors that are theoretically coaligned (Hair et al. 1992).

## C. Modeling coalignment within LISREL

Following similar studies by Venkatraman (1989, 1990), Venkatraman and Walker (1989), and Segars and Grover (1998), coalignment can be specified as a second-order factor where the first-order factors are the dimensions that are to be coaligned. The logic behind this modeling scheme is that the pattern of covariances among first-order factors can be explained by these separate and unobservable constructs. Such a conceptualization is readily operationalized and can be statistically evaluated within the framework of LISREL.

The analytical approach for establishing coalignment involves specification and testing of two competing models for explaining the covariances among first-order factors and the influence of coalignment on performance. The first of these models, a baseline or 'direct effects' model, specifies no second-order factor for explaining first-order correlations. An example of this model for three posited coaligned constructs ($\xi$) and a performance construct ($\eta$) is depicted in Fig. A.6. As shown, this model implies that each correlated dimension directly impacts the criterion (or performance) construct. In other words, each dimension is independent of the others in predicting performance.

The alternative or coalignment model specifies a second-order factor which governs the correlations among first-order factors. An example of this model is depicted in Fig. A.7. As shown, the three correlations among the first-order coalignment factors ($\phi$) are now represented by a second-order factor ($\xi$). This second-order factor is directly linked to the performance construct. It is important to note that the second-order factor is merely explaining the covariation among the first-order factors in a more parsimonious way (i.e. with more degrees of freedom). Therefore, even when the second-order factor is able to explain effectively the factor covariances, the goodness of fit can never be

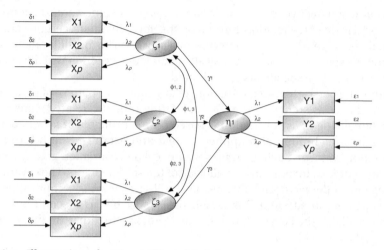

**Fig. A.6. Illustration of a Direct Effects Model**

better than a first-order model. In the present example, three correlations among first-order constructs ($\phi_1$, $\phi_2$, $\phi_3$) are not estimated in the coalignment model. However, an additional structural parameter ($\gamma_4$) is estimated between the second-order factor ($\xi$) and the performance construct ($\eta$). Therefore, the coalignment model captures the observed covariances with two additional degrees of freedom (or two fewer estimated parameters) than the baseline model.

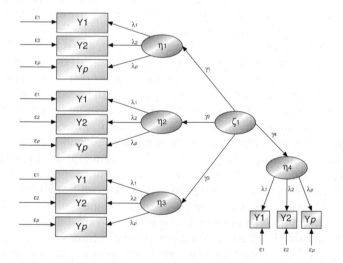

**Fig. A.7. Illustration of the Coalignment Model**

The comparison of fit between first- and second-order models is accomplished through examination of the Target coefficient $(T)$, as defined by Marsh and Hocevar (1985). This incremental fit measure is identical to Bentler and Bonnett's (1980) $\Delta$ in formulation and interpretation. If the model statistics of the coalignment model are not statistically different from the direct effects model (i.e. $T \geq .90$), then the coalignment model is chosen because of its parsimonious representation. Otherwise, the existence of coalignment is rejected. A complementary set of statistics is given by the significance of the parameters reflecting the second-order factor loadings ($\gamma_1$ to $\gamma_3$). If these are statistically significant, then they provide additional support for the existence of the 'second-order construct' of coalignment. The final structural parameter ($\gamma_4$) represents the impact of coalignment on performance. If significant, this parameter provides further support for coalignment and its performance implications.

## D. Model identification

As structural models become complex, there is no guaranteed approach for ensuring that model identification has been obtained (Bollen 1989). However, there are a number of diagnostics that can be utilized in gathering evidence of identification. Perhaps the most readily obtainable measure comes from the LISREL program itself. LISREL performs a simple test for identification during the estimation process and alerts the user to possible identification problems. However, as noted by Jöreskog and Sörbom (1989), this test is not robust in capturing all instances of unidentified models. In all models estimated in the present analysis, no such warnings were observed.

Another method of testing identification involves multiple estimation of the structural model with differing starting values. Programs such as LISREL, which estimate parameters of structural models, provide the researcher with a means of specifying an initial value for any coefficient. If a starting value is not specified, the program automatically computes it through likelihood or least-squares techniques (Jöreskog and Sörbom 1989). If the model is identified, the solution of each model should converge at the same point each time. Such an approach was undertaken in each of the estimated models of this analysis. In all cases, solutions converged at the same point and were identical, providing strong evidence of model identification.

In sum, this and previous sections have provided a frame within which the issues of interest are evaluated. Utilizing the covariation perspective, a theoretically truer and statistically more interpretable conceptualization of coalignment can be formed. Jöreskog and Sörbom's (1989) LISREL provides an analytical frame for empirically modeling these relationships. Utilizing both parsimonious fit indices and incremental model testing, formal assessment of the research questions is undertaken. Such an approach is consistent with current perspectives of structural modeling in the areas of marketing research

(Anderson and Gerbing 1988), psychology (Williams and Hazer 1986), and education (Jöreskog 1993).

## E. Information Orientation and performance: a coalignment perspective

The primary premiss for testing a higher-level construct such as Information Orientation is to establish a direct link between this construct and performance. In essence, the overarching premiss of our measurement model is that IT practices, information management practices, and information behaviors and values together, through a shared and more comprehensive indicator (Information Orientation), are better predictors of performance than any one or subset of these capabilities (dimensions). From a practical perspective, the contention is that superior performance is predicted by high levels of IT practices, information management practices, and information behaviors and values as captured in the common variation among these dimensions. This common variance forms a core that we term Information Orientation, which is directly associated with higher levels of business performance. To assess the validity of this contention, two path models must be estimated.

The first model implies that information management practices, information behaviors and values, and IT practices are independent in the prediction of performance. In other words, the three dimensions are not dependent upon each other when associated with performance.

The alternative model suggests that the three dimensions are coaligned or associated in their prediction of performance. This common core of variation is itself a definable source of variation (a second-order factor) that predicts performance more accurately than any unique variation among the first-order factors. In practical terms, this model suggests that an organization must score high on all three dimensions to realize superior performance. In other words, each of the dimensions is necessary but not sufficient for higher business performance. The dimensions form an orientation that is measured as the common core of the set of dimensions. This orientation, i.e. Information Orientation, is directly related to performance.

Given the establishment of Information Orientation in the prior section, we now turn our attention to establishing valid indicators of performance. Using the literature approach previously described, a four-item measure of performance was developed. As shown in Fig. A.8, the model estimates suggest that these items are relatively strong indicators of the performance construct. Importantly, it must be realized that performance measures contain inherently more error than other perceptual measures. Therefore, the estimated item reliabilities and measures of model fit (CFI=0.98, RMSEA=0.10) for this construct do seem robust in capturing important aspects of business performance (Cronbach's alpha of 0.74, all $t$-values are highly significant).

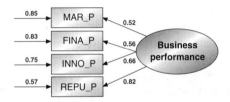

**Fig. A.8.   Factor Model of Business Performance**

*Note*: CFI=0.98; RMSEA=0.10.

Fig. A.9 and Fig. A.10 illustrate the measurement and structural model estimates of the SEM analysis for establishing the predictive power of Information Orientation. As shown in Fig. A.9, the direct paths from IT practices and information behaviors and values to performance are extremely low. The direct path from information management practices to business performance is even negative. In addition, the examination of the Target coefficient (*T*>.99) does not

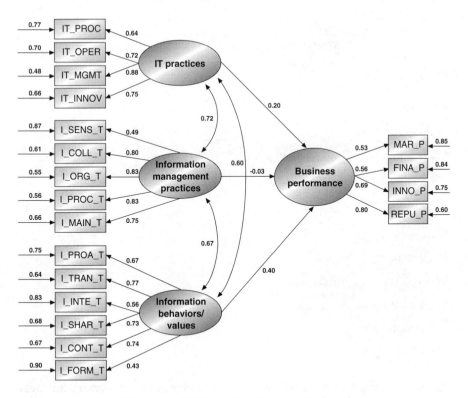

**Fig. A.9.   The Direct Effects Model Related to Business Performance**

*Note*: CFI=0.89; RMSEA=0.08.

show a statistical difference in terms of the model fit between the direct effects and coalignment models. Due to its better parsimonious representation, in this case we rejected the existence of the direct effects on business performance and accepted with more confidence the second-order, coalignment model as an accurate representation of the variation within the collected data.

Fig. A.10 illustrates the 'coalignment' model in which Information Orientation is positioned as a representation of the core variation, or 'interaction', among IT practices, information management practices, and information behaviors and values. As shown, this model is a vast improvement in terms of explaining the performance construct. The paths between first-order constructs and Information Orientation are very strong. In addition, measures of model fit (CFI=0.90, RMSEA=0.08) make it seem reasonable to accept the second-order model as an accurate representation of the variation within the collected data. Such results not only confirm the existence of Information Orientation, they suggest that this concept or construct is an important direct link in explaining business performance. As shown, the estimated path between

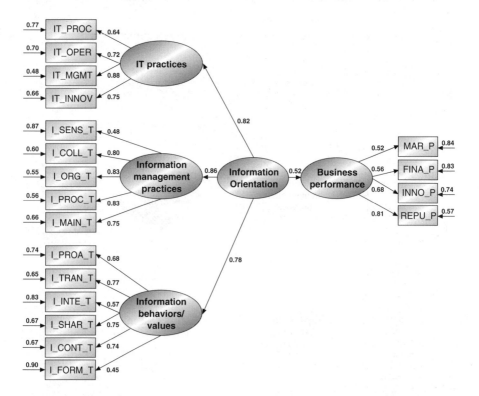

**Fig. A.10. Coalignment Model: Information Orientation Predicting Business Performance**

*Note*: CFI=0.90; RMSEA=0.08.

Information Orientation and performance is significant at 0.52. This result is strong, particularly given the difficulty of measuring performance and the complexity of the constructs that constitute Information Orientation.

From a practical perspective, these results suggest that while IT practices, information management practices, and information behaviors and values are distinct and valid dimensions, organizations that are advanced in managing IT practices, managing information practices, and creating behaviors and values that leverage the use of information tend to form a core of Information Orientation that is a major contributing factor to superior business performance. Second, these results show that Information Orientation represents a superior measure of effective information use, and should be practically applied in companies to diagnose and benchmark their current levels of information usage effectiveness. Finally, it can be surmised that, if a firm suboptimizes by over- or under-investing in any of these three dimensions, at the expense of one of the other dimensions, then sub-par business performance may result.

## F. Information Orientation and industry information leadership: a coalignment perspective

Along with assessing performance, the concept of industry information leadership is an important predictive test of the Information Orientation concept. In essence, this performance perspective looks beyond performance today and assesses the expectations of the firm to handle challenges in information use that may loom in the future. These challenges aim at creating information asymmetries (Desiraju and Moorthy 1997; Dewan and Min 1997; Nault 1998) in the marketplace, and make the company an industry leader in competing with information (Kettinger and Hackbarth 1999).

Accordingly, a literature review was conducted to establish important aspects of industry leadership. The result of this exercise suggested that three dimensions are important in depicting future industry leadership. These dimensions are:

1. *Leadership in the use of competitive information*—using information to better compete in the marketplace;
2. *Leadership in the use of customer information*—using information about customers, as well as interacting with customers, to provide better products and services and retain their business; and
3. *Leadership in the use of operational information*—using information that will boost operational effectiveness.

For these constructs, Cronbach's alpha values were 0.79 for competitive information, 0.86 for customer information, and 0.83 for operational information.

Similar to the development of Information Orientation, a second-order model was estimated to assess the efficacy of these measures in capturing the latent construct of future industry leadership.

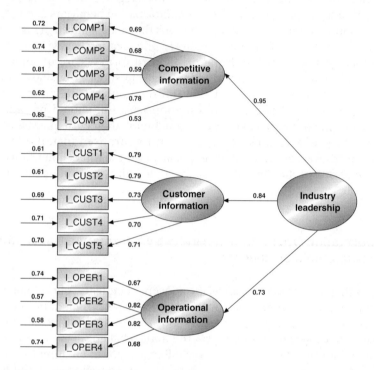

**Fig. A.11. Factor Model of Industry Leadership**

*Note*: CFI=0.97; RMSEA=0.05.

As illustrated in Fig. A.11, the results of model estimation strongly support the hypothesized model. Reliability estimates between item measures and first-order constructs are extremely high, as are path coefficients between the first-order dimensions and the second-order factor. Overall measures of model fit are very strong (CFI=0.97, RMSEA=0.05), also suggesting that this model is explaining a large amount of variation within the data. Since the *t*-values for each indicator are highly significant, convergent validity can also be concluded.

Similar to the Information Orientation construct, item measures of future industry orientation must be collapsed in order to use the construct as a performance criterion for Information Orientation. Therefore, factor scores were used to reduce the set of fourteen items to a set of three items (with an alpha value of 0.81).

Using the same framework of coalignment described in the previous section, two competing models were estimated to assess the predictive ability of

Information Orientation relative to future industry leadership in competing with information. Fig. A.12 and Fig. A.13 illustrate the results of this analysis. As shown in Fig. A.11, direct paths from the dimensions of information management practices, information behaviors and values, and IT practices are not significant in explaining industry leadership in competing with information.

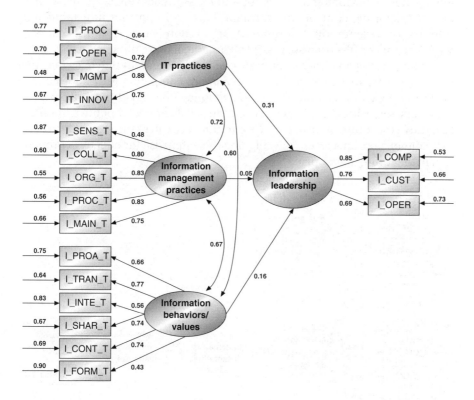

**Fig. A.12. The Direct Effects Model Related to Industry Leadership**

*Note*: CFI=0.90; RMSEA=0.08.

In contrast, the coalignment model depicted in Fig. A.13 provides a stronger fit for the observed data. In particular, the paths from first-order factors to Information Orientation are strong and overall model fit statistics (CFI=0.91, RMSEA=0.08) suggest good fit of the model to the data. Most importantly, the path from Information Orientation to industry leadership is strong, suggesting that Information Orientation is a significant factor in predicting industry leadership in competing with information.

From a practical perspective, the adoption of Fig. A.13 as an explanatory model of the observed data implies that the alignment or orientation of IT practices, information management practices, and information behaviors and values is a better predictor of industry leadership in competing with information than any single dimension or subset of dimensions. For managers, this suggests that good IT practices (described as process, operations, management, and innovation support), good information management practices (described as sensing, collecting, organizing, processing, and maintaining), as well as information behaviors and values (described as proactiveness, transparency, integrity, sharing, control, and formality) are all important in establishing Information Orientation. Information Orientation is a precondition of performance that results from successful alignment of these dimensions.

In sum, a focus on either IT or information management practices may not be sufficient for realizing industry leadership in competing with information. Further, a focus on IT and information management without information behaviors and values may result in less than satisfactory competitive information use in the future. Information Orientation recognizes the importance of all three dimensions in successfully aligning the enterprise for effective competition in the future marketplace.

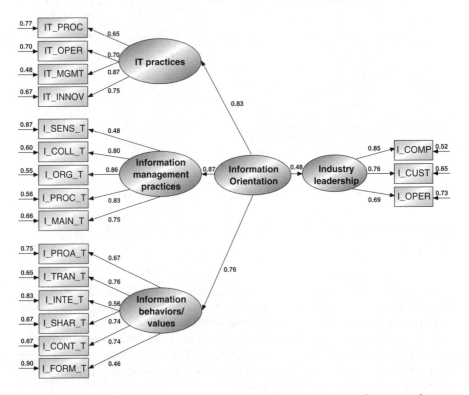

**Fig. A.13. Coalignment Model of Information Orientation Predicting Industry Leadership**

*Note*: CFI=0.91; RMSEA=0.08.

## G.  Cross-validation with two independent samples

While the findings in this Appendix have been reported based on one large sample of 1,009 senior managers, to further validate the strength of our findings in this section, we will demonstrate the IO model's invariance across two independent samples. By cross-validation we explicitly address a common concern about structural models with little or no regard for capitalization on chance factors or for generalizability to the population (e.g. Andersen and Gerbing 1988; Breckler 1990; Cliff 1983; Cudeck and Browne 1983).

Depending on the focus of one's study, there are different approaches to cross-validation in the analysis of covariance structures (Andersen and Gerbing 1988; Cudeck and Browne 1983). Our application is straightforward testing for evidence of multigroup invariance. Tests for invariance are applied to answer the question: does the factorial structure of a measuring instrument replicate across independent samples of the same population (Byrne 1994)? Answering this question addresses the issue of cross-validation. To conduct this test we applied the testing procedures provided by EQS from Multivariate Software Inc., since it allows for testing several assumptions about invariances multivariately at the same time.

The EQS approach tests the validity of equality constraints multivariately, rather than univariately, using the Lagrange Multiplier Test (LM Test). The incorporation of this strategy into the program, therefore, makes it unnecessary to compare a series of restrictive versus less restrictive models in order to identify the source of non-invariance in the model. As a consequence, it is also not necessary first to test for the equality of the measurement model and then to conduct tests of the structural model. All equality constraints can be put to the test simultaneously (Byrne 1994).

It is considered very appropriate to first establish baseline models for each group separately before testing hypotheses related to invariance. These models represent the best fitting ones to the data both from the perspective of parsimony and from the perspective of substantive meaningfulness. Hence, the models for IT practices, information management practices, and information behaviors and values were established for two independent samples separately ($N$=505, and $N$=504). In addition, baseline models for Information Orientation, IO predicting business performance, and IO predicting industry leadership in competing with information were established. All these models showed good model fit and very slight variation in factor loadings.

In the next step, simultaneous tests of the measurement and structural models were conducted for Information Orientation, IO predicting business performance, and IO predicting industry leadership. It is important to note that with these analyses, the equality of structural parameters is tested while concomitantly maintaining equality of measurement parameters across groups.

Again, the goodness-of-fit statistics were indicative of well-fitting models (CFI≥0.90 and RMSEA<0.65). While these findings suggest that cross-group equivalences generally hold, it is recommended to further investigate the LM $\chi^2$ test results bearing on the specified equality of the factor variances and covariances. Based on analyses of both univariate and multivariate LM $\chi^2$ statistics, it can be stated that all equality constraints on the three different models hold.

Given these findings of invariance, we can conclude that the factorial structure of our measuring instrument replicated satisfactorily across two large independent samples of the same population. This further supports the strong external validity of our findings.

## H.  Path analysis as causal analysis

To further investigate the causal relationships between the different dimensions of our structural equation models for discussion purposes and prescriptive suggestions in Chapter 8, four path models using SEM were tested. As indicated in Chapter 8, these path analyses were proposed and executed within each capability (dimension) of Information Orientation, IT practices (ITP, Model 1), information management practices (IMP, Model 2), and information behaviors and values (IBV, Model 3), and across these three capabilities (dimensions) using key sub-dimensions (Model 4). Test findings for 'goodness of fit' with all these four models show reasonable fit for all these models from 'moderate' (IMP—Model 2: CFI=0.89, RMSEA=0.08; IBV—Model 3: CFI=0.89, RMSEA=0.07) to 'good' (ITP—Model 1: CFI=0.92, RMSEA=0.09; cross-dimensions—Model 4: CFI=0.93, RMSEA=0.07). While the CFI for IMP and IBV models are slightly below the rigorous statistical standards applied in this study (CFI>0.90), further examination of other fit indices such as AGFI and RMSEA indicates that we can safely assume the reasonable fit of these models.

As we previously demonstrated in testing the causal relationship between Information Orientation and business performance in the coalignment model, path analysis using SEM provides possibilities for causal determination among sets of research variables. Unlike correlation analysis which can only measure the linear association between two variables, using path analysis it is possible to postulate a causal relationship and determine the directionality and strength of this relationship.

For example, in Fig. 8.1, depicting the causal path for ITP, the straight line running from IT for operational support to IT for business process support represents the direct influences of the IT for operational support variable upon IT for business process support . There are also indirect ways of influence, as illustrated in Fig. 8.1. Hence, variables recognized as effects of certain antecedent factors may, in turn, serve as causes for subsequent variables. For example, the IT for business process support and IT for innovation support factors are both caused by IT for operational support, which in turn influences IT for management support. Thus IT for management support is affected indirectly by IT for operational support, in addition to two direct effects from IT for innovation support and IT for business process support. As a result, IT for management support can be considered as the most consequent variable that is most influenced by other variables within this capability, and is probably most difficult to control due to its dependent nature on other antecedents. Or, stated in prescriptive terms, executives have to manage the antecedent sub-dimensions well in order to influence positively IT for management support.

Path coefficients in the models reflect the amount of direct contribution of a given variable on another variable when effects of other related variables are taken into account. Significance of these coefficients was tested using $t$-tests and all show statistical significance at the $p=0.01$ level. The relative magnitude $(0<\rho<1)$ of causal linkage can be observed through comparing the path coefficients. For example, we can conclude that IT for management support is more strongly influenced by IT for innovation support (0.64) than IT for business process support (0.35).

The technique of path analysis, however, is not a method of discovering causal laws, but a procedure for giving a quantitative interpretation of an assumed theoretical causal system as it operates within a given environment. Over-interpretation or generalization of the findings should be avoided. However, for practical and prescriptive purposes they represent a valuable starting point of discussion to guide an improvement program for effective information use in companies.

## I.  Correlational analysis

In a few cases, where exploratory as opposed to confirmatory objectives drove our analysis, we used correlational analysis. These correlations were executed within and between the different constructs of the study, and were calculated at the item and the composite factor score levels. Correlations are used to better understand the strongest relations between dimensions or items. It should be noted that correlation does not imply a causal relationship. A correlation indicates the extent of association between two variables. In essence, can it be reliably said that when one variable moves in a particular direction, another variable will move in a predictable direction? A correlation of 1 would mean that the two variables are perfectly correlated and always move in sync in a set direction. Given the uncertainty of nature such perfect correlation is almost unheard off. In the social sciences, where ideas and environments are much more complex and less easily controlled than the physical sciences, correlations above .5 are usually considered high association, above .4 fairly high association, and above .3 moderate association. Only correlations that were significant at the 0.01 level were examined.

## J.  Analysis group differences

To further examine our findings, we tested whether different groups of senior managers in our sample perceive IT practices, information management practices, and information behaviors and values differently. In particular, we were interested whether differences in perceptions exist between senior managers from Europe and North America, between senior managers from service versus production-oriented industries, and between senior managers that hold different positions in their companies.

### Analysis by region

To test whether senior managers coming from different geographical regions perceive IT practices, information management practices, and information behaviors and values differently, two-sample $t$-tests on the composite factor scores of the respective dimensions were conducted. Table A.7 depicts the respective group statistics.

**Table A.7.**  *Group Statistics for Regional Differences*

| Group | $N$ | Mean | Std. deviation | Std. error mean |
|---|---|---|---|---|
| IT practices | | | | |
|   Europe | 660 | 33.4287 | 7.4074 | .2883 |
|   North America | 218 | 32.6371 | 8.3689 | .5668 |
| Information management practices | | | | |
|   Europe | 660 | 42.8490 | 9.0992 | .3542 |
|   North America | 219 | 42.4829 | 9.7614 | .6596 |
| Information behaviors and values | | | | |
|   Europe | 641 | 50.9199 | 8.5970 | .3396 |
|   North America | 217 | 49.6849 | 8.8127 | .5982 |

Table A.8 shows the test results. Levene's Test for Equality of Variances, which tests whether the *spread* of the groups differs, is displayed first. The significance of this test directs the researchers to use the appropriate $t$-testing method. If the significance is lower than a specific cutoff value (we used 0.05), then a separate-variance $t$-test, which does not assume equal variances, should be used. Otherwise, the pooled-variance $t$-test (assuming equal variances) is appropriate. In this case, the separate-variance $t$-test has to be used for IT practices. The $t$-test significance values are far greater than 0.001, indicating that *there do not exist any differences* in perceptions of IT practices, information management

Table A.8.  *Independent Samples Test for Regions*

| | Levene's test for equality of variances | | t-test for equality of means | | | | | 95% confidence interval of the difference | |
| --- | --- | --- | --- | --- | --- | --- | --- | --- | --- |
| | F | Sig. | t | d.f. | Sig. (2-tailed) | Mean difference | Std. error difference | Lower | Upper |
| **IT practices** | | | | | | | | | |
| Equal variances assumed | 5.943 | .015 | 1.323 | 876 | .186 | .7916 | .5981 | −.3823 | 1.9656 |
| Equal variances not assumed | | | 1.245 | 336.418 | .214 | .7916 | .6359 | −.4593 | 2.0425 |
| **Information management practices** | | | | | | | | | |
| Equal variances assumed | 1.869 | .172 | .507 | 877 | .613 | .3661 | .7228 | −1.0524 | 1.7847 |
| Equal variances not assumed | | | .489 | 352.150 | .625 | .3661 | .7487 | −1.1063 | 1.8386 |
| **Information behaviors and values** | | | | | | | | | |
| Equal variances assumed | .630 | .428 | 1.817 | 856 | .069 | 1.2350 | .6795 | −9.87E−02 | 2.5687 |
| Equal variances not assumed | | | 1.795 | 364.815 | .073 | 1.2350 | .6879 | −.1177 | 2.5877 |

practices, and information behaviors and values between senior managers from Europe and North America.

### Analysis by industry

For analysis of industry differences, a comparison of companies from more production-oriented industries was made with companies from more information intensive service industries. Responses from senior managers in the chemical industry and electric and electronic equipment industries were combined to form a representative production-oriented industry group 'ChemElec'. As a comparison group, responses from companies in the banking and insurance industries where collapsed to establish the service-oriented industry group 'BankInsu'.

Similar to the analysis of regions, two-sample *t*-tests were executed to test for group differences on the dimensions IT practices, information management practices, and information behaviors and values. The group statistics are shown in Table A.9.

**Table A.9.** *Group Statistics for Industry Differences*

| Group | N | Mean | Std. deviation | Std. error mean |
|---|---|---|---|---|
| IT practices | | | | |
| BankInsu | 265 | 35.2751 | 8.4373 | .5183 |
| ChemElec | 156 | 29.8728 | 6.3647 | .5096 |
| Information management practices | | | | |
| BankInsu | 267 | 45.4222 | 9.6078 | .5880 |
| ChemElec | 157 | 39.8080 | 9.2601 | .7390 |
| Information behaviors and values | | | | |
| BankInsu | 258 | 52.6551 | 9.4542 | .5886 |
| ChemElec | 154 | 46.1867 | 7.1898 | .5794 |

Following the same line of argument as laid out in the previous discussion, we can conclude that senior managers from production and service-oriented companies *do perceive* IT practices, information management practices, and information behaviors and values somewhat differently (see Table A.10). The group means in Table A.9 show that the service-oriented industries tend to have higher factor scores on each of the dimensions. This finding can most likely be explained by higher information intensity within service-oriented industries. Firms in more information intensive industries may possess higher levels of Information Orientation as a result of a maturation process that that takes place

Table A.10. *Independent Samples Test for Industries*

| | Levene's test for equality of variances | | t-test for equality of means | | | | | 95% confidence interval of the difference | |
| --- | --- | --- | --- | --- | --- | --- | --- | --- | --- |
| | F | Sig. | t | d.f. | Sig. (2-tailed) | Mean difference | Std. error difference | Lower | Upper |
| IT practices | | | | | | | | | |
| Equal variances assumed | 13.052 | .000 | 6.920 | 419 | .000 | 5.4023 | .7806 | 3.8678 | 6.9367 |
| Equal variances not assumed | | | 7.432 | 394.009 | .000 | 5.4023 | .7268 | 3.9733 | 6.8312 |
| Information management practices | | | | | | | | | |
| Equal variances assumed | .676 | .412 | 5.888 | 422 | .000 | 5.6142 | .9535 | 3.7400 | 7.4884 |
| Equal variances not assumed | | | 5.945 | 336.849 | .000 | 5.6142 | .9444 | 3.7565 | 7.4719 |
| Information behaviors and values | | | | | | | | | |
| Equal variances assumed | 12.242 | .001 | 7.319 | 410 | .000 | 6.4684 | .8837 | 4.7312 | 8.2056 |
| Equal variances not assumed | | | 7.832 | 386.621 | .000 | 6.4684 | .8259 | 4.8446 | 8.0922 |

Table A.11.  *Group Statistics for Position Differences*

| | N | Mean | Std. deviation | Std. error | 95% confidence interval for mean | | Minimum | Maximum |
|---|---|---|---|---|---|---|---|---|
| | | | | | Lower bound | Upper bound | | |
| **IT Practices** | | | | | | | | |
| CEO | 205 | 34.2983 | 7.8208 | .5462 | 33.2213 | 33.3753 | 8.21 | 54.55 |
| CFO etc. | 138 | 32.0526 | 7.2345 | .6158 | 30.8348 | 33.2704 | 8.88 | 54.86 |
| CIO etc. | 115 | 32.5613 | 7.9568 | .7420 | 31.0915 | 34.0312 | 10.78 | 48.13 |
| Total | 458 | 33.1855 | 7.7348 | .3614 | 32.4752 | 33.8958 | 8.21 | 54.86 |
| **Information management practices** | | | | | | | | |
| CEO | 209 | 42.8539 | 9.3332 | .6456 | 41.5812 | 44.1266 | 10.91 | 70.29 |
| CFO etc. | 139 | 42.8304 | 8.4956 | .7206 | 41.4056 | 44.2552 | 19.05 | 64.57 |
| CIO etc. | 110 | 40.8482 | 10.2997 | .9820 | 38.9018 | 42.7946 | 15.58 | 69.49 |
| Total | 458 | 42.3650 | 9.3527 | .4370 | 41.5062 | 43.2239 | 10.91 | 70.29 |
| **Information behaviors and values** | | | | | | | | |
| CEO | 201 | 51.5596 | 9.0976 | .6417 | 50.2943 | 52.8250 | 10.90 | 71.40 |
| CFO etc. | 133 | 50.2051 | 8.5128 | .7381 | 48.7449 | 51.6652 | 29.22 | 67.63 |
| CIO etc. | 112 | 47.2664 | 9.5475 | .9022 | 45.4788 | 49.0541 | 23.59 | 65.28 |
| Total | 446 | 50.0776 | 9.1879 | .4351 | 49.2225 | 50.9326 | 10.90 | 71.40 |

as information intensive companies begin to measure, monitor, and improve on their information usage effectiveness to meet competitive pressures.

## Analysis by position

Last, we wanted to see whether senior managers who hold different positions in their company perceive IT practices, information management practices, and information behaviors and values differently. From the total sample of 1,009 senior managers, we extracted three groups. The 'CEO' group were those managers whose position-title explicitly included the term 'CEO', 'president', or 'managing director'. Second, the 'CFO etc.' group was formed by senior managers who were either CFOs or head of the finance or controlling function of their respective company or business unit. Third, we chose CIOs, CTOs, information systems, IT, and information management directors to establish the 'CIO etc.' group. Since three groups were to be compared, we used analysis of variance (ANOVA) to test for differences in means.

Table A.11 lists the descriptive statistics of the factor scores for IT practices, information management practices, and information behaviors and values for the three position groups. The slight differences in the group means are not significant, as can be concluded from reviewing the results in the ANOVA table presented in Table A.12. Only the $F$ statistic for the factor score of information

**Table A.12.**  *ANOVA Results for Position Differences*

|  | Sum of squares | d.f. | Mean square | $F$ | Sig. |
|---|---|---|---|---|---|
| IT Practices |  |  |  |  |  |
|   Between groups | 475.770 | 2 | 237.885 | 4.029 | .018 |
|   Within groups | 26865.297 | 455 | 59.045 |  |  |
|   Total | 27341.067 | 457 |  |  |  |
| Information management practices |  |  |  |  |  |
|   Between groups | 333.139 | 2 | 166.570 | 1.912 | .149 |
|   Within groups | 39641.768 | 455 | 87.125 |  |  |
|   Total | 39974.907 | 457 |  |  |  |
| Information behaviors and values |  |  |  |  |  |
|   Between groups | 1328.737 | 2 | 664.368 | 8.122 | .000 |
|   Within groups | 36237.110 | 443 | 81.799 |  |  |
|   Total | 37565.846 | 445 |  |  |  |

behaviors and values shows significance. The $F$ statistic for IT practices indicates significance level below the 0.02 level. Generally this finding indicates that senior executives do not differ significantly in their understandings of the three dimensions that make up IO.

## 6. FOLLOW-UP INTERVIEWS

To more fully understand the meaning and implications of the results of the quantitative survey research data, project researchers implemented an aggressive 'active learning' strategy. Companies in which survey results indicated particularly high or low scores in areas of study interest were contacted and invited to participate further in the research as case studies. A total of twenty-four companies have been involved in this effort. Contact has also been made by telephone with individual respondents to obtain further insights into important research findings. In addition, five companies requested project researchers to present their study findings to their corporate management group.

All of these opportunities have contributed to the richness of the study's findings and have added real world examples of their importance and implications which are offered in the book.

# BIBLIOGRAPHY

ABELL, DEREK F. (1993). *Managing with Dual Strategies: Mastering the Present. Preempting the Future.* New York: The Free Press.

ALPAR, P., and KIM, M. (1990). 'A Microeconomic Approach to the Measurement of Information Technology Value,' *Journal of Management Information Systems,* 7 (2): 55–69, Fall.

ALTER, STEVEN (1980). *Decision Support Systems: Current Practice and Continuing Challenges.* Reading, Mass.: Addison-Wesley Publishing.

ANDERSON, J. C. (1987). 'An Approach for Confirmatory Measurement and Structural Equation Modeling of Organizational Properties,' *Management Science,* 33: 525–41.

—— and GERBING, D. W. (1988). 'Structural Equation Modeling in Practice: A Review and Recommended Two-Step Approach,' *Psychological Bulletin,* 103: 411–23.

ANONYMOUS (1997). 'Productivity: Lost in Cyberspace,' *The Economist,* Sept. 13.

ANTHONY, ROBERT N. (1965). *Planning and Control Systems: A Framework for Analysis.* Boston: Harvard Business School Division of Research Press.

ARGYRIS, CHRIS, and SCHÖN, DONALD A. (1978). *Organizational Learning: A Theory of Action Perspective.* Reading, Mass.: Addison-Wesley Publishing.

ASHBY, W. R. (1956). *An Introduction to Cybernetics.* London: Chapman & Hall.

BAGOZZI, R. P., and PHILLIPS, L. W. (1982). 'Representing and Testing Organizational Theories: A Holistic Construal,' *Administrative Science Quarterly,* 27: 459–89.

—— YI, Y., and PHILLIPS, L. W. (1991). 'Assessing Construct Validity in Organizational Research,' *Administrative Science Quarterly,* 36: 421–58.

BAKER, G. (1997). 'Anatomy of a Miracle,' *Financial Times,* June 20: 17.

BANKER, R. D., and KAUFMAN, R. J. (1988). 'Strategic Contributions of Information Technology: An Empirical Study of ATM Networks,' *Proceedings of the 9th International Conference on Information Systems, Minneapolis, Nov. 30–Dec. 3* (Atlanta: ICIS Administrative Office), 28–45.

BANNISTER, R. J., and JESUTHASAN, R. (1997). 'Is your Company Ready for Value-Based Management?' *Journal of Business Strategy,* Mar.–Apr.: 12–15.

BARKI, HENRI, and HARTWICK, JON (1989). 'Rethinking the Concept of User Involvement,' *MIS Quarterly,* Mar.: 53–63.

BEARDEN, W. O., SHARMA, S., and TEEL, J. E. (1982). 'Sample Size Effects on Chi Square and Other Statistics Used in Evaluating Causal Models,' *Journal of Marketing Research,* 19: 425–30.

BECKER, THOMAS E. (1998). 'Integrity in Organizations: Beyond Honesty and Conscientiousness,' *Academy of Management Review*, 23 (1): 154–61.

BELL, DESMOND, MCBRIDE, PHILIP, and WILSON, GEORGE (1994). *Managing Quality.* Oxford: Butterworth-Heinemann Ltd.

BENDER, D. H. (1986). 'Financial Impact of Information Processing,' *Journal of Management Information Systems*, 3 (2): 23–32.

BENIGER, JAMES R. (1986). *The Control Revolution: Technological and Economic Origins of the Information Society.* Cambridge, Mass.: Harvard University Press.

BENTLER, P. M. (1995). *EQS Structural Equations Program Manual.* Encino, Calif.: Multivariate Software, Inc.

—— and BONNETT, D. G. (1980). 'Significance Tests and Goodness of Fit in the Analysis of Covariance Structures,' *Psychological Bulletin*, 88: 588–606.

BENTLER, R. I. (1986). 'Structural Modeling and Psychometrika: A Historical Perspective on Growth and Achievements,' *Psychometrika*, 51: 35–51.

BEST, DAVID (ed.) (1996). *The Fourth Resource: Information and its Management.* Aldershot: Aslib Gower.

BHARADWAJ, T., BHARADWAJA, S., and KONSYNSKI, B. (1999). 'Information Technology Effects on Firm Performance as Measured by Tobin q.,' *Management Science*, 45 (6): 1008–24.

BOLLEN, K. A. (1989). *Structural Equations with Latent Variables.* New York: John Wiley & Sons.

BOSTROM, R. P., and HEINEN, J. S. (1977a). 'MIS Problems and Failures: A Sociotechnical Perspective. Part 1: The Causes,' *MIS Quarterly*, 1 (3): 123–43.

—— (1977b). 'Part 2: The Application of Socio-technical Theory,' *MIS Quarterly*, 1 (4): 12–33.

BOURGEOIS, J. L. (1980). 'Performance and Consensus,' *Strategic Management Journal*, 1: 227–48.

—— (1984). 'Strategic Management and Determinism,' *Academy of Management Review*, 9: 586–96.

BRADY, T., CAMERON, R., TARGETT, D., and BEAUMONT, C. (1992). 'Strategic IT Issues: The Views of Some Major IT Investors,' *Journal of Strategic Information Systems*, 1 (4): 183–9, Sept.

BRECKLER, S. J. (1990). 'Applications of Covariance Structure Modeling in Psychology: Cause for Concern?' *Psychological Bulletin*, 107: 206–73.

BROADBENT, M., and LOFGREN, H. (1993). 'Information Delivery: Identifying Priorities, Performance, and Value,' *Information Processing and Management*, 29 (6): 683–701.

BROWN, CAROL V., and MAGILL, SHARON L. (1994). 'Alignment of the IS Functions with the Enterprise: Towards a Model of Antecedents,' *MIS Quarterly*, Dec.: 371–403.

BROWN, LESLEY (ed.) (1993). *The New Shorter Oxford English Dictionary.* Oxford: Oxford University Press.

BRYNJOLFSSON, ERIK (1993). 'The Productivity Paradox of Information Technology,' *Communications of the ACM* 36 (12): 67–77.

—— and HITT, LORIN (1996). 'Paradox Lost? Firm-Level Evidence on the Returns to Information Systems Spending,' *Management Science*, 42 (4): 541–58.

BYRNE, B. M. (1994). *Structural Equation Modeling with EQS and EQS/Windows: Basic Concepts, Applications, and Programming.* London: Sage Publications.

CAUDLE, SHARON L., and MARCHAND, DONALD A., with BRETSCHNEIDER, STUART I., FLETCHER, PATRICIA T., and THURMAIER, KURT M. (1989). *A National Study of State Government Information Resources Management*. Syracuse, NY: Syracuse University, School of Information Studies, Center for Science and Technology.

CAUDRON, SHARI (1997). 'Here's to You! For Becoming your Company's Most Important Partner,' *Workforce*, Jan: 72–81.

CECIL, J., and GOLDSTEIN, M. (1990). 'Sustaining Competitive Advantage from IT,' *McKinsey Quarterly*, 4: 20–7.

CHAN, YOLANDE E., HUFF, SID L., BARCLAY, DONALD W., and COPELAND, DUNCAN G. (1997). 'Business Strategic Orientation, Information Systems Strategic Orientation, and Strategic Alignment,' *Information Systems Research*, 8 (2): 125–50.

CHARAN, RAM (1991). 'How Networks Reshape Organizations for Results,' *Harvard Business Review*, 69 (5): 104–15.

CHARKRAVARTHY, B. S. (1986). 'Measuring Strategic Performance,' *Strategic Management Journal*, 7 (5): 437–58.

CHILD, J. (1972). 'Organization Structure, Environment, and Performance: The Role of Strategic Choice,' *Sociology*, 6: 1–22.

CHOO, CHUN WEI (1998). *The Knowing Organization: How Organizations Use Information to Construct Meaning, Create Knowledge, and Make Decisions*. New York: Oxford University Press.

CLEMONS, ERIC K. (1986). 'Information Systems for Sustainable Competitive Advantage,' *Information and Management*, 11 (3): 131–6.

—— (1991). 'Investment in Information Technology,' *Communications of the ACM* 34 (1): 22–36, Jan.

—— and ROW, MICHAEL C. (1991). 'Sustaining IT Advantage: The Role of Structural Differences,' *MIS Quarterly*, 15 (3): 275–92.

—— and WEBER, B. W. (1990). 'Strategic Information Technology Investments: Guidelines for Decision Making,' *Journal of Management Information Systems*, 7 (2): 9–28, Fall.

CLIFF, N. (1983). 'Some Cautions Concerning the Application of Causal Modeling Methods,' *Multivariate Behavioral Research*, 18: 115–26.

COOPER, ROBIN, and KAPLAN, ROBERT S. (1988). 'Measure Costs Right: Make the Right Decisions,' *Harvard Business Review*, 66 (5): 96–103.

CRON, W. L., and SOBOL, M. G. (1983). 'The Relationship between Computerization and Performance: A Strategy for Maximizing the Economic Benefits of Computerization,' *Information and Management*, 6 (3): 171–81, June.

CUDECK, R., and BROWNE, M. W. (1983). 'Cross–validation of Covariance Structures,' *Multivariate Behavioral Research*, 18: 147–67.

CURRIE, W. (1994). 'The Strategic Management of Large Scale IT Projects in the Financial Sector,' *New Technology Work and Employment*, 9 (1): 19–29.

CYERT, RICHARD M., and MARCH, JAMES G. (1963). *A Behavioral Theory of the Firm*. Englewood Cliffs, NJ: Prentice Hall.

DAS, S. R., ZAHRA, S. A., and WARKENTIN, M. E. (1991). 'Integrating the Content and Process of MIS Strategic Planning with Competitive Strategy,' *Decision Sciences*, 22 (1): 953–84.

D'Aveni, Richard A., and Gunther, Robert (1994). *Hyper-competition: Managing the Dynamics of Strategic Manœuvering.* New York: The Free Press.

Davenport, Thomas H. (1997). *Information Ecology: Mastering the Information and Knowledge Environment.* New York: Oxford University Press.

—— and Beers, Michael C. (1995). 'Managing Information about Processes,' *Journal of Management Information Systems,* 12 (1): 57–80.

—— Eccles, Robert G., and Prusak, Laurence (1992). 'Information Politics,' *Sloan Management Review,* Fall: 53–65.

Davis, Fred D., Bagozzi, Richard P., and Warshaw, Paul R. (1989). 'User Acceptance of Computer Technology: A Comparison of Two Theoretical Models,' *Management Science,* 35 (8): 982–1003.

Davis, Gordon B., and Olson, Margrethe H. (1974). *Management Information Systems: Conceptual Foundations, Structure, and Development.* New York: McGraw-Hill.

Davis, Keith (1967). *Human Relations at Work: The Dynamics of Organizational Behavior.* New York: McGraw-Hill.

de Geus, Arie (1997). *The Living Company.* Boston: Harvard Business School Press.

Dervin, B. (1992). 'From the Mind's Eye of the "User": The Sense-Making Qualitative-Quantitative Methodology,' in J. D. Glazier and R. R. Powell (eds.), *Qualitative Research in Information Management.* Englewood, Conn.: Libraries Unlimited, 61–84.

Deschamps, Jean-Philippe (2000). 'From Information and Knowledge to Innovation,' in D. Marchand (ed.), *Competing with Information,* London: John Wiley & Sons Ltd., 127–48.

Desiraju, Ramarao, and Moorthy, Sridhar (1997). 'Managing a Distribution Channel under Asymmetric Information with Performance Requirements,' *Management Science,* 43 (12): 1628–44.

Dess, G. G., and Robinson, R. B. (1984). 'Measuring Organizational Performance in the Absence of Objective Measures: The Case of Privately-Held Firms and Conglomerate Business Units,' *Strategic Management Journal,* 5: 265–73.

Dewan, Sanjeev, and Min Chung-ki Min (1997). 'The Substitution of Information Technology for Other Factors of Production: A Firm Level Analysis,' *Management Science,* 43 (12): 1660–75.

Downes, Larry, and Mui, Chunka (1998). *Unleashing the Killer App: Digital Strategies for Market Dominance.* Boston: Harvard Business School Press.

Drucker, Peter F. (1988). 'The Coming of the New Organization,' *Harvard Business Review,* 66 (1): 45–53.

—— (1989). *The New Realities.* New York: Harper & Row.

—— (1993). *Post-capitalist Society.* New York: Harper Business.

Earl, Michael J. (1999). 'Every Business is an Information Business,' *Financial Times,* London, Special Series on Mastering Information Management, Feb. 1.

Evans, Philip B., and Wurster, Thomas S. (1997). 'Strategy and the New Economics of Information,' *Harvard Business Review,* 75 (5): 71–81.

Farbey, B., Land, F. and Targett, D. (1992). 'Evaluating Investments in IT,' *Journal of Information Technology,* 7 (2): 100–12.

Fenny, D. F., Edwards, B. R. and Simpson, K. M. (1992). 'Understanding the CEO/CIO Relationship,' *MIS Quarterly,* 16: 435–48.

FLETCHER, PATRICIA T., BRETSCHNEIDER STUART I., MARCHAND, DONALD A., with ROSENBAUM, HOWARD, and BERTOT, JOHN CARLO (1992). *Managing Information Technology: Transforming County Governments in the 1990s.* Syracuse, NY: Syracuse University, School of Information Studies, Center for Science and Technology.

FRIEDRICKSON, J. W., and MITCHELL, T. R. (1984). 'Strategic Decision Processes: Comprehensiveness and Performance in an Industry with an Unstable Environment,' *Academy of Management Journal,* 27 (2): 399–423.

GALBRAITH, JAY R. (1973). *Designing Complex Organizations.* Reading, Mass.: Addison-Wesley Publishing.

—— (1977). *Organization Design.* Reading, Mass.: Addison–Wesley Publishing.

—— (1994). *Competing with Flexible Lateral Organizations.* Reading, Mass.: Addison-Wesley Publishing.

—— (1995). *Designing Organizations: An Executive Briefing on Strategy, Structure, and Process.* San Francisco: Jossey-Bass Publishers.

—— and LAWLER, EDWARD E., and associates (1993). *Organizing for the Future. The New Logic for Managing Complex Organizations.* San Francisco: Jossey-Bass Publishers.

GALLIERS, ROBERT. D. (1995). 'A Manifesto for Information Management Research,' *British Journal of Management,* 6, Special Issue 4: S45–S52.

GERTH, H. H., and MILLS, C. WRIGHT (eds.) (1946). *From Max Weber: Essays in Sociology.* New York: Oxford University Press.

GORRY, G. ANTHONY, and SCOTT MORTON, MICHAEL S. (1971). 'A Framework for Management Information Systems,' *Sloan Management Review,* 13 (1): 55–70.

—— (1989). 'A Framework for Management Information Systems,' *Sloan Management Review,* Spring: 49–61.

GRAY, S. J., and RADEBAUGH, L. H. (1997). *International Accounting and Multinational Enterprises.* New York: John Wiley & Sons.

GROVER, VARUN, and KETTINGER, WILLIAM J. (eds.) (2000). *Process Think: Winning Perspectives for Business Change in the Information Age.* Harrisburg, Ill.: Idea Group Publishing.

—— PREMKUMAR, G., and SEGARS, A. H. (1993), 'The Impact of Environmental Characteristics on Managerial Information Scanning: An Experimental Study,' *Journal of Management Systems,* 5 (1): 1–19.

—— JEUNG, SEONG, KETTINGER, WILLIAM J., and LEE, CHOONG (1993). 'The Chief Information Officer: A Study of Managerial Roles,' *Journal of Management Information Systems,* 10 (2): 737–66.

GURBAXANI, V., and WHANG, S. (1991). 'The Impact of Information Systems on Organizations and Markets,' *Communications of the ACM* 34 (1): 59–73.

HAGEL, JOHN, and ARMSTRONG, ARTHUR G. (1997). *Net Gain: Expanding Markets through Virtual Economies.* Boston: Harvard Business School Press.

—— and SINGER, MARC (1999). *Net Worth: Shaping Markets When Customers Make the Rules.* Boston: Harvard Business School Press.

HAIR, J. F., ANDERSON, R. E., TATHAM, R. L., and BLACK, W. C. (1992). *Multivariate Data Analysis with Readings.* New York: Macmillan Publishing.

HAMBRICK, DONALD C., and MASON, PHYLLIS A. (1984). 'Upper Echelon: The Organization as a Reflection of its Top Managers,' *Academy of Management Review,* 9 (2): 191–206.

HAMBRICK, DONALD C. et al. (1996). 'The Influence of Top Management Team Hetero-geneity on Firms' Competitive Moves,' *Administrative Science Quarterly*, 42 (4): 659–84.

HAMEL, GARY, and PRAHALAD, C. K. (1994). *Competing for the Future: Breakthrough Strategies for Seizing Control of your Industry and Creating the Markets of Tomorrow*. Boston: Harvard Business School Press.

HAMILTON, STEWART (1998). 'Accountants Gather Round Different Standards', Mastering Global Business Series, *Financial Times*, Mar. 20: 12–13.

HAMMER, MICHAEL, and CHAMPY, JAMES (1993). *Reengineering the Corporation: A Manifesto for Business Revolution*. London: Nicholas Brealey Publishing Ltd.

HARKNESS, W., KETTINGER, W. J., and SEGARS, A. H. (1996). 'Sustaining Process Improvements and Innovation in the Information Services Function: Lessons Learned at the Bose Corporation,' *MIS Quarterly*, 20 (3): 349–68.

HENDERSON, JOHN C., and VENKATRAMAN, N. (1989). 'Strategic Alignment: A Framework for Strategic Information Technology Management,' Center for Information Systems Research, Working Paper No. 190, Massachussetts Institute of Technology, Cambridge, Mass.; Aug.

HESKETT, JAMES L., SASSER, W. EARL, Jr., and SCHLESINGER, LEONARD A. (1997). *The Service Profit Chain: How Leading Companies Link Profit and Growth to Loyalty, Satisfaction, and Value*. New York: The Free Press.

HIGGINS, H. N. (1998). 'Analyst Forecasting Performance in Seven Countries,' *Financial Analyst Journal*, May–June: 58–62.

HITT, LORIN M., and BRYNJOLFSSON, ERIK (1996). 'Productivity, Business Profitability, and Consumer Surplus: Three Different Measures of Information Technology Value,' *MIS Quarterly*, 20 (2): 121–42.

HODGETTS, RICHARD M. (1993). *Blueprints for Continuous Improvement: Lessons from the Baldridge Winners*. Briefing of the AMA. New York: American Management Association.

HORTON, FOREST W. (1968). 'How to Harness Information Resources: A Systems Approach,' *Association for Systems Management*.

—— (1985). *Information Resources Management: Harnessing Information Assets for Productivity Gains in the Office, Factory, and Laboratory*. Englewood Cliffs, NJ: Prentice-Hall, Inc.

—— and MARCHAND, DONALD A. (1982). *Information Management in Public Administration*. Arlington, Va.: Information Resources Press.

HOSMER, LARUE TONE (1995). 'Trust: The Connecting Link between Organizational Theory and Philosophical Ethics,' *Academy of Management Review*, 20 (2): 379–403.

HREBINIAK, L. G., and JOYCE, H. F. (1985). 'Organizational Adaptation: Strategic Choice and Environmental Determinism,' *Administrative Science Quarterly*, 30: 336–49.

HUBER, G. P., and POWER, D. J. (1985). 'Retrospective Reports of Strategic-Level Managers: Guidelines for Increasing their Accuracy,' *Strategic Management Journal*: 171–80.

IVES, BLAKE, OLSON, MARGRETHE H., and BAROUDI, JACK J. (1983). 'The Measurement of User Information Satisfaction,' *Communications of the ACM* 26 (10): 785–93.

JARVENPAA, SIRKKA L., and IVES, BLAKE (1991). 'Executive Involvement and Participation in the Management of Information Technology,' *MIS Quarterly*, 15 (2): 205–27.

JOHNSON, H. THOMAS (1992). *Relevance Regained: From Top-down Control to Bottom-up Empowerment.* New York: The Free Press.

—— and KAPLAN, ROBERT S. (1987). *Relevance Lost: The Rise and Fall of Management Accounting.* Boston: Harvard Business School Press.

JÖRESKOG, K. G. (1971). 'Simultaneous Factor Analysis in Several Populations,' *Psychometrika*, 36: 409–26.

—— (1993). 'Testing Structural Equation Models,' in K. A. Bollen and J. S. Long (eds.), *Testing Structural Equation Models.* Newbury Park, Calif.: Sage Publications, 31–53.

—— and SÖRBOM, D. (1989). *LISREL 7: A Guide to the Program and Applications.* Chicago: SPSS, Inc.

KAPLAN, ROBERT S., and NORTON, DAVID P. (1992). 'The Balanced Scorecard: Measures that Drive Performance,' *Harvard Business Review*, 70 (1): 71–9.

—— —— (1993). 'Putting the Balanced Scorecard to Work,' *Harvard Business Review*, 71 (5): 134–42.

—— —— (1996a). 'Using the Balanced Scorecard as a Strategic Management System,' *Harvard Business Review*, 74 (1): 75–85.

—— —— (1996b). 'Linking the Balanced Scorecard to Strategy,' *Management Review*, 39 (1): 53–79.

—— —— (1996c). *The Balanced Scorecard: Translating Strategy into Action.* Boston: Harvard Business School Press.

KEEN, PETER G. W. (1988). *Measuring Business Value of Information Technology.* Washington: ICIT Press.

—— (1993). 'Information Technology and the Management Difference: A Fusion Map,' *IBM Systems Journal*, 32 (1): 17–39.

—— and SCOTT MORTON, MICHAEL S. (1978). *Decision Support Systems: An Organizational Perspective.* Reading, Mass.: Addison-Wesley Publishing.

KETTINGER, WILLIAM J., and GROVER, VARUN (1995). 'Towards a Theory of Business Process Change Management,' *Journal of Management Information Systems*, 12 (1): 9–30.

—— —— and SEGARS, ALBERT H. (1995). 'Do Strategic Systems Really Pay Off? An Analysis of Classic Strategic IT Cases,' *Information Systems Management*, Winter: 35–43.

—— and HACKBARTH, GARY (1999). 'Reaching the Next Level in E-commerce: A Framework for Strategy Development,' *Financial Times*, London, Special Series on Mastering Information Management, Mar. 15.

—— and LEE, CHOONG C. (1994). 'Perceived Service Quality and User Satisfaction with the Information Services Function,' *Decision Sciences*, 25 (5/6): 737–66.

—— —— (1999). 'Exploring the IS–User Gap in IT Innovation,' Working Paper: Center for Information Management and Technology Research, Darla Moore School of Business, University of South Carolina, Columbia, SC.

—— GROVER, VARUN, GUHA, SUBASHISH, and SEGARS, ALBERT H. (1994). 'Strategic Information Systems Revisited: A Study in Sustainability and Performance,' *MIS Quarterly*, 18 (1): 31–58.

KICHEN, S., and RUSSO MCCARTHY, T. (1995). 'Private Business,' *Fortune*, Dec. 4: 170–1.

KICHEN, S., and RUSSO MCCARTHY, T. (1997). 'Wall Street? No Thanks!' *Fortune*, Dec. 1: 180–3.

KING, DONALD W., and BRYANT, EDWARD C. (1971). *The Evaluation of Information Services and Products*. Washington: Information Resources Press.

KING, JOHN L., and KRAEMER, KENNETH L. (1988). 'Information Resource Management: Is It Sensible and Can It Work?' *Information and Management*, 15: 7–14.

KOENIG, M. (1992). 'The Importance of Information Services for Productivity "Under-recognized" and "Under-invested",' *Special Libaries*, Fall: 199–210.

KOTTER, JOHN P., and HESKETT, JAMES (1992). *Corporate Culture and Performance*. New York: The Free Press.

KOUZES, JAMES M., and POSNER, BARRY Z. (1993). *Credibility: How Leaders Gain and Lose It, Why People Demand It*. San Francisco: Jossey-Bass Publishers.

KUHLTHAU, C. C. (1991). 'Inside the Search Process: Information Seeking from the User's Perspective,' *Journal of the American Society for Information Science*, 42 (5): 361–71.

LACITY, M. C., and HIRSCHHEIM, R. (1993). *Information Systems Outsourcing: Myths, Metaphors, and Realities*. New York: Wiley.

LESTER, RICHARD K. (1998). *The Productive Edge*. New York: W. W. Norton & Company.

LINDBLOM, C. E. (1959). 'On the Science of "Muddling Through",' *Public Administration Review*, Spring: 81.

LIPNACK, JESSICA, and STAMPS, JEFFREY (1997). *Virtual Teams: Reaching across Space, Time and Organizations with Technology*. New York: J. Wiley and Sons.

LUCONI, FRED, MALONE, THOMAS W., and SCOTT MORTON, MICHAEL S. (1986). 'Expert Systems and Expert Systems Support Systems: The Next Challenge for Management,' *Sloan Management Review*, Fall: 354–73.

LUFTMAN, JERRY N., LEWIS, PAUL R., and OLDACH, SCOTT H. (1993). 'Transforming the Enterprise: The Alignment of Business and Information Strategies,' *IBM Systems Journal*, 32 (1): 198–221.

MCCONVILLE, DANIEL J. (1994). 'All about EVA,' *Industry Week*, 243 (8): 55–8.

MCFARLAN, F. WARREN (1984). 'Information Technology Changes the Way You Compete,' *Harvard Business Review*, 62 (3): 98–103.

MCGEE, JAMES, and PRUSAK, LAURENCE (1993). *Managing Information Strategically*. New York: John Wiley & Sons.

MACHLUP, F. (1979). 'Uses, Value, and Benefits of Knowledge,' *Knowledge: Creation, Diffusion, Utilization*, 1 (1): 62–81.

MCKEEN, J., SMITH, H., and PARENT, M. (1997). 'Assessing the Value of Information Technology: The Leverage Effect,' *Proceedings of the Fifth European Conference on Information Systems, Cork, June 9–12* (Atlanta: Association of Information Systems, Georgia State University), 22–41.

MCKENNA, REGIS (1997). *Real Time: Preparing for the Age of the Never Satisfied Customer*. Boston: Harvard Business School Press.

MCKINNON, SHARON M., and BRUNS WILLIAM J., Jr. (1992). *The Information Mosaic: How Managers Get the Information They Really Need*. Boston: Harvard Business School Press.

MARCHAND, DONALD A. (1999). 'The New Waves of Business Process Redesign and IT in Demand/Supply Chain Management: Hard Choices for Senior Managers,' *IMD Working Paper Series*, 99 (1): 1–24.

—— and HORTON FOREST W., Jr. (1986). *Infotrends: Profiting from your Information Resources.* New York: John Wiley & Sons.

—— and STANFORD, MICHAEL J. (1993). 'Focusing on the "I" in IT: A Manager's Guide to Assessing Information's Value to the Business,' *Manufacturing 2000,* Executive Reports Series No. 12, Nov., IMD International.

MARDIA, K. V. (1970). 'Measures of Multivariate Skewness and Kurtosis with Applications,' *Biometrika,* 57: 519–30.

MARSH, H. W., and HOCEVAR, D. (1985). 'Application of Confirmatory Factor Analysis to the Study of Self-Concept: First and Higher Order Factor Models and their Invariance across Groups,' *Psychological Bulletin,* 97: 562–82.

MASON, R. O., and, MITROFF, I. I. (1981). *Challenging Strategic Planning Assumptions: Theory, Cases and Techniques.* New York: John Wiley & Sons.

MAYO, ELTON (1933). *The Human Problems of an Industrial Civilization.* New York: Macmillan Publishing.

MEEK, G., and SAUDAGARAN, S. (1990). 'A Survey of Research on Financial Reporting in Transnational Context,' *Journal of Accounting Literature,* 9 (1): 45–82.

MINTZBERG, HENRY (1973). *The Nature of Managerial Work.* New York: Harper & Row.

—— (1975). 'The Manager's Job: Folklore and Fact,' *Harvard Business Review,* 53 (4): 49–61.

—— AHLSTRAND, BRUCE, and LAMPEL, JOSEPH (1998). *Strategy Safari: A Guided Tour through the Wilds of Strategic Management.* London: Prentice Hall Europe.

MUKHOPADHYAY, T., KEKRE, S., and KALATHUR, S. (1995). 'Business Value of Information Technology: A Study of the Electronic Data Interchange,' *MIS Quarterly,* 19 (2): 137–56.

MUMFORD, ENID, and WEIR, MARY (1979). *Computer Systems in Work Design: The ETHICS Method.* New York: Wiley.

MYERS, PAUL S. (ed.) (1997). *Knowledge Management and Organizational Design.* Boston: Butterworth-Heinemann.

NAULT, BARRIE R. (1998). 'Information Technology and the Organization Design: Locating Decisions and Information,' *Management Science,* 44 (10): 1321–35.

—— and DEXTER, A. S. (1994). 'Added Value and Pricing with Information Technology,' *MIS Quarterly,* 19 (4): 449–64.

NEGROPONTE, NICHOLAS (1995). *Being Digital.* New York: Alfred A. Knopf.

NOLAN, RICHARD L., and BRADLEY, STEPHEN P. (1998). *Sense and Respond: Capturing Value in the Network Era.* Boston: Harvard Business School Press.

NONAKA, IKUJIRO, and TAKEUCHI, HIROTAKA (1995). *The Knowledge-Creating Company: How Japanese Companies Create the Dynamics of Innovation.* New York: Oxford University Press.

O'REILLY, CHARLES (1989). 'Corporations, Culture, and Commitment: Motivation and Social Control in Organizations,' *California Management Review,* Summer: 9–25.

ORNA, ELIZABETH (1996). 'Valuing Information: Problems and Opportunities,' in D. P. Best (ed.), *The Fourth Resource: Information and its Management.* Aldershot: Aslib-Gower.

PFEIFFER, JEFFREY (1992). *Managing with Power: Politics and Influence in Organizations.* Boston: Harvard Business School Press.

PITT, L. F., WATSON, R., and KAVAN, C. B. (1995). 'Service Quality: A Measure of Information Systems Effectiveness,' *MIS Quarterly*, 19 (20): 173–88.

PORTER, MICHAEL E. (1980). *Competitive Strategy*. New York: The Free Press.

PRUSAK, LAURENCE (ed.) (1997). *Knowledge in Organizations*. Boston: Butterworth-Heinemann.

QUINN, JAMES BRIAN, BARUCH, JORDAN J., and ZIEN, KAREN ANNE (1996). 'Software-Based Innovation,' *Sloan Management Review*, Summer: 11–24.

RAPPAPORT, ALFRED (1987). 'Linking Competitive Strategy and Shareholder Value Analysis,' *Journal of Business Strategy*, 7 (4): 58–67.

—— (1992). 'CFOs and Strategists: Forging a Common Framework', *Harvard Business Review*, May–June: 84–91.

RAYPORT, JEFFREY F., and SVIOKLA, JOHN J. (1994). 'Managing in the Marketspace,' *Harvard Business Review*, 72 (6): 141–50.

—— (1995). 'Exploiting the Virtual Value Chain,' *Harvard Business Review*, 73 (6): 7585.

REICH, BLAIZE H., and BENBASAT, IZAK (1996) 'Measuring the Linkage between Business and Information Technology Objectives,' *MIS Quarterly*, Mar.: 55–82.

REPO, A. J. (1989). 'The Value of Information: Approaches in Economics, Accounting, and Management Science,' *JASIS* 40 (2): 68–85.

ROACH, STEPHEN S. (1991). *The Technology Imperative*. New York: Morgan Stanley & Co., Inc.

—— (1998). 'In Search of Productivity,' *Harvard Business Review*, 76 (5): 153–60.

ROBBINS, S. R., and DUNCAN, R. B. (1988). 'The Role of the CEO and Top Management in the Creation and Implementations of Strategic Vision,' in D. C. Hambrick (ed.) *The Executive Effect: Concepts and Methods for Studying Top Managers*. Greenwich, Conn.: JAI Press, 205–33.

ROBINSON R. B., Jr., and PEARCE, J. A. (1988). 'Planned Patterns of Strategic Behavior and their Relationship to Business-Unit Performance,' *Strategic Managment Journal*, 9: 43–60.

ROCKART, JOHN F. (1979). 'Chief Executives Define their Own Information Data Needs,' *Harvard Business Review*, 57 (2): 81–93.

—— and BULLEN, CHRISTINE V. (1986). *The Rise of Managerial Computing*. Homewood, Ill.: Dow Jones-Irwin.

—— and DELONG, D. W. (1988). *Executive Support Systems: The Emergence of Top Management Computer Use*. Homewood, Ill.: Dow Jones-Irwin.

ROGERS, EVERETT M., and AGARWALA-ROGERS, REKHA (1976). *Communication in Organizations*. New York: The Free Press.

SAMBAMURTHY, VIJAY, and POOLE, M. S. (1992). 'The Effect of Variations in Capabilities of GDSS Design on Management of Cognitive Conflict in Groups,' *Information Systems Research*, 3 (3): 224–51.

—— and ZMUD, ROBERT W. (1992). *Managing IT for Success: The Empowering Business Partnership*. Morristown, NJ: Financial Executive Research Foundation.

SCHEIN, E. H. (1985). *Organizational Culture and Leadership*. San Francisco: Jossey-Bass Publishers.

SCHOEMAKER, P. J. H. (1990). 'Strategy, Complexity and Economic Rent,' *Management Science*, 36: 1178–92.

SCHULER, RANDALL S. (1995). *Managing Human Resources*. St Paul, Minn.: West Publishing Company.

SEGARS, ALBERT H. (1997). 'Assessing the Unidimensionality of Measurement: A Paradigm and Illustrations within the Context of Information Systems Research,' *Omega*, 25 (1): 107–21.

—— and GROVER, VARUN (1993). 'Re-examining Ease of Use and Usefulness: A Confirmatory Factor Analysis,' *MIS Quarterly*, 17: 517–25.

—— (1998). 'Strategic Information Systems Planning Success: An Investigation of the Construct and its Measurement,' *MIS Quarterly*, 22 (2) 139–63.

SENGE, PETER M. (1990). *The Fifth Discipline: The Art and Practice of the Learning Organization*. New York: Doubleday Currency.

SIMON, HERBERT A. (1946). *Administrative Behavior: A Study of Decision-Making Processes in Administrative Organization*. New York: The Free Press.

—— (1960). *The New Science of Management Decision*. New York: Harper & Row.

SIMONS, ROBERT (1995). *Levers of Control: How Managers Use Innovative Control Systems to Drive Strategic Renewal*. Boston: Harvard Business School Press.

SLATER, STANLEY F., and OLSON, ERIC M. (1996). 'A Value-Based Management System,' *Business Horizons*, Sept.–Oct.

SPRAGUE, R. H., and CARLSON, E. D. (1982). *Building Effective Decision Support Systems*. Englewood Cliffs, NJ: Prentice-Hall.

—— and WATSON, HUGH J. (eds.) (1986). *Decision Support Systems: Putting Theory into Practice*. Englewood Cliffs, NJ: Prentice-Hall.

STAMPER, RONALD (1973). *Information in Business and Administrative Systems*. New York: John Wiley & Sons.

STEWART, G. BENNETT (1990). *The Quest for Value: The EVA Management Guide*. New York: Harper Business.

STEWART, THOMAS A. (1997). *Intellectual Capital: The New Wealth of Organizations*. London: Nicholas Brealey Publishing Ltd.

STRASSMANN, PAUL A. (1985). *Information Payoff*. New York: The Free Press.

—— (1990). *The Business Value of Computers: An Executive's Guide*. New Canaan, Conn.: The Information Economics Press.

STUBBART, C. I. (1989). 'Managerial Cognition: A Missing Link in Strategic Management Research,' *Journal of Management Studies*, 26: 325–47.

SVEIBY, KARL ERIK (1997). *The New Organizational Wealth*. San Francisco: Berrett-Koehler.

SYNNOTT, WILLIAM R. (1987). *The Information Weapon: Winning Customers and Markets with Technology*. New York: John Wiley & Sons.

—— and GRUBER, WILLIAM H. (1981). *Information Resource Management: Opportunities and Strategies for the 1980s*. New York: John Wiley & Sons.

TALLON, P., KRAEMER, K., and GURBAXANI, V. (1997). 'A Multidimensional Assessment of the Contribution of Information Technology to Firm Performance,' *Proceedings of the Fifth European Conference on Information Systems, Cork, June 9–12* (Atlanta: Association of Information Systems, Georgia State University), 42–55.

TAPSCOTT, DON (1996). *The Digital Economy: Promise and Peril in the Age of Networked Intelligence*. New York: McGraw-Hill.

Tapscott, Don and Caston, Art (1993). *Paradigm Shift: The New Promise of Information Technology.* New York: McGraw-Hill.

—— Lowy, Alex, and Ticoll, David (1998). *Blueprint for the Digital Economy.* New York: McGraw-Hill.

Taylor, Robert S. (1986). *Information in Decision Contexts: Value-Added Process in Information Systems.* Norwood, NJ: Ablex Publishing Corporation.

Taylor, R. S. (1968). 'Question-Negotiation and Information Seeking in Libraries', *College and Research Libraries,* 3 (29): 178–94.

Thompson, James (1967). *Organizations in Action.* New York: McGraw-Hill.

Turner, J. (1985). 'Organizational Performance, Size and the Use of Data Processing Resources,' Working Paper Number 58, Center for Research in Information Systems, New York University.

Vandenbosch, Betty and Huff, Sid L. (1997). 'Searching and Scanning: How Executives Obtain Information from Executive Information Systems,' *MIS Quarterly,* 21 (1): 81–108.

Vandermerwe, Sandra (1993). *From Tin Soldiers to Russian Dolls: Creating Added Value through Services.* Oxford: Butterworth-Heinemann Ltd.

Varian, Hal R., and Shapiro, Carl (1998). *Information Rules.* Boston: Harvard Business School Press.

Venkatraman, N. (1985). 'Strategic Orientation of Business Enterprises: The Construct and its Measurement.' Ph.D. Dissertation, University of Pittsburgh.

—— (1989). 'Strategic Orientation of Business Enterprises: The Construct, Dimensionality and Measurement,' *Management Science,* 35 (8): 942–62.

—— (1990). 'Performance Implications of Strategic Coalignment: A Methodological Perspective,' *Journal of Management Studies,* 27: 19–41.

—— (1994). 'IT-Enabled Business Transformation: From Automation to Business Scope Redefinition,' *Sloan Management Review,* 34 (2): 73–87.

—— and Camillus, J. C. (1984). 'Exploring the Concept of "Fit" in Strategic Management,' *Academy of Management Review,* 9 (3): 513–25.

—— and Grant, J. (1986). 'Construct Measurement in Organizational Strategy Research: A Critique and Proposal,' *Academy of Management Review,* 11: 71–86.

—— and Ramanujam, V. (1986). 'Measurement of Business Performance in Strategy Research: A Comparison of Approaches,' *Academy of Management Review,* 11: 801–14.

—— and Walker, G. (1989). 'Strategic Consistency: Theory and Analysis,' Unpublished Working Paper, Sloan School of Management, MIT, Cambridge, Mass.

Victor, Bart, and Boynton, Andrew C. (1998). *Invented Here: Maximising your Organization's Internal Growth and Profitability.* Boston: Harvard Business School Press.

von Krogh, Georg, and, Roos, Johan (eds.) (1996). *Managing Knowledge: Perspectives on Cooperation and Competition.* London: Sage Publications.

Weick, Karl E. (1979). *The Social Psychology of Organizing.* Reading, Mass.: Addison-Wesley Publishing.

—— (1995). *Sensemaking in Organizations.* London: Sage Publications.

Weill, P. (1989). 'The Relationship between Investment in Information Technology and Firm Performance in the Manufacturing Sector,' Unpublished Ph.D. Dissertation, New York University.

—— and OLSON, M. (1989). 'Managing Investment in Information Technology: Mini Case Examples and Implications,' *MIS Quarterly*, 13 (1): 3–18.

WILLCOCK, L. (1992*a*). 'IT Evaluation: Managing the Catch-22,' *European Management Journal*, 10 (2): 220–9.

—— (1992*b*). 'Evaluating Information Technology Investments: Research Finding and Reprisal,' *Journal of Management Information Systems*, 2 (3): 243–68.

—— and MARGETTS, H. (1993). 'Risk Assessment and Information Systems,' *European Management Journal*, 3 (2): 127–38.

WILLIAMS, J. C., and HAZER, J. T. (1986). 'Antecedents and Consequences of Satisfaction and Commitment in Turnover Models: A Re-analysis Using Latent Variable Structural Equation Models,' *Journal of Applied Psychology*, 71: 219–31.

WINSTON, J. S. (1984). *Artificial Intelligence.* Reading, Mass.: Addison-Wesley Publishing.

WISEMAN, C. (1988). *Strategic Information Systems.* Homewood, Ill.: Dow Jones-Irwin.

YE, L. R., and JOHNSON, P. E. (1995). 'The Impact of Explanation Facilities on User Acceptance of Expert Systems Advice,' *MIS Quarterly*, 19 (2): 157–72.

ZUBOFF, SHOSHANA (1984). *In the Age of the Smart Machine: The Future of Work and Power.* New York: Basic Books, Inc.

# INDEX